Praise for *Buffett's Early Investments*

"Kate Sanborn said that 'genius is 1% inspiration and 99% perspiration.' While the moniker 'The Oracle of Omaha' may conjure up the image of Warren Buffett being omniscient, he is human like the rest of us. His real genius is the remarkable amount of hard work he put into becoming the investor he is, as well as equanimity that would make Spock jealous. In Brett Gardner's outstanding *Buffett's Early Investments*, Brett does a masterful job of showing how the sausage was made. I first met Brett in 2011 after reading an analysis of a company he wrote on a blog and was immediately struck by his remarkably curious mind and love of detail. These traits made him a fantastic person to write this book. *Buffett's Early Investments* is for the investor's investor, as it tries to reconstruct the real analytical work done by Buffett when making some of the investments he made during his formative years. It is compelling reading for anyone who wants to better understand Warren Buffett the actual investor."

—Jonathan Bloom, President of Golden Mean Partnership LLC

"What could be more important to students of Warren Buffett than understanding the earliest years of his career during which he developed his strategy and learned invaluable lessons? Brett investigates the bedrock of Buffett's career with remarkable depth."

—Frederik Gieschen, Author of the Substack *The Alchemy of Money*

"Brett's intellectual curiosity and analytical prowess are on full display in this exploration of the seminal years of Warren Buffett. He channels his inner Warren and breathes life into the early days of the iconic value investing style Buffett became synonymous with."

—Vincent Aita, Ph.D., Chief Investment Officer and Managing Partner, Cutter Capital Management, LP

Buffett's
EARLY
INVESTMENTS

Buffett's
EARLY
INVESTMENTS

A new investigation into the decades when
Warren Buffett earned his best returns

Brett Gardner

HARRIMAN HOUSE LTD
3 Viceroy Court
Bedford Road
Petersfield
Hampshire
GU32 3LJ
GREAT BRITAIN
Tel: +44 (0)1730 233870

Email: enquiries@harriman-house.com
Website: harriman.house

First published in 2024.
Copyright © Brett Gardner

Hardback ISBN: 978-1-80409-057-2
eBook ISBN: 978-1-80409-058-9

British Library Cataloguing in Publication Data
A CIP catalogue record for this book can be obtained from the British Library.

Contents

Foreword

Just over a year ago, Brett shared with me that he was writing a book on the early investments of Warren Buffett. He sent me an early draft of this book, which I thoroughly enjoyed. For readers who may be less immersed in the world of finance, Buffett can be likened to the Beyoncé (wind machines and all) of value investing. We know that when Beyoncé sneezes on a beat the beat gets sicker. Likewise (especially later in his career) when Buffett eyes a company the company looks lovelier. The "halo effect" around Buffett the legend sometimes prevents us from developing a better understanding of Buffett the investment analyst.

This book seeks to peer beyond the halo and to examine a handful of Buffett's investments more closely, using only the information that was available to him at the time. For stock pickers, the book offers an opportunity to travel back in time, step into Buffett's shoes, and evaluate these investment opportunities through his eyes. We can ask ourselves: Would we have made the same decisions he did? If so, would we have sized the investments the way he did? Would we have sold the investments when he did? And if our decisions would have been different from his, why? In this manner, these case studies can help us not only understand who Buffett was as an investor at the time he made those investment decisions, but also who we are as investors today, at the present stage of our own investing evolution.

In typical Brett fashion, he was less interested in studying Buffett's later, higher-profile investments, because he believed that these have been well covered and well documented. Instead, he wondered what Buffett was like earlier on in his career, when he was still honing his craft and evolving his mental models. We can imagine the dots connecting in Buffett's head with each subsequent investment. This required Brett to conduct a lot of primary research. He could not simply ask ChatGPT how many passengers Union Street Railway had in 1944 (one could, but one won't get the answer). Brett's research for the book has involved, among other things, spending hours poring over copies of newspapers, magazines, manuals, and annual reports from various libraries to carefully reconstruct the information that was available to Buffett at the time of each investment profiled in this book. Brett's was a labor of love.

The result speaks for itself. This is a book for the investor's investor. It is chockful of historical anecdotes about a rather eclectic set of businesses, from hardware wholesalers to cooperage, as well as the people who ran them, the long and the short and the tall.

We get to "see" the young Buffett interact with his portfolio companies and grapple with issues at some of them. To modern senses and sensibilities, the corporate governance issues Buffett sometimes encountered can smell the way Disneyland looks on a dank, disappointed, rained-out day. We learn, yet again, that fat pitches are often only fat pitches with hindsight. We tend to look at the past with rose-tinted glasses, especially if things worked out well *a posteriori*. *A priori*, there are often things that can go wrong with every investment, and when such investment is available at a compelling price, it is usually because there is some kind of "hair" on it, or risk that has become patent. The challenge for any investor is to work out if it is worthwhile underwriting the "hair" and risks of the investment at such price, sometimes with dread hands and dread feet. On this subject, the chapters on American Express and Disney make for especially riveting reading, particularly for those unfamiliar with their histories.

Perhaps the chapter that was the most illuminating for me was the one on Philadelphia and Reading. We can almost see the straight line from Philadelphia and Reading to Berkshire Hathaway. I have often wondered how Buffett comes up with his creative, out-of-the-box ideas, from taking over a textile mill and converting it into a tax-efficient permanent-capital vehicle to managing the asset side of insurance-company balance sheets so differently from the rest of the insurance industry. Studying Philadelphia and Reading, we perchance get a glimpse into a source of inspiration for Buffett's Berkshire Hathaway.

I also appreciated Brett's focus on the balance sheets and select operating metrics of the companies discussed in this book. These are indispensable to securities analysis and yet are sometimes glossed over in favor of narratives. In today's era of (until recently) nearly free money, several of the case studies in this book are timely reminders that analyzing the right-hand side of balance sheets can be important. For example, the dual-class share structure at Greif affected the risk-reward of Buffett's investment. Likewise, understanding the potential claims of British Columbia Electric convertible debentures was relevant to assessing the risk-reward of Buffett's investment in British Columbia Power.

Finally, for those of us who are following in Buffett's daunting footsteps, it is comforting to see that the young Buffett sometimes made mistakes, as was the case with Cleveland Worsted Mills and Hochschild Kohn. However, in each case, the risk of permanent capital impairment in downside cases was bounded by the sizeable margin of safety afforded to Buffett at the price he paid. Such calibration matters. The very same company (with all its attendant opportunities and risks) can be a great investment at a low price, a mediocre investment at a higher price, and a terrible investment at a still higher price.

While Brett was still working on this book, I introduced him to Peter Kaufman, the Chairman and CEO of Glenair and editor of *Poor Charlie's Almanack*. Peter was characteristically gracious: He invited Brett to visit him in Glendale, California, and then to meet with Buffett's late business partner, Charlie Munger, in Charlie's home two months before Charlie's passing.

As Brett points out, Buffett and Charlie tend to serve as a Rorschach inkblot upon which investors superimpose their own investing biases and predilections, clothing them with immediate credibility. For example, Charlie's influence on Buffett to buy wonderful businesses at fair prices has, over the years, been co-opted by so many investors to justify paying insane prices for good businesses, thereby guaranteeing poor returns on such investments. Over time, as too much capital began chasing too few good businesses, the definition of "quality" changed so that investors began throwing insane money behind shockingly poor businesses with structurally challenged unit economics masquerading as "high-quality compounders." Intellectual straitjackets investing dogma can make. Of course, Buffett and Charlie themselves did not participate in the escalating insanity. Instead, they continued to be rare voices of common sense in our recent age of epic financial unreason.

I first learned about Buffett over two decades ago, and the discovery changed the course of my career. Fourteen years ago, I founded Discerene Group LP, a private investment partnership that invests globally, pursuing a fundamental, contrarian, long-term value investing philosophy. Even as we paint our own painting, we're still standing on Buffett's shoulders, just as he stood on those of Ben Graham, Phil Fisher, and others. Our unusual partnership structure allows us to invest with our portfolio companies generationally. We do not consider capital to be fungible; the *who* behind the capital, and the relationships we build with them, are core to our DNA. We hope to celebrate our 50th anniversary with a roomful of septuagenarians, octogenarians, and nonagenarians who have traveled with us on our investing journey. We would love to say, "Look at what we achieved together! Look what we learned! Look how much fun it was, and how profitable and worthwhile it's been!"

I first met Brett in 2011, when he was still at St. John's University, about a year after Discerene's founding. A Discerene team member read a blog he wrote about an off-the-radar company we were researching and thought that he had done interesting, original research. We had assumed that Brett was an analyst at another firm and were surprised that he was still in college and doing all this work from his dorm room. When he asked if he could intern with us, it was not hard to say yes. Unforgettably, his primary research on a deathcare company included getting pictures of their cemeteries, burial plots, and coffins from nightwatchmen. We still have these and hope to bust them out at our 50th-anniversary party.

After college, Brett went on to hone his research and investing skills at several other investment firms. We kept in touch over the years, and it has been no little pleasure to see him come into his own as a professional. Even as he has done so, Brett has retained the preternatural spark and slightly quirky "off-center" quality that many people with high capacity for independent-minded thinking have. He is still the restless, intrepid, questing, captain of his own ship as he navigates his personal investing voyage.

Brett also sought my advice on professional opportunities to explore once he finished this book. As it happened, we were hiring, and Brett expressed his interest in throwing his hat into the ring. Once again, it was not hard to say yes. So, a full 12 years since his internship, Brett rejoined Discerene as an investment analyst in April 2024. At a firm renowned for its robust, rigorous, resolve-testing recruiting rituals, Brett's two-scores-and-eight-seasons trek homeward may nevertheless mark a memorable, monumental milestone.

Charlie Munger said many memorable things, but my favorite quote of his is this modest one: "The best thing a human being can do is to help another human being know more." With this book, I believe that Brett has achieved the goal of helping us know more about perhaps the most closely studied investor in the world, and in an entertaining and accessible manner to boot. This is quite a feat.

Buffett declined to be interviewed for this book, which is too bad, because—you guessed it—it is not hard to say yes to Brett. However, Buffett sent Brett a kind note to say that this was the sort of project he would have enjoyed doing if he was far younger. I could say the same, so I am glad Brett undertook this passion project in the prime of his youth. I hope that *Buffett's Early Investments* will stand the test of time and become an august addition to the ambrosial anthology on Buffett. You'll be the judge!

Soo Chuen Tan, President of Discerene Group
Stamford, CT, May 2024

Preface

"He'd find something that was selling for one-fourth of liquidating value. He'd load up. So for a long period of time, he had a happy hunting ground. All he had to do was go through lists of liquid securities and slowly buy them, and he could get these ridiculous bargains."

—*Charlie Munger*[1]

Charlie Munger grossly oversimplifies Warren Buffett's early success in the quote above. Yes, it's true the young Buffett would often pounce on stocks trading at mouth-wateringly low valuations. But Munger, whom Buffett calls 'The Architect of Berkshire Hathaway', makes it all sound much easier than it actually was.[2] The idea that Buffett simply flipped through *Moody's Manuals* and *Standard & Poor's Stock Guides* and hoovered up bargains suggests any contemporary investor could have amassed a fortune doing the same thing.

The truth is far more interesting. Benjamin Graham, Buffett's mentor and the father of value investing, was less successful an investor than his devoted student. Graham wrote *The Intelligent Investor*, co-authored *Security Analysis*, taught classes on investing, and managed multiple investment vehicles throughout his career. Buffett worshipped his professor, calling *The Intelligent Investor*, "by far the best book about investing ever written." Discovering Graham's writings was "almost like he had found a god."[3] Graham was, without a doubt, the formative influence on Buffett's investment philosophy.

But Graham didn't do nearly as well as his pupil. A key tactic Graham deployed was buying stocks trading below net current asset value, a proxy for liquidation value. These investments, known as 'net-nets,' were theoretically worth more dead than alive: Selling all assets and paying off every obligation would result in higher proceeds than what the company was selling for in the stock market. While both Buffett and Graham used this system to select securities, simply picking up cheap stocks trading below their liquidation value wasn't the driving force behind Buffett's early outperformance. If it had been, Graham should have enjoyed a comparable level of success as his protégé merely by picking up net-nets.

In fact, Graham didn't beat the stock market indices for long periods throughout his career. The Ben Graham Joint Account, which operated from 1925 through 1935, returned around 6% versus the S&P 500's 5.8%—hardly an outstanding result. Graham's more famous investment fund, Graham-Newman Corp., earned approximately 14.7% annually from 1936 to 1956 versus the stock market's 12.2%. Graham-Newman underperformed the market for most of its life, however, delivering a 15.5% return from 1945 to 1956 compared to the S&P 500's 18.3%.[i] Although Graham achieved good returns, there were extended periods when the market bested him.[4]

In comparison to his professor, Buffett absolutely crushed the market during his 'partnership years.' This period began with the formation of Buffett Associates, Ltd., on May 5, 1956—the first of a series of partnerships the young investor created before merging them into Buffett Partnership, Ltd. in 1962.[5] These partnership years were when Buffett started building his professional investment track record. As Table 1 shows, the partnership produced astonishing results. He compounded capital at 29.5% annually from 1957–1969 versus the Dow's 7.4%. $1 invested in the partnership at the start of 1957 turned into $28.94 at the end of 1969 versus only $2.52 for the Dow over the same period. In other words, Buffett obliterated the market in a way Graham simply couldn't match.

These years were the beginning of the greatest investment track record of all time. But oddly, Buffett, like Munger, would often speak about his early days as if picking stocks was almost effortless, with fat bargains just waiting for an enterprising capitalist to pick up. I was skeptical that investing was as simple and easy as the two often made it sound. Therefore, I started researching some of Buffett's earliest stock purchases. I discovered that his investments were not as straightforward as he liked to make them seem. For instance, some that looked to be sure winners at the start didn't work out so well, while others that at first blush seemed risky turned out to be enormously successful. Buffett's own overly simplistic characterization of his investments often did a disservice to the intensity of the work he performed to amass his early fortune.

Broadly, Buffett's career can be thought of in two stages. The first was when he bought the 'cigar-butt' stocks that traded below asset value. This phase was primarily shaped by Ben Graham. The second stage was when Buffett started buying better businesses, where he was heavily influenced by Charlie Munger and *Common Stocks and Uncommon Profits* author Phil Fisher. The investments in the first stage had more of their value derived from the balance

---

i   Devoted Graham students should note this excludes the GEICO investment, which Graham-Newman was forced to distribute to shareholders as SEC rules forbade investment companies from owning more than 10% of an insurance company.

Table 1: Buffett Partnership results

Year	Overall Results From Dow	Partnership Results	Limited Partners Results'
1957	-8.4%	10.4%	9.3%
1958	38.5%	40.9%	32.2%
1959	20.0%	25.9%	20.9%
1960	-6.2%	22.8%	18.6%
1961	22.4%	45.9%	35.9%
1962	-7.6%	13.9%	11.9%
1963	20.6%	38.7%	30.5%
1964	18.7%	27.8%	22.3%
1965	14.2%	47.2%	36.9%
1966	-15.6%	20.4%	16.8%
1967	19.0%	35.9%	28.4%
1968	7.7%	58.8%	45.6%
1969	-11.6%	6.8%	6.6%

On a cumulative or compounded basis:

Year	Overall Results From Dow	Partnership Results	Limited Partners' Results
1957	-8.4%	10.4%	9.3%
1957–58	26.9%	55.6%	44.5%
1957–59	52.3%	95.9%	74.7%
1957–60	42.9%	140.6%	107.2%
1957–61	74.9%	251.0%	181.6%
1957–62	61.6%	299.8%	215.1%
1957–63	94.9%	454.5%	311.2%
1957–64	131.3%	608.7%	402.9%
1957–65	164.1%	943.2%	588.5%
1957–66	122.9%	1156.0%	704.2%
1957–67	165.3%	1606.9%	932.6%
1957–68	185.7%	2610.6%	1403.5%
1957–69	152.6%	2794.9%	1502.7%
Annual Compounded Rate	7.4%	29.5%	23.8%

Source: Warren Buffett, "The Superinvestors of Graham and Doddsville," *Hermes* (Fall 1984).[ii]

ii   1957–1961 combines the results of all predecessor limited partnerships operating throughout the entire year.

sheet, while the companies bought in the later stage had more value dependent on the ability of the business to generate and grow free cash flow. In this second stage, business quality—the ability to sustainably earn high returns on invested capital—mattered more than in the first stage. There is no clear demarcation of when this evolution happened (Buffett himself has remarked, "I evolved, I didn't go from ape to human or human to ape in a nice, even manner"[6]), but the years I write about are primarily in the first phase.

In this book, I write about ten investments Buffett made in the 1950s and 1960s. This period, when Buffett earned his highest returns, is an understudied component of the billionaire's career. While researching these investments, I discovered that there were other reasons for Buffett's success rather than the idea he simply feasted on immature and inefficient financial markets.

I concluded that the following four factors drove Buffett's outperformance in this period of his career.

First, Buffett's use of activism helped him generate spectacular profits. He took significant positions in companies and influenced management teams to change corporate policy to help close the price-to-value gap.

Second, Buffett ran a highly concentrated portfolio, occasionally investing more than 20% of his fund in a single investment idea. Great investment ideas are rare; Buffett seized on them whenever he uncovered them.

Third, Buffett was a tenacious and creative researcher, traveling extensively to learn about companies and industries, pushing his understanding of business beyond what he could learn from the documents. While he was certainly a voracious reader, he also applied similar ferocity to uncovering information through people.

Fourth, Buffett possessed a remarkable filter. His ability to sift through investment opportunities quickly, something he has honed throughout his career, allowed him to seize on the best ideas and concentrate his efforts on wringing the most profit out of those.

Layering these factors onto the value investing philosophy made Buffett rich. Moreover, these early years studying bad companies helped inform his later career, where he focused on better businesses with high returns on capital and defensive competitive positions. Trudging through mediocre but cheap companies in dying industries helped him learn how to uncover and appreciate the truly advantaged gems.

This book is split in two parts: the pre-partnership and partnership years. The division shows how Buffett developed as an investor and helps explain why his application of the value investing philosophy was much different than Ben Graham's. The pre-partnership investments taught him lessons that sharpened his strategy when he started his own investment firm.

I chose the ten investments I write about in this book based on three criteria. First was my ability to secure the proper documents for the investments. Could I get my hands on the necessary annual reports or *Moody's Manuals*? The second filter was whether I thought my research was differentiated enough. I wanted to write about investments that added value to existing Buffett research. For example, I chose not to write about famous investments from these years, such as GEICO, Dempster Mill, or Sanborn Map because Buffett himself and others have written sufficiently about these. The last criterion was my assessment of how interesting the story behind the investment was. Did the purchase contain important lessons or a compelling story? Were there misconceptions that deserved correcting?

While this is a Buffett book first and foremost, it is also a business history book. Anyone with a passing interest in Buffett or investing generally can get something out of this. Many of the companies I write about are now defunct. But at one point, they were thriving firms that were critical to their communities—and, in some cases, the country as a whole. I lucked out, as local libraries often had extensive corporate archives and other documents to help me better understand the histories of the businesses I wanted to study. I provide a brief overview of their corporate histories within the chapters to help contextualize the companies. While some of these industries and companies have faded away, seeing how corporations grow, thrive, and die is helpful as we analyze our own investments.

While I don't have Buffett's trade data, I use the documents he would have used when he invested in these businesses. Additionally, I supplement my analysis with articles and books about the companies and industries to help readers understand the backdrop surrounding the investments. These case studies not only demonstrate how Buffett earned such remarkable returns but also illustrate the intense work and creative approaches Buffett took to uncover unique insights into the companies he purchased. The original research in this book reveals new information about the individual investments themselves—piercing through misconceptions and uncovering new facts—to reveal how Buffett produced such remarkable results. By the end of the book, I hope you see that Buffett did not come out of the womb blessed with the ability to allocate capital. Rather, through tenacity and determination, he learned and grew as a securities analyst, portfolio manager, and businessman throughout his career to develop into the world's greatest investor.

The Pre-Partnership Years

In the early stages of his journey as a value investor while studying at Columbia in 1950 and 1951, Buffett exhibited remarkable potential. He was the sole student to earn an A+ in Ben Graham's security analysis course and was already producing profitable stock picks and writing thoughtful articles on his favorite investments. Prior to starting Buffett Associates, Ltd., Buffett invested for himself and through a 50–50 partnership with his father, Howard.

However, his post-graduation path was not without challenges, as Graham rejected Buffett's offer to work at Graham-Newman for free. At the time, Graham only hired Jewish workers to counteract discrimination on Wall Street. As a result, Warren joined the stock brokerage firm his father had co-founded, Buffett-Falk. In this role, Buffett worked as a stockbroker, selling securities to clients rather than actively picking and investing in stocks. He worked at his father's firm until Graham finally relented and hired him—with pay—at Graham-Newman in 1954.

As Table 1 illustrates, investors benefited from a favorable investing environment during this period. The S&P 500 only had one down year, a small single-digit decline, with the index nearly quadrupling over these six years. Economic growth was robust, buoyed by the Korean War beginning in 1950, and was only briefly interrupted by the post-war recession. Inflation was also generally low outside of 1951 when prices popped due to war-related shortages. Interest rates, as indicated by the three-month treasury bill, were low.

Table 1: Market and economic data

	S&P 500	Real GDP	CPI	3-month Treasury bill yearly average
1950	30.8%	8.7%	1.1%	1.2%
1951	23.7%	8.0%	7.9%	1.5%
1952	18.2%	4.1%	2.3%	1.7%
1953	-1.2%	4.7%	0.8%	1.9%
1954	52.6%	-0.6%	0.3%	0.9%
1955	32.6%	7.1%	-0.3%	1.7%

Source: Federal Reserve Bank of Minneapolis; Bureau of Economic Analysis; NYU Stern, Historical Returns on Stocks, Bonds and Bills: 1928–2023; Federal Reserve Bank of St. Louis.

There are some interesting investments Buffett made during this period that I do not discuss. While Buffett fanatics may be familiar with them, a brief overview should be helpful as we journey ahead:[iii]

- GEICO: On a Saturday, Buffett takes the train from New York to Washington, D.C. to try and better understand the business. A guard answers Buffett's knock on the door. After Buffett introduces himself and mentions he's a student of Ben Graham's, the guard goes upstairs and finds GEICO's financial vice president (and future CEO) Lorimer Davidson working. Davidson tells the guard to let Buffett in and teaches him about auto insurance. Thinking the company had a unique competitive position with attractive growth characteristics and an undemanding valuation, Buffett bought the stock, making it more than half his portfolio at the end of 1951. The 21-year-old wrote about the stock in an article for *The Commercial and Financial Chronicle* in 1951 and would later buy the whole company when running Berkshire Hathaway.[7]

- Western Insurance Securities: Buffett wrote this stock up for *The Commercial and Financial Chronicle* in 1953. The stock was selling for less than 2.0x earnings and at around 0.45x book value when he bought it.[8]

[iii] For more reading on these fascinating stories, please see: the Berkshire Hathaway 1988 chairman's letter for a discussion on Rockwood, the December 6, 1951 edition of *The Commercial and Financial Chronicle* for Buffett's GEICO write-up, and the April 9, 1953 edition of *The Commercial and Financial Chronicle* for Buffett's Western Insurance Securities write-up. A query on your favorite internet search engine should help you find these. If you're having trouble, e-mail me at Brett@BuffettsEarlyInvestments.com, and I'd be happy to send them to you. *The Snowball* also offers vivid accounts of each.

- Rockwood: Buffett bought this arbitrage opportunity when working at Graham-Newman. This Brooklyn chocolate products company used a quirk in the tax code to distribute its inventory to shareholders on a tax-free basis. The company exchanged its shares for cocoa beans as it eliminated one of its businesses. Jay Pritzker controlled the company and masterminded the transaction. In contrast to Graham, who merely played the Rockwood arbitrage, Buffett kept his stock, allowing him to enjoy the security's rise from $15 to $100 following the completion of the arbitrage.[9]

Despite his gifts, not everything Buffett touched turned to gold. He had some unsuccessful investments and embarrassed himself in front of people he admired. The first three investments in this book were not big money-makers for Buffett. But they were inexpensive stocks purchased at a discount to asset value, which helped protect against losses. However, the fourth and fifth investments explored emerge as big winners due to significant changes in the companies' capital allocation.

None of the five companies in this section were quality businesses when Buffett purchased their stocks. But he was able to make a killing on two of them—and these two were probably the weakest businesses of the bunch. Though in the beginning stages of his development as a value investor, the precocious capital allocator was learning how to wring profits out of bad businesses. And he would carry these lessons forward when he started his partnership.

Marshall-Wells: 1950

"They'd been working here for thirty years building up this business and all they would have had to run it was this kid named Warren Buffett. He's the best they could come up with. And who'd want to ride with him?"

—Louis Green[10]

Twenty-year-old Warren Buffett was a graduate student in New York, choosing to attend Columbia University because his idol Ben Graham taught there. The precocious student learned that one of the companies he invested in, Marshall-Wells, was hosting its annual meeting across the river in Jersey City. He asked his professor, Graham's *Security Analysis* co-author David Dodd, if he could skip class to attend. Buffett had purchased 25 shares of the hardware wholesaler's stock in a partnership with his father a few months prior at $200 a share and wanted to check in on the company. Dodd approved, so the young investor set off with his friend and fellow student Fred Stanback.[11]

Buffett viewed the annual meeting as a time for management to account for its performance. But this was not what he saw while there, as the leadership viewed the gathering only as a necessary legal obligation to fulfill. Shareholders didn't seem to care much, either, with only a handful of folks in the room.

Despite the limited crowd, the room contained a couple of riveting people. One of those in attendance was Walter Schloss, who seemed to upset the company's leadership with his pointed questions. Buffett initiated a conversation with Schloss and was ecstatic when he learned that Schloss worked for his hero at Graham-Newman. The two would later work together when Buffett joined the firm in 1954.[iv]

Schloss wasn't the only interesting person Buffett encountered at the event. Louis Green, an investor at Stryker & Brown and an associate of Graham's, was also there.[v] Green knew Buffett's mentor well; the two investors bought similar

---

iv   Schloss would also go on to start his own highly successful investment fund after Graham-Newman closed.

v   Stryker was the market maker in Marshall-Wells' stock.

stocks and served on boards together. After the meeting, Green took Buffett and Stanback to lunch. The older investor asked Warren why he had bought Marshall-Wells. When Buffett replied that he purchased it because Ben Graham owned the stock, Green was repulsed, condescendingly retorting, "Strike one!" In reality, Buffett did not buy Marshall-Wells merely because Graham held it—he had done his own work on the investment.[12]

Buffett's failure to explain his rationale would lead Green to dismiss his abilities at Graham-Newman's final shareholders' meeting in 1956, where he uttered the sneering quote that opens this chapter. This blow came at a crucial time for Buffett, as he was just beginning to raise capital for his partnership. Although he may have sourced the idea from a list of Graham's holdings, Graham-Newman only owned 100 shares of Marshall-Wells in January 1950, accounting for a mere 0.3% of the portfolio.[vi] Graham-Newman was a highly diversified investment fund, owning around a hundred securities—in contrast, Buffett held only a few stocks, and Marshall-Wells accounted for about a quarter of his net worth in 1950.[13] Even if he did source the idea from Graham, he performed his own analysis to justify such a significant stake in his portfolio.

Marshall-Wells wasn't some way-off-the-map company that no one had ever heard of. It was North America's largest hardware wholesaler and was big enough to make the Fortune 500 when the list of largest US companies was introduced in 1955, coming in at number 339.[14]

So why did Buffett buy the stock? Simple, because it was really cheap. Marshall-Wells was a deep value investment, trading below net current asset value and at a salivating earnings multiple. Any analyst looking at this investment would instantly grasp how inexpensive it was. However, Buffett did not hold onto the stock for long—and it wasn't a winner for him.

Let's see what happened.

The development of the Marshall-Wells Company

Albert Morley Marshall purchased a controlling interest in the Duluth-based Chaplin-Wells Company in 1893. The Chaplin-Wells founders embraced the fresh capital Marshall furnished, as well as the relevant experience he brought from working at a different hardware merchant. Shortly after his purchase, Albert changed the company's name to the Marshall-Wells Hardware Company. Unfortunately, the untimely deaths of his two partners, C.W. Wells and F.C

---

vi   Others have speculated that Buffett got the idea from *Security Analysis*. However, the edition mentioning Marshall-Wells did not come out until 1951, when the company was included in a table titled "Six Common Stocks Undervalued in 1949".

Stone, forced Marshall to take complete control of the business shortly after purchasing his stake.[15]

Duluth, Minnesota was a small city in the 1890s, with a population of about 5,000. Located on the north shore of Lake Superior, Duluth was a convenient transportation hub that enabled lumber and other goods to be easily moved by boat.[16] Minnesota had developed as a major center of hardware wholesaling because of its accessibility and dense population relative to other Midwestern states. The North Star state flourished as a distribution hub and became the third-largest hardware wholesale state in the United States in 1948, trailing only New York and California.[17]

But the young firm confronted a terrible economic environment. Albert Marshall persevered through the 1893 Depression, choosing to send salesmen into new geographies and increase building capacity. After the turn of the century, the company extended its footprint, building new branches and distribution centers, setting itself on a path to become the largest hardware wholesaler in North America.[18]

In its early days, the firm supplied hardware for the logging camps and iron mines of northern Minnesota and parts of Michigan, eventually expanding to offer general hardware for retail stores.[19] To further enhance the relationship with retailers, Albert's son Seth—who had become president in 1918 after his father ascended to the chairmanship—crafted the Marshall-Wells Stores plan in 1928, a program where independent retail hardware stores operated under the Marshall-Wells name.[20]

Marshall-Wells did not own these retailers but played an intimate role in developing their businesses, helping them set up their stores and select merchandise.[21] In exchange, the stores agreed to buy a 'satisfactory volume' from the company, providing a predictable outlet for its inventory.[22] A study in the early 1950s surveying 12 dealers under the plan—a small sample since there were more than 600—found that, on average, the stores associated with the program bought 86% of their products from Marshall-Wells.

When Buffett invested in the company, Marshall-Wells sold hardware goods—tools, electric appliances, paint, sporting goods, and more—into the northwestern states of the United States, Alaska,[vii] and the western provinces of Canada (Image 1 lays out the company's geographic coverage).[23] The company's 1949 revenue was split evenly between the United States and Canada. While Marshall-Wells was primarily a wholesaler, it also housed some manufacturing subsidiaries such as Western Paint & Varnish and Zenith Machine Co.[24]

vii   Alaska did not become a state until 1959.

Image 1: Marshall-Wells geographic coverage

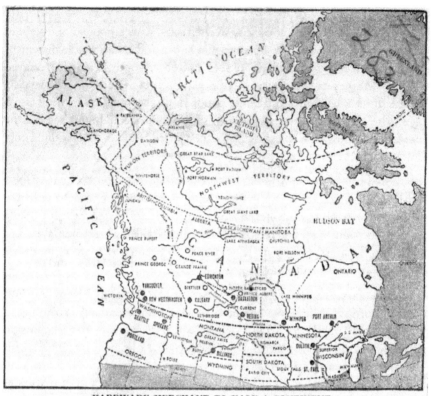

HARDWARE MERCHANT TO HALF A CONTINENT

Dots are major warehouses in Marshall-Wells sales territory; circles, supplementary stocks

Source: *Minneapolis Sunday Tribune.*

John Moore, the company's president when Buffett bought the stock, thought focusing on hard-to-reach, agriculturally focused geographies gave the company a unique advantage over other wholesalers. In his mind, these sparsely populated rural areas could only be reached by an intermediary, and only a large firm like Marshall-Wells could serve them well.

The company had three primary customers: the stores under its plan, industrial enterprises, and independent hardware retailers. Independent dealers were the largest segment of the business, comprising about half of the business, but the stores associated with the program were growing as a percentage of the company's overall sales and accounted for about 30% of revenue. The remainder of the company's sales came from industrial customers.[25] And while Marshall-Wells was the biggest hardware wholesaler in North America, hardware wholesaling was still highly fragmented, with Marshall-Wells accounting for only a low-single-digit percentage of the United States hardware wholesaling market in the late 1940s.[26]

Hardware wholesaling wasn't a particularly enthralling business, but the company occupied a critical segment of the value chain. Wholesalers bought, sold, stored, and transported goods, serving as an intermediary between the manufacturer of the goods and the retailer who eventually sold them to customers.[27] With a diverse set of manufacturers and a fragmented group of retailers, wholesaling served a vital role within the hardware industry.

Why did Buffett invest in Marshall-Wells?

Buffett bought 25 shares of Marshall-Wells in 1950 at $200 per share for a total investment of $5,000. Buffett made the investment through a 50–50 partnership with his father, making his attributable stake $2,500, about a quarter of his net worth. Marshall-Wells had an $11.4 million market capitalization at his purchase price, and with net cash on the books, only a $7.0 million enterprise value.

Having just read Graham's writings, Buffett was in the early days of his journey as a value investor. At this point, he was most focused on the quantitative aspects of an investment. And Marshall-Wells' valuation was tantalizing. Table 1 presents the metrics, illustrating that the company sold for a significant discount to its tangible book value and net current asset value, as well as at a ridiculously low price-to-earnings multiple. The stock traded at a 40% discount to net current asset value and only 1.93x EV/1949 EBIT. It was an unbelievable bargain.

Table 1: Valuation metrics

	Market capitalization	Enterprise value	P/TB	P/NCAV	EV/1949 EBIT	1949 P/E	5-year average	
							EV/EBIT	P/E
Marshall-Wells	11,352	6,986	0.46x	0.60x	1.93x	5.53x	1.23x	3.95x

Source: *Moody's Manuals* and Author's Calculations. Dollar figures in thousands.

The asset composition, found in Table 2, was appealing: Cash and government securities were 20.3% of total assets, and current assets were 81.9% of total assets. Inventories were the most crucial item at 43.4% of total assets. The goods Marshall-Wells sold—hardware tools, housewares, farm equipment, and so on—were all non-perishable items, carrying minimal obsolescence risk.

Liabilities and preferred equity were small relative to the assets: only $5.3 million of current liabilities, a $0.4 million reserve, and $2.3 million of preferred stock, totaling $8.0 million of liabilities and senior equity. The company's net current

Table 2: Asset composition

	1949	% of total assets
Cash	4,786	14.6%
U.S. and Canadian Government securities	1,884	5.7%
Accounts receivable, less reserve	5,469	16.7%
Inventories	14,232	43.4%
Prepaid expenses	463	1.4%
Total current assets	26,833	81.9%
Cash surrender value of life insurance	534	1.6%
Sundry other investments	67	0.2%
Land, buildings and equipment, less reserve	5,346	16.3%
Total assets	32,780	100.0%

Source: *Moody's Manuals* and Author's Calculations. Dollar figures in thousands.

asset value was $331.42 per share—65.7% more than the $200 Buffett paid for the stock. The valuation was clearly cheap, so Buffett snatched the stock up.

The income statement was also encouraging. Over the decade preceding Buffett's investment, the company was able to grow revenue and earnings—it was not a company meandering along or struggling. Table 3 shows that Marshall-Wells' recent financial performance since 1939 was strong; sales more than tripled and earnings before interest and taxes (EBIT) increased by more than six-fold. The company grew sales most years, with a big post-war bump in 1946 and 1947. 1949—the last year financials were available before Buffett's investment—was a down year for Marshall-Wells. The recession caused revenue to contract 8.9% as consumers' income fell within Marshall-Wells' territories, damaging margins and returns on invested capital. Costs associated with opening a new branch in Seattle also hurt operating income, but the company was still profitable. In fact, Marshall-Wells hadn't had a losing year since 1933.

Despite the tough 1949, the near-term prospects for the business were positive. J.M. Dain & Company—a Minneapolis-based investment banking firm—published equity research reports on Marshall-Wells in 1950 and 1951 that discussed its optimistic view of the firm:

> Over the long term, it is probable that further cyclical fluctuations in earnings, such as occurred in 1949, will be experienced, and that profit

Table 3: Marshall-Wells' summary financials

	1940	1941	1942	1943	1944	1945	1946	1947	1948	1949	CAGR since 1939
Revenue	27,060	33,859	37,805	42,612	44,963	48,881	70,208	84,177	87,778	79,989	12.8%
Gross profit	3,778	5,307	6,373	7,353	7,765	8,259	12,736	14,484	14,517	11,514	13.8%
EBIT	1,000	2,006	2,713	3,399	3,568	3,723	6,977	7,499	6,570	3,620	20.0%
Net income[1]	625	1,314	1,122	1,169	1,226	1,203	3,678	4,089	4,072	2,190	18.1%
Earnings per share[2]	5.98	17.61	14.36	15.22	18.36	17.98	59.88	69.60	69.30	36.15	30.9%
Net working capital—excluding cash	6,324	7,311	8,481	5,921	6,023	6,926	9,303	9,782	13,350	14,846	9.3%
Property, plant, and equipment	5,571	5,355	5,074	4,809	4,490	4,424	4,850	5,341	5,336	5,346	-0.7%
Total invested capital	11,895	12,666	13,555	10,731	10,513	11,350	14,153	15,124	18,686	20,191	5.5%
Days NWC	84	73	76	62	48	48	42	41	48	64	
Revenue growth	13.2%	25.1%	11.7%	12.7%	5.5%	8.7%	43.6%	19.9%	4.3%	-8.9%	
Gross margin	14.0%	15.7%	16.9%	17.3%	17.3%	16.9%	18.1%	17.2%	16.5%	14.4%	
EBIT margin	3.7%	5.9%	7.2%	8.0%	7.9%	7.6%	9.9%	8.9%	7.5%	4.5%	
Net income margin	2.3%	3.9%	3.0%	2.7%	2.7%	2.5%	5.2%	4.9%	4.6%	2.7%	
Pre-tax ROIC	8.4%	16.3%	20.7%	28.0%	33.6%	34.1%	54.7%	51.2%	38.9%	18.6%	
Post-tax ROIC	5.3%	10.7%	8.6%	9.6%	11.5%	11.0%	28.8%	27.9%	24.1%	11.3%	

Source: *Moody's Manuals*, Marshall-Wells' annual reports, and author's calculations. [1] Net income excludes preferred stock dividends and surplus credits and deductions. [2] Earnings available for common shareholders, includes preferred stock dividends and surplus credits and deductions. Dollars figures in thousands, other than per share data.

margins will be lower than those of the bonanza years of 1946–1948. Under these conditions, more intensive efforts will be required to maintain and expand earning power, but the continued economic development of the territory should provide opportunities for the profitable employment of building funds "earmarked" already for future expenditure and of the capital which should be realized from reinvestment of earnings. The ability of the management to utilize advantageously such opportunities has already been demonstrated.[28]

It was clear the peak post-war years were outliers, with the note alluding to a more competitive environment: "more intensive efforts will be required to maintain and expand earning power." But, the threat from other forms of hardware distribution didn't seem imminent when Buffett purchased the stock. And the equity was clearly inexpensive—one J.M. Dain report observed, "Marshall-Wells common stock is currently selling at an exceptionally low ratio to earnings and asset value. For the investor willing to subordinate current income and marketability to longer term possibilities, we believe that this stock affords an unusual value."[29] *Anyone analyzing the stock could tell it was cheap.*

There were, of course, risks to the investment. As J.M. Dain noted, the business was already showing signs of returning to normalcy after World War II. The seller's market that persisted after World War II allowed Marshall-Wells to continue producing excellent returns as shortages allowed wholesalers to keep prices elevated. The stabilization of the hardware market offered a two-punch blow: First, margins would fall, as evidenced by a decline in Marshall-Wells' EBIT margins more than halving from 9.9% in 1946 to 4.5% in 1949. Second, working capital investment would increase, as shown by days net working capital rising from a low of 41 in 1947 to 64 in 1949. The combined factors of earnings normalization and additional capital requirements would lead to deteriorating returns for the business.[30]

As the industry stabilized, competitive vigor would increase. And some tenacious adversaries were looming, such as specialty-line and dealer-owned wholesalers and vertically integrated chain stores.[viii] While these competitors had been around for a while, they were more cost-competitive than an old-line wholesaler such as Marshall-Wells. It was unclear how the Duluth-based company would fare once the environment normalized. The company compounded this risk

---

viii   In a dealer-owned cooperative, the individual retailers each owned a fraction of the cooperative wholesaler—the wholesaler under this program was a non-profit and distributed its earnings to its retailer owners. Specialty line wholesalers earned a major portion of their dollar volume in a single line or narrow range of merchandise.

by continuing to invest heavily, opening new branches and refreshing old warehouses. Increased investment amidst a foggy outlook was a bit concerning.

Further, Marshall-Wells was a closely held stock with limited float available to investors, making it difficult for an investor to intervene if management allocated capital poorly. But the family's ownership and company's governance mitigated this risk. Albert Marshall's son Seth was still chairman (Albert had passed away in 1926) and John Moore was the company's president. Moore had joined Marshall-Wells in 1933 when the firm was experiencing financial hardship at the request of a group of banks, so he was likely to be disciplined given his background.[31] And with shares concentrated in the Marshall family's hands, they were incentivized to maximize value.

The probability that these risks would impair the investment seemed low when Buffett invested. Plus, the stock was incredibly cheap, so an investor was well compensated for these risks.

Buffett's result and Marshall-Wells' demise

Buffett didn't hold the stock long, both buying and selling it in 1950, jettisoning the security at a 1% loss. However, with the company paying a $12 per share dividend that year, he may have made some money that his year-end statement didn't reflect. Buffett had a strong view of how employees should be accountable to the business's owners, and Marshall-Wells' leadership did not seem to fit the bill. Management's lackadaisical approach towards shareholders likely turned the young investor off. And he simply found other investments. At the end of 1950, Buffett owned stocks such as Parkersburg Rig & Reel and two closed-end funds: Selected Industries and U.S. & International Securities.[32]

The United States' entrance into the Korean War in 1950 prolonged the seller's market, helping Marshall-Wells earn $61.99 per share vs. $36.15 in 1949. At Buffett's purchase price of $200, the stock would trade at 1.08x EV/EBIT and a 3.23x P/E on 1950 numbers. However, the buyer's market returned in 1952 and 1953, inflicting damage upon Marshall-Wells' financial performance. As we see from Table 4, the company's sales fell in 1952, stagnated in 1953, and fell again in 1954 before returning to growth in 1955.[33]

The industry's legacy manufacturer-to-wholesaler-to-retailer system had become inefficient. Competition increased as department stores, discount houses, and mass merchandisers all sold hardware, leading to traditional hardware retailers ceding share throughout the 1950s.[34] Marshall-Wells tried replicating some of its competitors' methods, but its legacy overhead costs proved problematic.[35] Dealer-owned cooperatives and specialty wholesalers started taking substantial

Table 4: Marshall-Wells financial summary through 1956

| | 1945 | 1946 | 1947 | 1948 | 1949 | 1950 | 1951 | 1952 | 1953 | Post-Buffett investment | | |
										1954	1955	1956
Revenue	48,881	70,208	84,177	87,778	79,989	90,239	93,748	89,057	89,389	81,919	87,824	104,045
Gross profit	8,259	12,736	14,484	14,517	11,514	15,166	15,885	13,815	13,595	12,307	n/a	n/a
EBIT	3,723	6,977	7,499	6,570	3,620	6,454	5,986	4,186	3,783	3,004	2,877	2,910
Net income[1]	1,203	3,678	4,089	4,072	2,190	3,642	2,867	1,986	1,900	1,516	1,333	1,601
Earnings per share[2]	17.98	59.88	69.60	69.30	36.15	61.99	48.62	33.09	31.57	24.81	28.14	25.94
Net working capital—excluding cash	6,926	9,303	9,782	13,350	14,846	16,533	17,311	18,644	19,342	19,840	23,744	24,835
Property, plant, and equipment	4,424	4,850	5,341	5,336	5,346	5,726	5,763	6,081	6,942	6,625	6,691	8,083
Total invested capital	11,350	14,153	15,124	18,686	20,191	22,259	23,074	24,725	26,283	26,465	30,435	32,919
Days NWC	48	42	41	48	64	63	66	74	78	87	91	85
Revenue growth	8.7%	43.6%	19.9%	4.3%	-8.9%	12.8%	3.9%	-5.0%	0.4%	-8.4%	7.2%	18.5%
Gross margin	16.9%	18.1%	17.2%	16.5%	14.4%	16.8%	16.9%	15.5%	15.2%	15.0%	n/a	n/a
EBIT margin	7.6%	9.9%	8.9%	7.5%	4.5%	7.2%	6.4%	4.7%	4.2%	3.7%	3.3%	2.8%
Net income margin	2.5%	5.2%	4.9%	4.6%	2.7%	4.0%	3.1%	2.2%	2.1%	1.9%	1.5%	1.5%
Pre-tax ROIC	34.1%	54.7%	51.2%	38.9%	18.6%	30.4%	26.4%	17.5%	14.8%	11.4%	10.1%	9.2%
Post-tax ROIC	11.0%	28.8%	27.9%	24.1%	11.3%	17.2%	12.7%	8.3%	7.4%	5.7%	4.7%	5.1%

Source: *Moody's Manuals* and Marshall-Wells' annual reports. [1] Net income excludes preferred stock dividends and surplus credits and deductions. [2] Earnings available for common shareholders includes preferred stock dividends and surplus credits and deductions. Dollars figures in thousands, other than per share data.

Note: Marshall-Wells acquired Kelley-How-Thomson Co. in November 1955, which explains the 1956 revenue increase.

share, with specialty wholesalers growing from 15.5% of the market in 1948 to more than half in 1963.[ix,36] Dealer-owned cooperatives also stole share, although they were still minor players, increasing from 2.1% of hardware wholesale sales in 1948 to 6.2% in 1963.[37]

Old-line wholesalers responded to this competition by changing their product mix (often becoming specialty-line wholesalers themselves), lowering prices, and offering additional services such as prepaid freight. These changes led to this group's after-tax net profit margins declining from north of 4.0% in 1946 to 1.9% in 1953 before falling below 1.0% in 1960. Table 4 shows that Marshall-Wells did better than its peers but suffered from the same trend, with net income margins falling from 5.2% in 1946 to 2.1% in 1953. Hardware wholesalers' profits remained flat from 1946 to 1963 despite sales quadrupling. The industry's retailers were also squeezed, with profit margins falling from 4.5% in 1950 to below 1.0% in 1960.[38]

Ambrook Industries, led by Hyman Sobiloff, purchased the Marshall family's 43% stake in Marshall-Wells in May 1955, reportedly for $375 per share. Ambrook picked up additional shares in the open market to gain control.[39] Sobiloff initially had no thoughts of liquidating the company, as evidenced by Marshall-Wells' November 1955 purchase of competitor Kelley-How-Thomson, another Minnesota-based hardware wholesaler. Sobiloff planned to increase the number of dealers in the Marshall-Wells Stores Plan, expand geographically, and reach $200 million of sales by 1960.[40]

But these plans were halted as the business deteriorated, with the company earning only 5.1% on its capital in 1956, leading Ambrook to begin liquidating parts of the business. In early 1957, Ambrook sold Marshall-Wells' Canadian operations in return for a controlling interest in Barker Bros., a California furniture company. Marshall-Wells diversified, acquiring multiple companies that year. The company produced a modest loss in 1957 before losing over a million dollars in 1958.[41]

The business was then sold off in pieces once the recession hit in 1958.[42] The Duluth warehouse was closed in January 1959. While Sobiloff retained the Marshall-Wells name, he moved the offices to New York and installed

---

ix   Dealer-owned cooperatives had three key cost advantages vs. the legacy wholesalers. First, they were dealer-owned—they rebated their profits to the retailers. Second, they were not-for-profit, which meant they paid no taxes (this part would be modified in 1962, after much complaining from old-line wholesalers). Third, they were more efficient, with no costly traveling salesmen or bloated warehouse branches. These advantages led to significantly lower costs compared to the legacy players. Specialty wholesalers were smaller and more nimble than old-line wholesalers.

a banker as president. After Ambrook merged with Barker Bros., Marshall-Wells became a holding company.[43] The corporate entity continued on for a few additional years, eventually merging into Larchfield, Ambrook's successor company, in 1965.[44]

A final note on the Minnesota hardware wholesaler

Marshall-Wells was a good investment for shareholders at Buffett's purchase price; an investor would have earned a mid-to-high-teens internal rate of return (IRR) if he sold at the price Ambrook paid in 1956.[x,45] The investment is a good illustration of the value investment approach Ben Graham espoused proving effective; the hard assets offered downside protection and provided a margin of safety, allowing the investor to earn a good return despite mediocre future business performance.

The price Ambrook paid in 1955 was still cheap on 1954 asset value: 0.64x tangible book and 0.80x net current asset value, but a healthier 15.11x 1954 earnings multiple. While the $375 price was above the 1949 net current asset value per share of $331.42, it was a discount to the 1954 net current asset value. An arms-length buyer of a significant amount of the stock did not, in fact, think the stock was worth net current asset value.

Despite Marshall-Wells' stock doing well, Buffett produced a 75.8% return in 1951, 144.8% in 1954, and 29.5% annually throughout his partnership years.[46] Marshall-Wells is one of the cheapest stocks discussed in this book, but it wasn't a big winner for Buffett. Investments like this were not why Buffett did so spectacularly. As discussed in the preface and explored in detail later in this book, Buffett's biggest winners in the 1950s and 1960s usually had an extra kicker—a shift in capital allocation that drove superb returns.

Brand new competitors didn't undo the company; the specialty-line and dealer-owned wholesalers had been around for decades. Post-war shortages provided a fleeting boost to the industry, allowing everyone to do well. As the market returned to normal, competition took its toll.[47] Marshall-Wells was in a challenging strategic position; the company didn't really have an attractive path to change course. The retailers Marshall-Wells catered to needed additional services to operate their businesses more efficiently, resulting in a higher cost structure. As chain store hardware retailers became more prominent,

---

x   Marshall-Wells' stock price became increasingly hard to find after the sale, which is why the return analysis ends in 1955. Graham-Newman marked the stock at $352—below the price Ambrook paid—in January 1956. Walter Schloss said it was one of his biggest winners in 1958 but didn't provide additional details.

Marshall-Wells' customers faced an uphill battle against these price-advantaged competitors. Add in that alternative forms of wholesaling were eating away at Marshall-Wells' business, and the company was destined to struggle.[48]

Up next, we explore Greif Bros. Cooperage. Like Marshall-Wells, this barrel maker was another cheap stock. But, in contrast to Marshall-Wells, management deftly navigated challenging circumstances, facilitating a shift from a dying business to one that continues flourishing to this day.

The Greif Bros. Cooperage Corporation: 1951

"My wife and kids went back to Omaha just ahead of me. I got in the car, and on my way west checked out companies I was interested in investing in. It was due diligence. I stopped in Hazleton, Pennsylvania, to visit the Jeddo-Highland Coal Company. I visited the Kalamazoo Stove & Furnace Company in Michigan, which was being liquidated. I went to see what the building looked like, what they had for sale. I went to Delaware, Ohio, to check out Greif Bros. Cooperage. (Who knows anything about cooperage anymore?) Its chairman met with me. I didn't have appointments; I would just drop in. I found that people always talked to me. All these people helped me."

—Warren Buffett[49]

Warren wasn't the only Buffett with a connection to this barrel maker. His father, Howard, recommended the stock to Phil Carret, the head of the Pioneer fund and the author of multiple investment books, in the 1940s. Carret bought the security and would hold it for the rest of his life.

Ben Graham was a client of Buffett-Falk, and Warren would work orders for his mentor prior to joining Graham-Newman as an employee in 1954. The younger Buffett would always try and impress his professor by discussing stocks he liked. Buffett later explained his reasoning for pitching stocks by saying, "If I wanted to be starting quarterback on the Washington Redskins, I'd try to get them to watch me throw a few passes."[50] In a correspondence with his professor about an order for the Baldwin Company, Buffett mentioned Greif Bros. Cooperage as a company he thought Graham should take a look at. But before writing Graham about the company and dropping in on its chairman, Buffett bought the stock in the partnership with his father in 1951. At the end of that year, Greif was his second-largest investment, with $3,650 allocated to the position (see Table 1). Buffett, who went out into the world to perform proprietary research rather than just depend on the documents,

Table 1: Warren Buffett's portfolio at the end of 1951

	Shares	Price	Value	Percent of total assets
Buffett-Falk & Co.			$292.63	1.18%
Dividends receivable			140.00	0.56%
Government Employees Insurance	350	$37.50	13,125.00	52.74%
Timely Clothes	200	$13.00	2,600.00	10.45%
Baldwin Co.	100	$22.00	2,200.00	8.84%
Greif Brothers Cooperage "A"	200	$18.25	3,650.00	14.67%
Des Moines Railway 5's - 1955			330.00	1.33%
Thorp Corp	200	$12.75	2,550.00	10.25%
Total			$24,887.63	
Less: bank loan			($5,000.00)	
Less: loss on Cleveland Worsted Mills	25	$95.00	($150.00)	
NET ASSETS			$19,737.63	
Net increment in investment account			$9,933.93	
Less: capital additions			(2,500.00)	
Net gain from investments			$7,433.93	
12/31/1950 Net assets			$9,803.70	
Percentage gain on 12/31/50 net assets			75.8%	

Source: Kilpatrick, A. (2020). *Of Permanent Value: The Story of Warren Buffett.*

spent hours chatting about barrels with a worker who ran a Greif outpost to better understand the business.[51]

Cooperage, the company's primary source of income in 1950, is the business of manufacturing wooden staves, headings, barrels, and kegs. Greif Bros. called itself 'The Largest Cooperage Company in the World' in the early 1900s, a label that likely remained true when Buffett bought the stock. However, cooperage was a declining industry throughout the 20th century, as alternative containers started stealing share.[52] And it was clear that this trend would continue.

While the stock was inexpensive, Greif's success in transitioning away from cooperage was still in doubt. While company leadership responded proactively to the decline in its legacy business, the outlook for its alternative container products was cloudy. Yet, Buffett liked the company enough to buy the stock and pitch it to his idol. Let's see what the young investor liked about this barrel-maker.

The history of Greif Bros.

William Greif and Albert Vanderwyst founded the Cleveland-based Vanderwyst and Greif in 1877. William's three brothers—Charles, Louis, and Thomas—joined the small cooperage shop shortly after its formation.[53] Cooperage was fueled by the growth of the sugar refining and petroleum industries, with the two accounting for about half the cooperage trade at the turn of the century.[54] The company prospered and became the world's largest cooperage in the early 1900s.

There were two classes of barrels in the cooperage industry: tight and slack. Tight barrels were made to hold liquid, such as whiskey and beer, while slack barrels were used to store dry products, such as sugar, flour, fruit, and vegetables.[55] Cooperages typically specialized in one or the other because they each had different customer bases and wood requirements. They were often located in major towns to be close to their customers. Slack cooperage demand was more fragmented than tight cooperage, and therefore had a more diverse customer base. While most of the industry was tight cooperage, Greif focused on slack, with the company having the most slack capacity of any player. The cooperage industry had grown increasingly concentrated over time, with the top four companies' share of total production increasing from 26% in 1935 to 47% in 1947.[56]

John Raible acquired control of the company from the Greif brothers in 1913. Raible was a wealthy investor, not terribly interested in the cooperage business. But his leadership was valuable, helping the company grow revenue from $1 million when he took over to $10 million when he took Greif public in 1926. But Raible's reign came to an end in 1947, undone by a fellow board member. John Dempsey, an accountant in his early 30s, had joined the firm as a director and company secretary in 1946. After Raible tried to buy shares held by Dempsey's wife and mother-in-law at a price the young accountant thought too cheap, Dempsey accumulated enough voting shares to take control of the company. Dempsey, claiming to be motivated by Raible calling Greif 'my wood company,' purchased over 50% of the voting shares and made himself chairman.[57]

But cooperage was a dying business when Dempsey took over. Some commodities, such as nails, small hardware, and gunpowder, were still shipped in coopered containers due to a lack of acceptable substitutes. However, most of the container industry was shifting away from cooperage. Large cloth and paper sacks, fiber, steel, and aluminum drums and barrels were all taking share from cooperage barrels and kegs.[58] While 1950 had been a decent year for the industry, with output increasing and capacity utilization rising, the long-term trends were clearly negative.[59]

Fortunately for Greif, John Dempsey didn't sit idle while the industry's decay eroded profits. He was already shifting the company away from cooperage and into other container products, such as cartons, wire products, and steel and fiber drums. Table 2 shows that Greif was consistently profitable and earned a good return on invested capital in the decade prior to Buffett's purchase. While the company's revenue and net income had fallen from their 1947 highs, they generally grew over the prior decade. And while it was unclear how successful this transition would be, Greif already possessed the necessary customer relationships from its cooperage business. These buyers still needed containers for their products. End demand for container products was, in fact, growing: It seemed like Greif's odds of succeeding were good.

Barreling ahead to valuation

Greif had a quirk in its share structure that presented a valuation challenge. The company had two shares of stock, Class A and Class B, but only the A shares were publicly traded. The B shares were closely held and not exchange-traded. Like most companies with dual-class share structures, they had differing voting rights.

Unlike most companies with dual-class share structures, the classes were entitled to differing dividend distributions and liquidation proceeds. The A shares—the class Buffett bought—had first rights to liquidation proceeds and dividends. Plus, the A shares were entitled to cumulative dividends while the B shares were not. The A shares would only gain voting rights if the company failed to pay the A's entitled dividend for four quarters. However, the Class B shares received a higher split of additional dividends once the distribution exceeded a certain rate. This made calculating market capitalization figures difficult since there was no price readily available for the Class B shares.

Fortunately, the asset valuation was relatively simple. The A shares had priority payment until they received $12.50 per share. Then the B shares got the next $12.50. After that, each class shared equally. Since the company's net current asset value and tangible book exceeded these thresholds, the two could be viewed equally on a per-share basis when analyzing the company through the assets, putting the net current asset value per share at $20.47 and the tangible

Table 2: Greif 10-year financial summary

Fiscal year ending October 31; dollar figures in thousands.	1941	1942	1943	1944	1945	1946	1947	1948	1949	1950	10-year CAGR
Revenue	16,056	22,258	25,826	27,254	26,059	26,077	31,731	28,505	26,891	29,351	9.9%
Gross profit	2,836	5,209	5,063	5,036	3,567	3,495	6,227	4,628	4,540	5,370	11.7%
EBIT	1,716	3,832	3,525	3,323	1,971	1,847	3,465	1,815	1,760	2,529	11.7%
Net income	815	849	478	577	718	1,156	2,024	1,277	1,215	1,625	8.5%
Net working capital—excluding cash	3,908	2,897	2,414	3,305	3,236	4,476	4,750	5,960	4,912	4,486	2.6%
Property, plant, and equipment	2,709	3,091	3,607	3,428	3,259	3,921	5,017	5,351	5,124	5,234	9.9%
Total invested capital	6,617	5,989	6,021	6,733	6,494	8,397	9,766	11,311	10,037	9,720	5.9%
Days NWC	84	56	38	38	46	54	53	69	74	58	
Revenue growth	41.2%	38.6%	16.0%	5.5%	-4.4%	0.1%	21.7%	-10.2%	-5.7%	9.1%	
Gross margin	17.7%	23.4%	19.6%	18.5%	13.7%	13.4%	19.6%	16.2%	16.9%	18.3%	
EBIT margin	10.7%	17.2%	13.7%	12.2%	7.6%	7.1%	10.9%	6.4%	6.5%	8.6%	
Net income margin	5.1%	3.8%	1.9%	2.1%	2.8%	4.4%	6.4%	4.5%	4.5%	5.5%	
Pre-tax ROIC	28.3%	60.8%	58.7%	52.1%	29.8%	24.8%	38.2%	17.2%	16.5%	25.6%	
Post-tax ROIC	18.8%	46.2%	45.7%	40.9%	25.8%	17.6%	22.5%	11.4%	11.3%	16.0%	

Source: The Greif Bros. Cooperage Corporation annual reports and author's calculations.

book value per share at $39.60. With the A shares trading at $18.25 at the end of 1951, the stock traded at a slight discount to the company's net current asset value but at more than a 50% discount to its tangible book value.[60]

As Table 3 lays out, most of the assets were current assets. While holding inventory in a declining industry might be cause for concern, Greif only had around two and a half months of inventory on hand, so this was a reasonably safe asset.

Table 3: Asset composition

	1950	%
Cash	2,966	16.8%
U.S. government savings notes	1,322	7.5%
Trade notes and accounts receivables	2,358	13.3%
Inventories	4,652	26.3%
Total current assets	11,298	63.9%
Property, plant, and equipment	5,234	29.6%
Investments and other assets	234	1.3%
Insurance fund	769	4.4%
Intangibles	2	0.0%
Prepaid insurance	134	0.8%
Total assets	17,672	100.0%

(Dollars in thousands)

Source: The Greif Bros. Cooperage Corporation annual reports.

The most significant individual component of assets—property, plant, and equipment—included 239 manufacturing plants, 11 divisional offices, timber tracts, and logging equipment.[61] With the firm transitioning away from the cooperage business, the legacy plant and equipment would become less valuable over time. The company, in fact, was closing down mills and assembly shops.[62] While these buildings and machinery might not be worth much, 44.2% of the property, plant, and equipment line item came from valuable timber properties that would undoubtedly retain value as the container industry gravitated towards fiber drums and boxes that would make use of the wood.[63] Even if one were to write the buildings and machinery down to zero, the stock was still selling at more than a 40% discount to tangible book value.

But the attractiveness of the balance sheet numbers wasn't all the stock had going for it. When Buffett wrote to Graham about Greif, he said:

> You might be interested in checking into the Greif Brothers Cooperage Company. The "A" stock is traded on the Midwest Stock Exchange and, since we are not members, you would want to buy it through your regular broker. It looks like a situation where there is plenty of value in excess of market price. The chairman of the board died a year or two back and the company bought in about 30% of the total stock outstanding. This had the effect of raising the book value about $12.40 in one year on the "A" stock which sells around 17. You would also find it interesting to check the prices on slack barrels, steel, etc. at the time the company went on "Lifo" accounting compared with present cost price.[64]

The 21-year-old Buffett noted not only that the company had bought back a lot of stock, but that Greif's balance sheet understated the value of its inventory as a result of prices rising since the company adopted LIFO accounting in 1942.[xi] Buffett did get one detail incorrect: Raible, the *former* chairman, died in 1948, but Dempsey had already usurped him in that role by then.[65]

Valuing the company on an earnings basis was a bit more challenging because of the discrepancy in dividend rights between the share classes. The Class A shares were entitled to annual cumulative dividends of $0.80. The B shares were entitled to noncumulative dividends of up to $0.40 each year. Additional distributions above these rates were to be split 60–40 in favor of the B shares.[66] Each class had its pluses and minuses, but with the A shares receiving most of the distributions—$0.90 to the B's $0.55—in 1950, they were worth more at the time.

Furthermore, it would be great for the Class A shares if the B shares ever got more than them. The A shares would receive an additional $0.70 per share for the two classes to share in the distributions equally on a per-share basis. And while Greif was paying above the entitled $0.80 per share on the A shares in fiscal 1950, the company wasn't paying out all of its income to shareholders. If Greif distributed all of its $1.6 million 1950 net income, the Class B shares would receive the majority of the dividends. In this case, the B shares would be getting paid more—but the A shares would be sporting more than a 20% yield at the 1951 year-end price.

---

xi   LIFO (Last in, first out) inventory accounting results in lower valuations when prices increase compared to average-cost or FIFO (first in, first out) accounting. FIFO typically more accurately reflects the actual movement of inventory, meaning the inventory values on the balance sheet could be understated under LIFO accounting.

However, the specific valuation for the Class B shares didn't really matter—the stock was insanely cheap on all earnings multiples regardless of the value assigned to the B shares. Table 4 lays out the valuation metrics on three bases, from lowest to highest, which values the B shares on a per-share basis at:

- The same discount as the per-share dividend discrepancy in 1950 (38.9%).

- Equal value.

- 50% higher, the highest amount it could get.[xii]

Table 4: Earnings-based valuation metrics

	Market Cap	Enterprise Value	1950		5-year average		10-year average	
			EV/EBIT	P/E	EV/EBIT	P/E	EV/EBIT	P/E
B's discounted(1)	4,970	2,738	1.08x	3.06x	1.20x	3.41x	1.06x	4.63x
A and B shares equal(2)	6,078	3,847	1.52x	3.74x	1.68x	4.16x	1.49x	5.66x
B shares 50% higher	7,504	5,272	2.08x	4.62x	2.31x	5.14x	2.04x	6.99x

Source: *Moody's Manuals* and The Greif Bros. Cooperage Corporation annual reports. (1) B shares valued at a 38.9% discount to the A's (to match the dividend discrepancy between the A's and B's). (2) A and B shares valued equivalently. Dollar figures in thousands.

Seeing this valuation, it becomes clear why Buffett bought into Greif. There was downside protection through the assets—the company would fetch more in a liquidation than it sold for in the stock market—and was trading at ridiculously cheap multiples on earnings.

(Fiber) drumming along

With Dempsey transitioning Greif away from cooperage and into other container products, the most salient risk was that Greif wouldn't be able to replace the earnings of the cooperage business. After Buffett's purchase, the assault on cooperage continued, with Greif's slack barrel sales falling by more than half from 1947 to 1952. Dempsey was clear-eyed about the trends and converted, sold, and dismantled idle facilities, and continued investing in alternative container products. Table 5 shows that Greif's transition was

---

xii   The initial dividend discrepancy meant that it would never quite reach 50%, of course. In 1953, the company would buy some of the Class B shares at $12.50 per share, below the range for the A shares that year of $15.13–$19.00, supporting the idea that the A shares were worth more at the time.

Table 5: Greif's performance after Buffett's investment

	1950	1951	1952	1953	1954	1955	1956	1957	1958	1959	1960	10-Year CAGR
Revenue	29,351	34,435	29,420	31,278	28,086	31,921	37,458	38,217	34,941	40,507	42,797	3.8%
Gross profit	5,370	6,706	4,904	4,743	4,459	4,911	6,058	6,111	6,317	7,599	7,407	3.3%
EBIT	2,529	2,982	1,596	1,403	1,343	1,713	2,651	2,566	2,840	3,760	2,974	1.6%
Net income	1,625	1,241	1,140	912	932	1,123	1,700	1,538	1,638	2,426	1,742	0.7%
Net working capital—excluding cash	4,486	5,452	5,150	5,081	3,455	4,191	5,589	7,278	6,411	5,837	7,421	5.2%
Property, plant, and equipment	5,234	5,840	5,085	4,018	3,980	4,026	4,677	5,516	5,930	7,001	7,850	4.1%
Total invested capital	9,720	11,292	10,235	9,098	7,435	8,217	10,266	12,793	12,341	12,838	15,271	4.6%
Days NWC	58	53	66	60	55	44	48	61	71	55	57	
Revenue growth	9.1%	17.3%	-14.6%	6.3%	-10.2%	13.7%	17.3%	2.0%	-8.6%	15.9%	5.7%	
Gross margin	18.3%	19.5%	16.7%	15.2%	15.9%	15.4%	16.2%	16.0%	18.1%	18.8%	17.3%	
EBIT margin	8.6%	8.7%	5.4%	4.5%	4.8%	5.4%	7.1%	6.7%	8.1%	9.3%	6.9%	
Net income margin	5.5%	3.6%	3.9%	2.9%	3.3%	3.5%	4.5%	4.0%	4.7%	6.0%	4.1%	
Pre-tax ROIC	25.6%	28.4%	14.8%	14.5%	16.2%	21.9%	28.7%	22.3%	22.6%	29.9%	21.2%	
Post-tax ROIC	16.0%	14.2%	9.0%	9.4%	11.3%	14.4%	18.4%	13.3%	13.0%	19.3%	12.4%	
Class A stock price—high	$13.50	$19.50	$19.50	$19.00	$25.00	$30.50	$39.00	$42.50	$52.00	$58.50	$66.50	17.3%
Class A stock price—low	$11.00	$13.38	$15.00	$15.13	$16.00	$24.50	$30.00	$34.13	$35.00	$50.00	$56.25	17.7%
Class A stock price—midpoint	$12.25	$16.44	$17.25	$17.06	$20.50	$27.50	$34.50	$38.31	$43.50	$54.25	$61.38	17.5%
Class A dividends per share	$1.10	$1.10	$0.90	$0.90	$0.90	$1.00	$1.20	$1.60	$1.60	$1.90	$1.80	
Class B dividends per share	$0.85	$0.55	$0.25	$0.55	$0.55	$0.55	$1.00	$1.60	$1.60	$0.40	$1.90	

Source: *Moody's Manuals* and The Greif Bros. Cooperage Corporation annual reports. Dollar figures in thousands except stock price data. Financial data is for the fiscal year ending October 31; stock price and dividend data is for the calendar years.[xiii]

xiii   Eagle-eyed readers will note that the dividends differ from the aforementioned split for the Class A and Class B shares in some years—this is simply due to the timing of payments, as this dividend per share data is for the calendar year while Greif had an October fiscal year end. The dividends aligned with the stated distribution on a fiscal year basis.

successful, with the company producing record sales and profits in 1959.[67] The historical customer relationships from the cooperage business made the shift far easier than it would have been for an entrant starting from scratch. And the company's former secretary did a tremendous job steering the ship.

While Buffett's sale activity isn't known, he kept tabs on the company for years. Not only did he buy the stock and write to Graham about it in 1951, but he dropped in on the company and met John Dempsey after leaving Graham-Newman in 1956.[68]

Dempsey's intervention led to the company's successful shift away from the legacy cooperage business and into alternative containers. As of this writing in 2023, Greif continues as a leader in industrial packaging products and services, trading on the New York Stock Exchange with a $3.4 billion market capitalization.

Nevertheless, this wasn't a gigantic winner for Buffett. Even if he top-ticked the sale in 1956, he would have earned around a 20% annual return on the investment from year-end 1951, including dividends.[xiv] In contrast, he would earn 144.8% in 1954 and later compound capital at 29.5% throughout his partnership years.[69]

Phil Carret, the money manager who bought the stock on Howard Buffett's recommendation in 1946, owned it all the way to his passing at the age of 101 in 1998. Carret grew to admire Greif, calling it the best-managed company he knew of. Buffett would later call Carret a hero of his. Greif was a successful investment for Carret, as the stock went from a split-adjusted $0.68 when he bought it to $36.50 when he passed.[70]

Around the same time he invested in Greif, Buffett bought Cleveland Worsted Mills, another net-net. Its business, too, was under severe pressure. But the company's leadership took a different approach than Dempsey, and would infuriate Buffett in the process.

---

xiv   He may have bought the stock earlier in the year when it was trading a little cheaper, so his return could have been a bit better than this.

Cleveland Worsted Mills: 1952

"I called it Cleveland's Worst Mill after they cut off paying the dividend."

—*Warren Buffett*[71]

Buffett's thesis on Cleveland Worsted Mills was straightforward. The stock sold for below its net current asset value and at a bargain P/E multiple. The worsted manufacturer was consistently profitable and paid a fat dividend. By 1952, having graduated from Columbia and now an employee at Buffett-Falk, Buffett liked the stock enough to write a brief report on it, stating, "The $8 dividend provides a well-protected 7% yield on the current price of approximately $115."[72]

The stock had been cheap for some time. Buffett, in fact, had held the stock in 1951, selling at a slight loss as he invested his capital in companies like GEICO and Timely Clothes. Ben Graham also liked the stock, having made the Cleveland firm a 1.5% position in the Graham-Newman fund and including the company in the 1951 edition of *Security Analysis* in a table titled "Six Common Stocks Undervalued in 1949," along with Marshall-Wells.[73]

Despite the obvious cheapness, the investment did not work out the way Buffett anticipated. In a move that surprised him, Cleveland Worsted Mills slashed its dividend in half. Buffett was distraught—not only did he own the stock personally, he had advised clients to buy it, too—and his frustration prompted him to take a trip to Cleveland to figure out what happened.[xv]

---

xv   Readers should note that your author has a tinge of anxiety in selecting 1952 as the analytical year for Buffett's purchase. A footnote in *The Snowball* states Buffett's memo on Cleveland Worsted Mills was dated September 19, 1952, although some of the facts seem to better fit a 1951 publication. Buffett's year-end 1951 statement shows he sold the stock that year. However, he did experience the pain of the dividend cut, which happened in 1954. The thesis would remain the same whether I'm a year early or late, however. Years prior to deciding to write this book, I asked Buffett for the memorandum but was told that the document was not readily available.

History of the Cleveland Worsted Mills Company

Cleveland Worsted Mills manufactured woolen and worsted yarn and cloth. At its peak, the company was the second largest worsted manufacturer in the United States. The textile firm sold its products to factories that turned the merchandise into ready-to-wear clothing. These manufacturers then sent the apparel to retail stores, who were responsible for selling it to the end customer. The company's largest customers included other Cleveland-based firms, such as Joseph & Feiss and Richman Brothers. The latter had its own chain of clothing stores and counted on Cleveland Worsted Mills as one of its major suppliers.[74]

The firm's journey began in 1878 when Joseph Turner and his sons leased a cotton mill in Kent, Ohio. Turner had been part-owner of an alpaca mill in Jamestown, New York, but moved to Ohio thinking the Midwest was a less competitive market than the more established eastern state. While the construction of railroads helped form a national distribution system, the woolen textile industry was still a regional trade. Turner realized that Ohio's quality delaine wool and rapid urbanization would provide a suitable raw material source and ample customer base for his young firm.

Unfortunately, Joseph did not live long enough to see his vision play out, passing two short years after the company's founding. His sons Joshua and John took control of the business and incorporated the firm as Joseph Turner and Sons Manufacturing. The Turner heirs wisely introduced worsted cloth to the product line. Worsted fabric had become popular in the early 1870s as style-conscious customers enjoyed the weave pattern and finish. Technological innovations, tariff protection, and changes in fashion trends helped the industry blossom. Worsteds would surpass woolens as the most essential branch of fabric production by the end of the 20th century.[75]

After a contract dispute with the owner of their original mill, the Turners chose to relocate from Kent to Cleveland in 1889. The mill thrived in these early days and added employees and plant to meet expanding demand. However, the company used debt to fund this growth. The Panic of 1893 wreaked havoc on the nation's economy, leading to the company missing its debt payments. Lender banks seized control of the business and installed their own management to fix the company. An employee of one of the lenders, Oliver Stafford, assumed the presidency in 1894.

While the Turners continued on as executives, the banks thwarted the brothers' decisions. Frustrated at constantly being overruled, they resigned. Bank executives reorganized the firm and changed its name to Turner Worsted Company, reflecting the fact that its principal product was now worsted cloth.

The change in ownership helped the firm blossom into one of the largest worsted manufacturing operations in the country. Instead of penny-pinching or selling off assets, as many debt holders would be inclined to do, the banks expanded capacity and diversified the company's product line. With the firm having relocated to Cleveland and the Turners no longer involved in the company, the banks saw fit to change the name to Cleveland Worsted Mills.[76]

During World War I, increased demand required textile firms to substantially raise output by increasing the production schedule. After the war, the mills continued this practice, leading to an oversupply of goods and a textile depression. In contrast to the general prosperity of American business, the textile industry struggled throughout the 1920s. The increased efficiency that allowed firms to meet wartime needs resulted in overproduction when demand fell.[77]

The appeal of heavy woolen clothing, such as worsted, declined during the 1920s as automobiles and central heating shifted consumers to lighter fabrics. Men's suits became slimmer and vestless, while women's outfits became less strict and more revealing, reducing the demand for heavy woolen clothing. Excess capacity and falling demand led to a textile depression in the 1920s. By the end of the decade, there was enough machinery to produce three times as much fabric as there was demand for.[78]

Cleveland Worsted Mills was not immune to the industry's general malaise. A regime change engineered by Louis Poss would alter the course of the company. Its president, Oliver Stafford, once served as Poss's Sunday school teacher. After Poss had experienced success owning and managing a couple of businesses, Stafford appointed him to the boards of his companies, including Cleveland Worsted Mills in 1917. After the older Stafford passed in 1929, his son became president. While the company's largest owners were the families of Poss, Stafford, and Hodgson (Cleveland Worsted Mills' chairman), Poss didn't own enough stock to engineer a takeover himself. He had to build credibility with shareholders through his work as company vice president, where he embarked on an aggressive cost-cutting initiative. By consolidating facilities and abandoning unprofitable mills, he garnered sufficient stockholder support to seize the presidency in 1931.[79]

Despite stealing the company from his mentor's son, the new leader's control proved excellent for the firm. When Poss took charge, the company had excess inventory. Instead of selling this supply, Poss wisely hung on to it and had ample product on hand when the market improved in 1935. Cleveland Worsted Mills capitalized on rising prices as the economy recovered from the bottom of the Great Depression.[80] World War II also helped boost profits as worsted demand skyrocketed. While Poss abhorred President Roosevelt's interventionalist policies and focused on producing goods not regulated by the government, the company benefited as orders for military uniforms increased the need for worsteds.[81]

After World War II, the company was in a position to launch a capital improvement plan in 1947. The plant needed refreshment as wartime restrictions prevented the company from replacing its equipment, prompting Poss to allocate $2.7 million towards new machinery from 1947 through 1950. This modernization plan helped reassert Cleveland Worsted Mills' prominence within the industry, with one writer remarking that the company had the most modernly equipped textile plant in the nation once the efforts were complete. 1950 seemed to be the beginning of a promising decade.[82]

Why did Buffett buy Cleveland Worsted Mills?

Buffett's 1952 memo on Cleveland Worsted Mills mentioned that the stock traded below net current asset value and had "several well-equipped mills."[83] He thought the company had ample earnings to cover the dividend, a view supported by the summary financials found in Table 1. The company paid $8.00 a share out to shareholders, and the last year the company earned below this figure was 1945.[xvi]

The income and return on capital figures were a little concerning. Like Marshall-Wells in the first chapter, Cleveland Worsted Mills was coming off the post-World War II highs and falling back to earth, earning a respectable but not extraordinary return on invested capital in 1951. Worsted was a commodity product, with shortages the sole reason for the company's previously rising income and returns on capital. As the market normalized, the company was unlikely to earn above-average returns on capital in the future.

But the company didn't need to produce superior returns for the stock to do well. Average returns would still provide shareholders with a quality result. Despite competition from foreign and southern mills, Cleveland Worsted Mills seemed well-positioned when Buffett pitched the stock in 1952, with the company having just completed its modernization plan.

And the valuation, as Table 2 illustrates, was exceptionally attractive. Every valuation metric was appealing. The thesis was straightforward: The stock sold in a range of $84 and $100 in 1952 and had net current assets of $149.05 per share and tangible book value of $184.69 per share at the end of 1951. The earnings metrics were also tantalizing: The company traded for 1.91x EV/1951 EBIT and only a 5.15x P/E. The company paid its stockholders a hefty dividend, with a

---

xvi   The company did not report revenue in its annual reports. An employee later said 1951 sales were $29 million, which would have resulted in a 16.6% operating margin.

Table 1: Cleveland Worsted Mills summary financials

	1942	1943	1944	1945	1946	1947	1948	1949	1950	1951
Gross profit	4,259	4,951	4,438	3,262	6,692	8,324	9,871	5,523	7,567	6,082
Operating profit	3,393	3,999	3,561	2,595	5,790	7,295	8,603	4,187	6,025	4,802
Net income	994	1,146	1,005	686	3,458	4,560	5,379	2,608	3,569	2,415
Earnings per share	7.20	8.31	7.28	4.97	25.06	33.04	39.19	19.08	26.30	17.88
Dividends per share	1.00	1.00	1.50	2.00	6.00	6.00	7.50	8.00	8.00	8.00
Dividend payout ratio	13.9%	12.0%	20.6%	40.3%	23.9%	18.2%	19.2%	42.0%	30.5%	44.8%
Pre-tax ROIC	55.7%	74.4%	68.3%	39.9%	67.1%	68.1%	62.0%	26.4%	32.9%	22.4%
Post-tax ROIC	51.1%	21.2%	63.0%	35.7%	41.7%	42.3%	38.5%	16.4%	19.2%	11.2%
Net working capital—excluding cash	3,712	2,338	3,404	4,822	7,258	8,518	12,719	11,745	17,315	16,867
Property, plant, and equipment	2,376	2,319	2,369	2,427	2,745	2,894	3,611	3,642	3,895	4,786
Total invested capital	6,088	4,658	5,773	7,249	10,003	11,412	16,330	15,388	21,210	21,652

Source: Cleveland Worsted Mills annual reports and *Moody's Manuals*. Dollar figures in thousands.

Table 2: Cleveland Worsted Mills valuation metrics

	Market Capitalization	Enterprise Value	EV/EBIT		P/E		P/NCAV	P/TB
			1951	5-year average	1951	5-year average		
Cleveland Worsted Mills	12,428	9,161	1.91x	1.48x	5.15x	3.35x	0.62x	0.50x

Source: *Moody's Manuals* and Cleveland Worsted Mills annual reports. Dollar figures in thousands. Market capitalization and enterprise value figures are calculated using the midpoint of the stock's high and low prices in 1952.[xvii]

yield north of 8.7% at the midpoint of the stock's 1952 high and low. With a payout ratio below 50%, the dividend seemed safe.

The dividend cut

Unfortunately, the low payout ratio proved illusory. The company's fortunes were deteriorating as Buffett bought the stock, with earnings per share falling 71.7% to $5.05 in 1952. The company had to dip into the cash on its balance sheet to maintain the $8.00 per share distribution. While 1953 was a little better, with earnings increasing to $5.91 per share, it was still not enough to cover the dividend. But the business imploded in 1954, leading to the company cutting its dividend in half that year as net income fell to a minuscule $0.45 per share.

Buffett, who bought the stock himself and got his clients to buy it, was aggravated at the dividend cut, prompting him to go to the annual meeting:

> I went to an annual meeting of Cleveland's Worst Mill, and I flew all the way to Cleveland. I got there about five minutes late, and the meeting had been adjourned. And here I was, this kid from Omaha, twenty-two years old, with my own money in the stock. The chairman said, "Sorry, too late." But then their sales agent, who was on the board of directors, actually took pity on me, and so he got me off on the side and talked to me and answered some questions.[84]

The stock plummeted to as low as $60 per share in 1954, well below the $84 and $100 range the stock traded in 1952. It's unclear whether Buffett sold the stock at this point. Judging by his frustration, he probably did. But shareholders who held on would be richly rewarded.

---

xvii   During 1952, the stock traded between $84 and $100, a tight range.

Poss liquidates

Cleveland Worsted Mills workers chose to strike in August 1955, seeking higher pay and a union contract. Poss thought the 1954 earnings were the beginning of a negative trend, with the shift to synthetic fibers and low-cost competitors dimming the business' prospects. On December 31, 1955, Poss announced he intended to liquidate, with shareholders solidifying the plan in a vote the following month.[85]

The liquidation was wildly successful for shareholders. In 1957, the company sent $185.00 per share to shareholders, exceeding the $178.05 of tangible book value at the end of 1955. Some additional payments trickled through over the following years, with $10.00 sent in 1959, $3.00 in 1960, and $0.63 in 1961, totaling $198.63 of liquidating distributions.[86] A holder who purchased the security at the midpoint of the 1952 range would have earned a 21.0% IRR through the end of the liquidation.

Someone who bought the stock after the 1954 dividend cut would have done even better, earning around a 50% annual return. Seventy-six-year-old Poss, who owned about 22% of the company and had other business interests, had no need to carry on. Making the financially rational decision for the company was easy for him, as he was aligned with shareholders and had no need to collect a salary from the company. Cleveland Worsted Mills was selling a commodity product whose demand was falling due to alternative products. Plus, the company was competing against southern and foreign mills that were more cost competitive. Fortunately, the company possessed valuable buildings and high-quality equipment, such as weaving machines and looms, that it could sell. The newer equipment was sold to firms in West Germany, while the older equipment was sold to companies in Mexico and Argentina.[87]

Despite Buffett's frustrations, Cleveland Worsted Mills worked out really well for shareholders. The young stockbroker, of course, made an analytical error when he thought the dividend was secure. But he was right about the company's assets being worth much more than what the company was selling for in the market.

The company had traded at a discount to net current assets and tangible book value for some time, as Table 3 demonstrates. But the stock had done well in the years prior to Buffett's purchase, nearly doubling from 1947 to 1951 at the midpoint of the range for each year while paying out $37.50 per share in dividends over this period. As the stagnant P/NCAV and P/TB multiples illustrate, the stock performed well over this period because the company generated substantial earnings, not because of asset-based multiple expansion.[xviii] Cleveland Worsted Mills produced $18.5 million of profit during the five years ending in 1951, more than the company's market capitalization at any point over this period, which fluctuated between $6.3 million and $17.4 million.

Table 3: Historical valuation metrics

	1947	1948	1949	1950	1951	1952
P/NCAV	0.65x	0.68x	0.53x	0.64x	0.75x	0.64x
P/TB	0.53x	0.55x	0.44x	0.53x	0.61x	0.51x
P/E	1.76x	1.99x	3.51x	3.52x	6.26x	18.21x
EV/EBIT	0.59x	0.89x	0.88x	1.68x	2.47x	4.78x
Dividend Yield	10.3%	9.6%	11.9%	8.6%	7.1%	8.7%
High stock price	70.00	96.00	78.00	109.00	129.00	100.00
Low stock price	46.00	60.00	56.00	76.00	95.00	84.00
Average	58.00	78.00	67.00	92.50	112.00	92.00

Source: *Moody's Manuals*, Cleveland Worsted Mills annual report, and author's calculations. Multiples and dividend yields are calculated using the midpoint of the stock price range.

The company plowed this income into the business, increasing invested capital by $11.6 million from year-end 1946 to 1951. ($5.1 million of dividends were paid from 1947 to 1951, and the rest of the income was used to build up cash and for other small items.) And that capital was now earning much less than it did in the 1940s, with returns falling to single digits in 1952 and 1953 and then below 1% in 1954. The 1955 strike led to the property plant and equipment sitting idle and the firm's operations losing money (a tax credit put the income statement in the black, but operating income was negative).

In Berkshire Hathaway's 1989 letter, Buffett talked about some mistakes he had made. The first one he listed was the purchase of another textile manufacturing company, Berkshire Hathaway. He wrote,

> If you buy a stock at a sufficiently low price, there will usually be some hiccup in the fortunes of the business that gives you a chance to unload at a decent profit, even though the long-term performance of the business may be terrible. I call this the "cigar butt" approach to investing. A

---

xviii   With net income falling from $4.6 million in 1947 to $0.7 million in 1952, earnings-based multiples were bound to increase even if the stock didn't rise.

cigar butt found on the street that has only one puff left in it may not offer much of a smoke, but the "bargain purchase" will make that puff all profit.

Unless you are a liquidator, that kind of approach to buying businesses is foolish. First, the original "bargain" price probably will not turn out to be such a steal after all. In a difficult business, no sooner is one problem solved than another surfaces—never is there just one cockroach in the kitchen. Second, any initial advantage you secure will be quickly eroded by the low return that the business earns. For example, if you buy a business for $8 million that can be sold or liquidated for $10 million and promptly take either course, you can realize a high return. But the investment will disappoint if the business is sold for $10 million in ten years and in the interim has annually earned and distributed only a few percent on cost. Time is the friend of the wonderful business, the enemy of the mediocre.[88]

Cleveland Worsted Mills is a perfect example of a liquidation working out well. The company could have meandered along, trying to earn a mediocre return in a competitive business, but the company chose to close up shop instead. Shareholders were lucky to have Poss at the helm (workers, not so much). He was a significant shareholder and didn't have the patience to deal with striking employees. He shut down, liquidated, and provided shareholders with a good return.

Early in his journey as a business analyst, Buffett made the mistake of thinking the current level of Cleveland Worsted Mills' earnings was sustainable. The gross margins tightened as competition increased. As a commodity textile business up against cost-advantaged competitors, the company would not generate a good return on invested capital—especially as demand for worsteds fell.

Around the time Cleveland Worsted Mills was cutting the dividend, Buffett was buying the Union Street Railway. This bus company was selling for less than the cash on its balance sheet. It was another cheap stock. But Buffett had to work hard to accumulate shares. And he would visit management after doing so. This New Bedford-based company would offer the young investor valuable insight into how influencing corporate policies can impact shareholder returns.

Union Street Railway: 1954

"The ordinary type of 'horseless carriage' is at present a luxury for the wealthy, and although its price will probably fall in the future, it will never, of course, come into as common use as the bicycle."

—*The Literary Digest, 1899*[89]

Warren Buffett initially purchased Union Street Railway's stock from Graham-Newman while he was still working as a stockbroker in Omaha. A minor mistake led Graham's firm to reject the order for the security. Since Buffett found the stock cheap, he kept it for himself.

Union Street Railway was a New Bedford, Massachusetts-based bus company. With the equity trading below the net cash on the company's balance sheet, Union Street was a classic net-net when Buffett bought the stock. This was a small, thinly traded company with a market capitalization below $1 million. The small float meant acquiring stock required a bit of work and persistence by the young, enterprising investor.

Like the other stocks discussed so far, it was cheap. But in contrast to the previous investments discussed in this book, this one was actually losing money at the time of Buffett's purchase. Yet this stock would be a huge winner for Buffett, yielding him a dollar profit worth more than 4.5x the average household yearly income at the time. After accumulating a meaningful stake in the company, Buffett took a trip to Massachusetts to meet with the company's president. While he did not run a proxy contest or take aggressive action to prompt a capital return, the company paid a substantial dividend shortly after his visit.[90] Union Street Railway was an early lesson in how positive changes in capital allocation can lead to windfall profits.

From horses to streetcars to buses

The New Bedford & Fairhaven Street Railway had commenced horsecar service in 1872. The young firm thrived as New Bedford's population grew and the city's textile industry developed. Unfortunately, this success attracted competition, and the Acushnet Street Railway was formed in 1884. The two companies realized the city of New Bedford was too small for both to thrive independently, so they merged to create the Union Street Railway Company in 1887.[91]

Electric street railway lines started popping up across America after the first successful system began operating in Richmond in 1888.[92] Union Street Railway started running electric lines two years later over the objections of many New Bedford residents (including the city's mayor) who worried that the electric lines would scare horses and lead to accidents.[93] The success of the Richmond system sparked the development of electric lines across America, as electric railways were faster and more comfortable than horsecar service. Streetcars, also known as trolleys or trams, quickly supplanted the horsecar as the predominant means of public transportation.[94]

The Massachusetts street railway industry experienced explosive growth in its early days, with street railway mileage nearly tripling between 1890 and 1900. During this growth stage, street railway promoters played a significant role in the industry's development, raising funds to build new electric lines throughout the state. These promoters would occasionally keep the most promising lines for themselves but would more frequently sell railway securities to the less-sophisticated public and take a cut of the proceeds. The promoters' primary interest was in raising capital, and their success in doing so led to an oversupply of lines and the creation of unprofitable systems.[95]

Overbuilding in the growth stage led to consolidation during the first decade of the 1900s. Many lines, particularly outside the city center, were unprofitable as standalone operations, requiring them to either shut down or merge.[96] Unlike other railway companies, Union Street abstained from acquiring less profitable country lines and remained close to a pure city system. This route structure allowed Union Street to sustain profitability after many Massachusetts street railway peers fell into the red.[97]

During the 1910s, rising costs put additional pressure on the railways, a dire burden since the Massachusetts Public Service Commission limited the industry's ability to raise prices. Furthermore, competitive threats started encroaching on ridership as motor competition began stealing traffic around 1915. Not only was the top line under pressure as the companies had no pricing power and competitors stole passengers, but rising wages increased operating costs. Despite early signs of increasing competition, Union Street Railway more than doubled passengers and revenue during the decade. But the firm was only able to grow net income from $234,094 in 1911 to $287,630 in 1920 due to the cost pressures.[98]

The impact of motor competition, from both car and bus, accelerated during the 1920s. Between 1920 and 1930, the number of motor vehicles registered in Massachusetts more than tripled. Buses offered a viable alternative to public transit riders, while rising private automobile ownership allowed potential riders to avoid the hassles of public transport altogether. Buses were more efficient carriers over routes with relatively low traffic density, possessed superior route flexibility, and required much lower capital investment. Rising costs and declining passenger numbers led to bankruptcies and line abandonments, resulting in Massachusetts street railway track miles halving between 1918 and 1930. Although buses wouldn't surpass streetcar ridership until 1940, the loss of passengers was problematic for an industry that already produced pedestrian profits.[99]

Union Street reacted to these trends by starting its own bus service in 1923.[100] However, the company experienced some bad luck later in the decade, as the 1928 New Bedford textile workers' strike reduced ridership. The work stoppage permanently impaired the industry, accelerating the decline of New Bedford's textile industry as mill customers found other suppliers. Shortly after the strike, the Great Depression hit, with textile mill employees declining by 40% between 1930 and 1932. [101]

Despite offering its own bus service, Union Street Railway's total ridership took a big hit throughout the 1920s. Passengers peaked in 1920 at 31.7 million but dropped to 14.5 million a decade later, and fell to 10.3 million in 1933.[102] In 1935, the company adopted a five-year plan to convert its operations to buses and end all trolley operations by the end of 1940. However, Union Street had to delay the transition as the firm wasn't in a position to make the needed investment.[103] World War II provided a temporary boon, as the government handicapped motor competition by rationing gasoline and rubber tires during the war. Ridership recovered, jumping from just shy of 11 million in 1937 to 27 million in 1946. In contrast to the 1930s, where the company lost money most years, Union Street was profitable every year from 1941 to 1950.[104]

The company's bus plans resumed after the war concluded in 1945, leading to the end of street railway service in New Bedford, with Union Street's final trolley service running on May 3, 1947.[105] As Figure 1 shows, the United States streetcar industry was on its last legs by this point. No new streetcars were purchased or manufactured in the United States after 1952. And by 1960, only ten United States cities had any street railway operations at all.[xix,106]

---

xix   Some cities have since brought back streetcar service. For example, Memphis launched a streetcar line in 1993 and Portland established a line in 2001.

Figure 1: United States electric interurban railway passenger miles in service

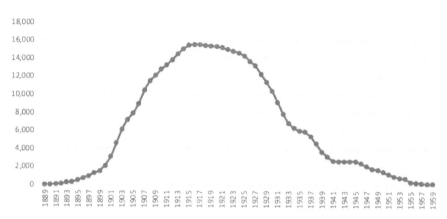

Source: Hilton, G. W., & Due, J. F. (2000). *The Electric Interurban Railways in America*. Stanford University Press.

When Buffett started looking at the company, Union Street Railway operated 113 buses and served 120,000 people in New Bedford, Fairhaven, Dartmouth, Fall River, and surrounding areas.[107] Table 1 shows Union Street's passenger (which included both railway and bus passengers for the applicable periods) and revenue figures plummeting following World War II, with net income dwindling over this period before finally turning negative.

Buffett buys a dollar for 50 cents

Buffett's thinking was simple: He bought the stock because it sold for less than its net cash. Union Street Railway was a tiny company, selling for a $643,000 market capitalization and an enterprise value of negative $327,000. Discussing his rationale, he said:

> It had a hundred sixteen buses and a little amusement park at one time. I started buying the stock because they had eight hundred thousand dollars in treasury bonds, a couple of hundred thousand in cash, and outstanding bus tickets of ninety-six thousand dollars. Call it a million dollars, about sixty bucks a share. When I started buying it, the stock was selling around thirty or thirty-five bucks a share.[108]

First, comparing Buffett's comments—made about 50 years after the purchase—to the summary balance sheet found in Table 2 demonstrates his superb memory, with his recollection remarkably close on most figures. Second,

Table 1: Union Street ten-year passengers and revenues

Year	Passengers	Gross revenues	Net income
1942	20,315,794	$1,493	$258
1943	26,118,921	$1,890	$225
1944	26,281,061	$1,904	$192
1945	26,831,720	$1,959	$192
1946	27,002,614	$1,988	$148
1947	26,146,932	$1,773	$70
1948	24,224,891	$1,972	$79
1949	21,209,982	$1,804	$84
1950	19,823,933	$1,673	$11
1951	18,736,420	$1,626	($49)
1952	15,354,504	$1,636	$52
1953	13,896,955	$1,484	($78)
1954	12,080,308	$1,372	($17)
1955	10,153,201	$1,344	$80

Source: *Moody's Manuals*. Dollar figures in thousands.

the table shows that at $30 to $35 a share the stock traded at a significant discount to the $48.13 of net cash on the balance sheet.

But the company had some additional items besides the net cash. Buffett noted the outstanding tickets. All sold—but unused—tickets were a liability; they were a form of deferred revenue. The company had received the cash, but the tickets were not yet redeemed. The value of this liability remained unchanged from 1952 to 1953, suggesting the tickets were very unlikely to be utilized. Plus, since the marginal cost of an additional passenger was zero, no cash expenditure would be incurred even if a passenger used the ticket. Therefore, it was appropriate to treat the cash as 'earned' and to write the liability down to zero, adding another $1.61 of value.

Then there were the long-term assets. While the property and equipment might be worth less than their value on the company's books, special deposits and insurance trusts had real value that would likely be released over time. These two items would add another $53.72 of value. With the stock trading below net cash, these assets were all gravy.

Table 2: 1953 summary balance sheet value

	Value	Per Share
(+) Cash	169	$9.22
(+) U.S. Government securities	800	$43.57
(-) Total liabilities	86	$4.66
Net cash	884	$48.13
(+) Outstanding tickets liability	30	$1.61
Net cash + outstanding tickets	$913	$49.74
(+) Accounts receivable	17	$0.91
(+) Net equipment	288	$15.67
(+) Net land and buildings	373	$20.30
(+) Special deposits	386	$21.04
(+) Accidental insurance trust	600	$32.67
(+) Maturities and supply	23	$1.28
(+) Prepayments	30	$1.65
Adjusted tangible book value	$2,631	$143.27

Source: *Moody's Manuals*. Dollar figures in thousands, other than per share numbers.

While the business lost $4.27 per share in 1953 as ridership continued to fall, accounting losses likely exceeded cash burn, as depreciation likely outstripped additional capital expenditures. Plus, this was a business where operating expenses could be toggled to meet demand—Union Street was unlikely to perpetually burn cash as they could cut costs by adjusting routes or changing service over time to mitigate the financial impact of ridership decline.

The stock was an obvious bargain—anyone looking at the *Moody's Manuals* could tell it was cheap. But this was a small company, and its stock was hard to find. Even Buffett, with a net worth of around $100,000 at this point, had to be resourceful to source enough shares to build a meaningful position. So he ran ads in the local newspaper to find holders that would sell to him. But the company knew its stock was cheap, and it ran competing ads. Since Union Street Railway was a public utility, Buffett was eventually able to get the list of largest shareholders from the Massachusetts public utility commission. These efforts allowed him to source 576 shares, 3.1% of the company's 1953 shares outstanding.[xx,109]

xx   The 576 share number is from the end of 1956, so there is a slight date mismatch.

The journey to New Bedford

Union Street's efforts to repurchase its stock were also successful. By 1955, the company shrunk its share count by 23% since 1953. Buffett now owned 4.1% of the company. And as Table 3 shows, the company's net cash position improved, both on an absolute and per-share basis. Union Street converted some of its special deposits (a long-term asset) into liquid cash. Liabilities also decreased as the outstanding tickets were written down to zero and the company's reserves declined. The bus company also returned to profitability, earning $5.67 per share in 1955. The stock rose in response to these developments, trading between $50 and $61 in 1955, but was still trading at a considerable discount to tangible book value.

Table 3: 1955 Balance sheet valuation

	Value	Per Share
(+) Cash	88	$6.23
(+) U.S. Government securities	1,099	$77.71
(-) Total liabilities	23	$1.63
Net cash	1,164	$82.32
(+) Outstanding tickets liability	-	$0.00
Net cash + outstanding tickets	$1,164	$82.32
(+) Accounts receivable	13	$0.90
(+) Net equipment	41	$2.89
(+) Net land and buildings	356	$25.20
(+) Special deposits	184	$13.04
(+) Accidental insurance trust	600	$42.44
(+) Maturities and supply	21	$1.52
(+) Prepayments	23	$1.62
Tangible book value	$2,402	$169.92

Source: *Moody's Manuals*. Dollar figures in thousands, other than per share numbers.

Buffett went to see the company's president, Mark Duff. Buffett said,

> I got up at about four a.m. and drove up to New Bedford. Mark Duff was very nice, polite. Just as I was about ready to leave, he said, "By the way, we've been thinking of having a 'return of capital' distribution to

shareholders." And I said, "Oh, that's nice." And then he said, "Yes, and there's a provision you may not be aware of in the Massachusetts statutes on public utilities that you have to do it in multiples of the par value of the stock." And I said, "Well. That's a good start." Then he said, "Bear in mind, we're thinking of using two units." That meant they were going to declare a fifty-dollar dividend on a stock that was selling at thirty-five or forty dollars at that time.[xxi,110]

While Buffett was unsure of whether his visit prompted the distribution, it's likely his actions did trigger the capital return. He held over 4% of the company and was proactive in acquiring his stock, with him and the company each placing competing ads in the local newspaper to solicit shares. Further, the company had maintained a significant net cash balance for years—yet it did not make a meaningful distribution until Buffett showed up.

After the $50 distribution, the stock sold between $15 and $21 throughout the rest of 1956. Buffett held onto it, thinking it still offered good value, saying:

> I got fifty bucks a share, and I still owned stock in the place. And there was still value in it. The bus companies hid assets in these so-called special reserves and land and buildings and car barns where they kept the old streetcars. And I'll never know whether my trip up there precipitated that or not.[111]

Union Street still owned $119.92 of tangible book value per share pro forma for the distribution. While Buffett's sale data isn't public, he held 576 shares through at least the end of 1956, when the stock traded for $20, worth $11,520.[112]

The valuation analysis was simple—anyone could see the stock was incredibly cheap. But it had been traded below net cash for several years before the company distributed cash to shareholders. Returning the cash was the critical factor in driving excellent returns. Assuming Buffett bought the stock in 1954 at $35 and sold in 1957 (having received the $50 per share distribution and a few dollars extra in dividends) when it traded between $20 and $28, he would have more than doubled his money and earned around a 30% IRR.[113] The stock didn't work because it was cheap—it worked because management returned capital to shareholders. The other securities discussed in this book were also incredible bargains—but it took action to drive wonderful returns for shareholders.

---

xxi   Buffett's recollection of the par value on the stock was incorrect—the par value was $100, not $25. It's unclear what statute he was referring to. This selective disclosure to Buffett would not be allowed today.

Union Street's life as a standalone company ended when the Eastern Massachusetts Street Railway Company acquired the firm in 1962 for $50 per share.[114] Like Union Street Railway, the Eastern Massachusetts Street Railway Company was a streetcar company that had transitioned to bus operations, ceasing its streetcar operations in 1948.[115]

Buffett would later have a famous skirmish with one of Union Street Railway's board members. The company's railway lines had run right near the Hathaway Mills, dropping off textile employees on their way to work. Seabury Stanton, the Hathaway Manufacturing Company president, served on Union Street's board. After Hathaway merged with Berkshire Fine Spinning Associates in 1955, Stanton would become vice chairman of the combined company, which was renamed Berkshire Hathaway. A couple of years after the merger, Stanton became its president.[116]

Buffett started buying Berkshire in 1962. The stock was another cheap net-net. Two years after Buffett's initial purchase, Seabury Stanton met with Buffett and asked what price he would need to tender his shares. Buffett agreed to tender at $11.50. Shortly after, Buffett received a letter from Berkshire offering $11.375. This 1/8 differential made him so angry that he started ferociously buying more Berkshire stock. He was on a mission to accumulate as many shares as possible, snapping at friends who tried to ride his coattails.[117]

Emotion may have driven Buffett's response to the Stanton deception. He later stated, "Looking back, it's interesting, that tender offer, I didn't realize it, but it happened about five days after my dad had died, and whether that had affected me or not, I don't know."[118] By 1965, Buffett controlled the company, using this power to fire Stanton and take a seat on the board of directors. These actions put the textile firm on a path to becoming one of the most valuable enterprises in the world. If not for Stanton's deceit, Berkshire Hathaway probably would have wound up as a forgotten old textile mill.

About a decade prior to his initial purchase of Berkshire Hathaway shares, Buffett stumbled upon the Philadelphia and Reading Coal and Iron Company. Like both Union Street Railway and Berkshire Hathaway, the stock was trading at a significant discount to its tangible book value and needed a change in its capital allocation policies. In contrast to the bus company, however, a change in *control* at P&R was necessary to spark this transformation. This anthracite coal company, the subject of our next chapter, provided Buffett with insights that he would use for the rest of his career.

Philadelphia and Reading: 1954

"Immature poets imitate; mature poets steal."

—*T.S. Eliot*

Anthracite coal was vital to America's energy output in the 1800s and early 1900s, contributing nearly one-fifth of the country's energy production at its peak. By that point, hard coal, as it was known, had a near-monopoly in the home heating market. Just one region in northeastern Pennsylvania, spanning roughly 500 square miles, accounted for virtually the entire national production of this essential resource.[119]

To help transport anthracite coal from the mines where it was produced to the cities where it was consumed, the state of Pennsylvania issued a charter to the Philadelphia and Reading Railroad Company (the predecessor to the Reading Railroad) to build a railroad from Reading to Philadelphia, Pennsylvania, in 1833.

The Reading was initially prohibited from owning coal lands or operating mines.[xxii] However, this changed when Pennsylvania lifted the restriction in 1868. Once liberated from these restrictive laws, the Reading formed a coal subsidiary in 1871 that became the Philadelphia and Reading Coal and Iron Company. The Reading Railroad's then-president Frank Gowen began scooping up coal lands, making his company the largest anthracite coal operator in the country.

For railroads, ownership of coal lands was a way to stabilize an industry levered to economic volatility and weather, with warmer winters depressing demand. The vertical integration of railroads and miners also helped the players control production and shipments. The industry became highly concentrated, with seven railroad companies controlling over 90% of the coal production in the region. This oligopoly occasionally entered into collusive arrangements and tried to manipulate the price of this critical energy source.

---

xxii   The Reading Railroad is the first railroad players encounter on a standard Monopoly board.

Despite these advantages, the Reading Railroad's spending spree eventually led to trouble, as the combination of leverage, competition, and economic volatility caused the company to declare bankruptcy three times between 1880 and 1896.[120] The Reading finally experienced financial success in the early 1900s, only to confront a new problem: The federal government was now determined to curb the power of the railroad and its peers. Congress began to enact legislation designed to split anthracite coal producers from railroads. These early attempts were easily circumvented by the anthracite giants.

In 1915, however, the Supreme Court started ruling that the railroad companies violated anti-trust law. In 1920, the Court banned the stock control of coal companies outright, which finally forced some of the largest anthracite operators, including the Reading Railroad, to separate their coal and railroad operations.[121] The split took three years, with the Philadelphia and Reading Coal and Iron Corporation (P&R) becoming a standalone coal producer, separate from the Reading Railroad, in December 1923.[122]

The government's timing could not have been worse for the hard coal companies, as the industry's production had peaked in 1917. From that point on, competing fuels such as oil, gas, and bituminous coal—which were either cheaper or more convenient to use—began rapidly stealing share from anthracite. Competition was not the industry's only problem. Since the most accessible anthracite had already been retrieved, the marginal coal became more challenging to mine. Furthermore, coal sizes (which were difficult for miners to control during the breakage process) were getting smaller. Larger coal was used for home heating—some heaters could not burn the smaller sizes—and therefore had greater demand and fetched a higher price per ton. So not only was total demand slowing but there was also a shift to less profitable sizes.[123]

As anthracite production fell after the divorce from the railroad, P&R's management raised debt to try and minimize the decay through capital investment, thinking new facilities could help the company remain competitive. But industry conditions worsened, and the Great Depression decimated economic activity, leading to significant losses for P&R throughout much of the 1930s. These results culminated in a declaration of bankruptcy in 1937.[124] It took eight years for the company to emerge, but the reorganized firm possessed a leaner balance sheet, better prepared to withstand the declining market.[125]

Ultimately, it didn't matter, as alternative fuel competition was simply overwhelming. As Figure 1 illustrates, production of hard coal eventually fell nearly 70%, dropping from 99.6 million tons from its 1917 peak all the way down to 30.9 million in 1953. Coal prices rose, mitigating the volume decline

47

(as seen in Figure 2). But there was no hope that the industry would return to its former glory; anthracite coal was in an irreversible decline.

This was the seemingly hopeless situation that confronted the young Warren Buffett, still in his early 20s, when he began looking at Philadelphia & Reading. Yet he started buying P&R stock at around $19 per share in 1952. When the stock soon plummeted to $9, Buffett, unphased by the decline, loaded up. By the end of 1954, he had invested $35,000 into the company, making it his largest personal position.[126]

Figure 1: Production (net tons)

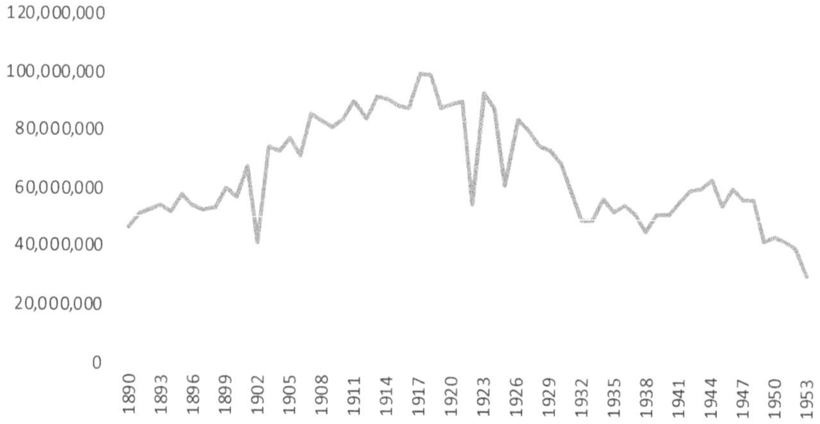

Source: *Minerals Yearbook 1953*, published by the United States Bureau of Mines.

Figure 2: Value of production (in thousands of dollars)

Source: *Minerals Yearbook 1953*, published by the United States Bureau of Mines.

Buffett's biggest bet

It was impossible for an investor to get excited about P&R's income statement. As seen in Table 1, after a few good years following the end of World War II, Philadelphia and Reading's volume, sales, and revenue were all falling over the five years ending in 1953, and the company was barely profitable.

The balance sheet told a different story. Selling for $13.38 per share at the end of 1954—an $18.8 million market capitalization—P&R traded close to its net current asset value of $9.16 per share, a figure that included significant excess inventory. While this alone was not enough to make the stock cheap, P&R also had an off-balance-sheet asset known as culm banks, a waste material accumulated from anthracite mining which was thought to have value as a fuel source. Buffett believed this asset could be worth around $8 per share.[127]

The net current asset value and the culm banks combined were worth $17 a share, enough to give Buffett confidence that the stock was cheap. But, as Table 2 shows, the company also had substantial property, plant, and equipment. These fixed assets were almost certainly worth less than their carrying value, as the industry had deteriorated since the company last valued them when it emerged from bankruptcy in 1945. While it wasn't clear what they were worth, they were certainly worth something.

Finally, and ultimately most importantly, Ben Graham was on P&R's board of directors, becoming a member after purchasing the stock in 1952. Buffett, who had discovered the stock on his own, would join Graham's firm in 1954. While Graham had not taken any significant action as a board member by then, Buffett sensed that his professor, mentor, and now boss would eventually make something happen. As he later stated, "I was just a peon sitting in the outer office… I was not in the inner circle, but I was terribly interested, knowing something was going on."[128]

Some big pluses

Ben Graham first bought P&R stock at $18 per share from the Baltimore and Ohio Railroad.[xxiii] He increased his position in 1954, and between his two main investment vehicles—the public fund known as Graham-Newman and a private partnership he ran called Newman & Graham—he held north of 5% of the

xxiii   There is some dispute over what Graham paid for the stock. Walter Schloss has stated it was $14. P&R's stock was trading around $18 at the time of Graham's purchase. Graham-Newman likely got a discount since it bought the block from B&O, but a 20%+ discount seems excessive. Interestingly enough, B&O is also on the standard Monopoly board.

Table 1: Philadelphia and Reading financial summary since emerging from bankruptcy

	1945	1946	1947	1948	1949	1950	1951	1952	1953
Volume of solid fuel sales, net tons	8,996,018	10,900,388	10,969,682	10,831,274	7,833,731	7,872,691	8,739,453	7,815,329	6,157,558
Volume year-over-year change	n/a	21.2%	0.6%	-1.3%	-27.7%	0.5%	11.0%	-10.6%	-21.2%
Net sales	56,021	73,415	77,811	87,764	65,748	69,721	73,379	67,696	57,134
Sales year-over-year change	-4.4%	31.0%	6.0%	12.8%	-25.1%	6.0%	5.2%	-7.7%	-15.6%
Pre-tax income	1,869	8,370	6,243	9,557	5,232	6,774	5,557	2,986	60
Pre-tax income margin	3.3%	11.4%	8.0%	10.9%	8.0%	9.7%	7.6%	4.4%	0.1%
Net income	1,486	5,506	4,468	6,176	3,682	4,800	4,346	2,836	100
Net profit margin	2.7%	7.5%	5.7%	7.0%	5.6%	6.9%	5.9%	4.2%	0.2%
Earnings per share	1.04	3.84	3.12	4.31	2.58	3.36	3.04	2.01	0.07
Net working capital	9,839	11,878	8,723	10,126	10,982	11,695	15,282	14,908	15,203
Tangible book	31,270	34,652	36,254	39,107	40,290	42,638	44,271	44,904	44,154
Tangible book value per share	21.82	24.18	25.30	27.38	28.21	29.86	31.00	31.87	31.33

Dollar figures in thousands, other than per share data.

Source: *Moody's Manuals*, Philadelphia and Reading annual reports, and author's calculations. Dollar figures in thousands other than per share data.

Table 2: P&R summary 1953 balance sheet

	Value	% of assets
Cash and cash equivalents	1,591	3.1%
Notes and accounts receivable	8,167	15.8%
Inventories	10,623	20.6%
Current assets	$20,381	39.5%
Long-term notes and accounts receivable	316	0.6%
Other long-term investments	400	0.8%
Special deposits	894	1.7%
Property, plant, and equipment	17,600	34.1%
Deferred charges	12,043	23.3%
Total assets	$51,634	100.0%
Total liabilities	7,480	
		Per Share
Tangible book	$44,154	$31.33
Net current asset value	$12,901	$9.16

Source: Philadelphia and Reading 1953 annual report. Dollar figures in thousands other than per share numbers.

stock.[xxiv] Graham-Newman, like Buffett, made P&R its largest position at nearly 11% of the fund's portfolio.[xxv,129]

In 1954, a group of Baltimore investors led by former magazine writer Thomas Hyland accumulated around 11% of the stock. Hyland was frustrated with P&R's board, made up mostly of Philadelphia businessmen who owned almost no stock, and he felt the company's strategy of continuing to dig for more coal was foolish. He approached Graham seeking an alliance in November 1954. An

xxiv   Graham's funds owned 5.29% of the company in February 1954. By the same time next year, he increased his stake within Graham-Newman by 50%. Newman & Graham, the private fund which owned nearly twice as much P&R than Graham-Newman did in 1954 did not publish its holdings. Assuming Graham increased his stake proportionally in both funds, he would have owned around 8% of the stock.

xxv   Buffett stated that his net worth was $127,000 at the end of 1955, and he owned $35,000 worth of the stock. P&R was almost certainly worth more than 30% of his portfolio at the end of 1954.

additional group of investors sympathetic to the Hyland-Graham cause invested in P&R as well. In 1955, the Baltimore and Graham-Newman parties owned or spoke for nearly 30% of the stock.[130]

Ironically, Graham himself was the pessimist of the group. After his initial purchase, Buffett's mentor asked for two seats on the board but settled for one, which he took himself. As a board member, Graham was frustrated like Hyland but hesitant to shake things up; he was already rich by then and did not like the reputation Graham-Newman was gaining as a takeover firm. He even considered selling the P&R position entirely, acknowledging that he had overvalued the company's coal assets. It was Micky Newman, the 34-year-old son of Ben's partner Jerome, who talked him out of it. Micky was more optimistic about the excess inventory P&R had piled up. Moreover, he saw an opportunity to apply some high finance to this industrial company. "Ben wanted to sell at a loss, but we persuaded him not to because I could see some big pluses," Micky later said. "I could see a huge potential tax loss due to abandonment of deep mines, and in addition, P&R coal had piled up small and unusual amounts of coal."[131]

In early 1955, P&R reported a $7.3 million loss for 1954, $5.3 million of which was attributable to write-offs related to the abandonments of mines.[132] The big loss gave the Baltimore/Graham-Newman group a chance to increase its control over the company's corporate governance: Hyland's broker, Benjamin Palmer, joined the board in February, and Micky Newman joined him three months later. Along with Ben Graham himself, the Baltimore and Graham-Newman shareholder group now controlled three of nine board seats. As a sign of things to come, P&R changed its name and amended its charter to allow the organization to engage in activities other than coal mining. The company dropped the reference to coal from its name, transitioning from the Philadelphia and Reading Coal and Iron Company to the Philadelphia and Reading Corporation.[133]

Micky took the initiative to transform the company. His plan was to use the cash P&R generated from liquidating its excess inventory to acquire profitable businesses, whose income would be shielded from future taxes by P&R's existing tax loss position. He sourced a deal to buy Union Underwear, then the country's largest manufacturer of men's and boys' underwear, operating as a licensee of the Fruit of the Loom trademark. Union's owner, Jack Goldfarb, was concerned about estate planning. But when he talked with Wall Street firms about taking his company public, they discouraged him, arguing that investors were not interested in garment companies. The bankers tried putting him in touch with other potential buyers, but Goldfarb was nervous about what they would do to his pride and joy. On the other hand, Micky Newman, who had met Goldfarb once or twice and followed up to express interest in Union, struck the older man as trustworthy and likable.

Despite Goldfarb having better offers monetarily, the two privately reached a deal for P&R to buy Union in June 1955. The agreement infuriated P&R's board when Newman reported back about it. Micky believed the directors were being obstinate not because they disliked the deal, but because it was becoming clear he wanted to run the company. One director insisted that the shareholders vote on the acquisition, even though the company's bylaws did not require this. The vote proceeded anyway—and shareholders wisely approved the deal.

P&R acquired Union Underwear for $15 million. The deal was a big swing for P&R, with the purchase price equal to 35% of its beginning-of-the-year assets. But beneath the big headline number, there were several factors that reduced risk. The deal was done at a salivating valuation: Union was earning $3 million in pre-tax profits—one-fifth of the purchase price—that would be partially sheltered by P&R's tax loss. Moreover, P&R structured the compensation of Union's management in an attractive manner: The company provided Goldfarb with a five-year management contract as well as a bonus of 10% of the subsidiary's operating profits (subject to both a minimum and a cap), ensuring he stayed on and incentivizing him to grow the business.[134] Finally, the deal's consideration was also interesting, which Buffett later reminisced about in the 2001 Berkshire Hathaway chairman's letter:

> The [Union Underwear] company possessed $5 million in cash—$2.5 million of which P&R used for the purchase—and was earning about $3 million pre-tax, earnings that could be sheltered by the tax position of P&R. And, oh yes: Fully $9 million of the remaining $12.5 million due was satisfied by non-interest-bearing notes, payable from 50% of any earnings Union had in excess of $1 million. (Those were the days; I get goosebumps just thinking about such deals.)[135]

Although the P&R board had approved the Union acquisition, Ben Graham was angered by its conservatism and pushed to add more directors. The other members obliged, ceding five additional seats to Graham allies. Jack Goldfarb and Louis Green of Stryker & Brown—the same Louis Green from the Marshall-Wells chapter—were among those added. Thomas Hyland had joined the board as well, replacing his broker. On January 1, 1956, Ben Graham became chairman, and Micky Newman was named company president.[136] The shareholder group now had a clear board majority and full management control.

The Graham-Newman investment firm would wind down later that year, distributing P&R shares to its investors.[137] But Ben Graham and Micky Newman continued their transformation of P&R, acquiring Acme Boots in February for $3.2 million. Like Union, the boot manufacturer was purchased at a low valuation, around 4x earnings. And like Union, Acme was bought with a mix of cash and non-interest-bearing notes tied to Acme's profits. And like Union, management was given a similar compensation arrangement.[138] The two deals proved tremendously successful; P&R earned $7.06 per share in 1956, $3.02 of which was attributable to the tax loss carryforward benefit.[139] By this point, Buffett had nearly made back in earnings what he had paid for the stock in 1954.

While he worked to allocate capital towards new businesses, Micky Newman also allocated away from the company's legacy coal operations, whose volumes had more than halved but whose administrative payroll had remained the same. He hired Roger Kelly as executive vice president. Kelly was a partner in an accounting firm that had previously done work for Graham-Newman. Together, they slashed costs, shut down losing operations, continued selling excess inventories, and updated the company's cost and reporting techniques.

The coal business earned a surprising $5.7 million in pre-tax profits for P&R in 1957, which allowed P&R to pay $1.60 a share in dividends in 1958. But Micky had another high finance trick up his sleeve: That year, P&R sold coal properties to Reading Anthracite, its wholly owned subsidiary, taking equity and debt in return. Instead of bringing up operating profit, P&R accounted for the proceeds as debt repayment from Reading Anthracite and paid it out as a mostly tax-free distribution. This allowed the operating profits at the subsidiary to be upstreamed to the parent not as a dividend, but rather as repayment of intercompany debt, which in turn allowed the distribution by the parent to shareholders to be treated as a mostly tax-free distribution.[140]

Then Newman kept making deals, acquiring a clothing manufacturer and a seller of toys, among other businesses. In 1961, the coal subsidiary sold its producing properties and business, freeing up $10 million while retaining nearly all of the culm coal waste banks. Having refashioned P&R as "business and financial generalists," Newman continued his acquisition efforts. That year, he bought the Fruit of the Loom company itself, uniting licensor and licensee and thereby saving $700,000 in annual licensing fees, since around 85% of Union's output carried the label.

Newman preferred to buy businesses whose management would stay in place to run their companies as subsidiaries of P&R. And he preferred to use his network to source deals rather than rely on investment bankers. Jack Goldfarb introduced the P&R president to Carroll Rosenbloom, a friend of his who ran a handful of companies that manufactured work clothes, men's shirts, and sports clothes. Newman scooped up Rosenbloom's businesses, paying with a mix of cash and P&R stock.

Buffett himself also contributed: In late 1963, he found Lone Star Steel, a fully integrated producer whose biggest business was selling pipe to the oil industry. Buffett scooped up 300,000 shares between $9 and $14 in his partnership and then reached out to P&R to discuss the idea, saying it was "something I thought would be interesting for them to look at." Micky Newman agreed and borrowed money to buy 73% of the company in 1965 for about $64 million.[141]

This purchase was another big swing, with the acquisition amount equivalent to 44% of P&R's beginning-of-the-year assets. But it set the stage for another explosion in earnings growth for the conglomerate, with earnings more than doubling from 1964—the year prior to the acquisition—to 1967. In 1968, a company called Northwest Industries purchased all of P&R, ending Micky Newman's tenure as a control investor.

Buffett's blueprint

We do not know exactly when Warren Buffett sold his P&R shares. We do know, however, that he dipped back into the stock in the 1960s while running his partnership.[142] We also know that he maintained his friendships with his former colleagues Ben Graham and Micky Newman throughout their lives. And we know that, as Table 3 shows, the long-term record of Graham and Newman as activist and later control shareholders of P&R was outstanding, with sales and earnings exploding and the stock consistently appreciating. A single share that Buffett was buying for less than $10 in 1954 became worth more than $200 before Northwest Industries acquired the company in 1968.

Finally, we know that Buffett's relationship with both Fruit of the Loom and Acme Boots did not end with his investment in P&R. Northwest Industries was itself acquired by businessman William Farley in 1985.[143] Farley took the Fruit of the Loom subsidiary public in 1987. In the same 2001 chairman's letter in which he discussed his investment in P&R, Buffett mentioned that Fruit of the Loom went on to achieve annual pre-tax earnings of over $200 million. However, the company ran into trouble about a decade later, which led to a bankruptcy filing in 1999 that was resolved when none other than Berkshire Hathaway bought the company out of receivership in 2002, where it remains today.

Acme Boots, for its part, experienced tremendous early success as a P&R subsidiary, both before and after Northwest Industries bought P&R, and it grew its profits to multiples more than P&R's original $3.2 million purchase

Table 3: P&R financials through 1967

	1953	1954	1955	1956	1957	1958	1959	1960	1961	1962	1963	1964	1965	1966	1967	CAGR 1953–1967
Sales	57,134	46,457	47,677	79,154	80,446	76,279	139,101	147,378	153,795	189,014	177,775	221,225	285,549	327,824	311,325	12.9%
Earnings before extraordinary items	100	(2,807)	(1,387)	4,948	6,625	7,256	8,724	7,385	8,956	6,310	7,762	9,901	14,013	19,125	23,905	47.8%
Per common share (after preferred dividends)	0.07	(1.99)	(1.02)	4.04	5.71	6.19	6.27	5.32	6.47	4.55	5.63	7.35	10.38	13.36	16.56	
Cash dividends on common stock	845	-	-	-	-	1,871	2,653	2,836	2,883	2,941	2,996	3,150	3,571	3,592	4,514	12.7%
Per share	0.60	-	-	-	-	1.60	1.92	2.03	2.08	2.12	2.16	2.32	2.65	2.65	3.31	
Working capital	15,203	15,576	21,895	26,001	28,406	32,388	44,137	52,823	45,486	61,796	81,849	84,011	156,228	137,580	152,427	17.9%
Total assets	51,634	42,828	51,821	58,175	64,330	68,104	89,452	95,649	121,756	151,255	151,167	145,049	336,163	298,592	318,612	13.9%
Common stockholders' equity	44,154	36,830	33,066	38,898	43,696	49,305	66,593	66,176	72,296	75,585	85,283	89,824	100,479	105,406	123,951	7.7%
Per Share	31.33	26.14	24.25	31.74	37.64	42.05	47.85	47.78	52.22	54.61	61.87	66.64	74.42	77.66	90.53	
Stock Price—high	18.75	14.00	19.00	29.38	31.50	72.00	114.75	99.96	175.83	171.92	90.38	89.43	127.25	160.37	219.71	19.2%
Stock Price—low	8.88	7.50	12.25	17.00	21.50	27.13	80.58	53.04	69.97	56.24	71.71	66.24	71.21	75.35	86.67	17.7%
P/B—high	0.60x	0.54x	0.78x	0.93x	0.84x	1.71x	2.40x	2.09x	3.37x	3.15x	1.46x	1.34x	1.71x	2.06x	2.43x	
P/B—low	0.28x	0.29x	0.51x	0.54x	0.57x	0.65x	1.68x	1.11x	1.34x	1.03x	1.16x	0.99x	0.96x	0.97x	0.96x	
P/E—high	263.14x	n/m	n/m	7.27x	5.52x	11.63x	18.30x	18.78x	27.18x	37.79x	16.05x	12.16x	12.26x	12.00x	13.27x	
P/E—low	124.55x	n/m	n/m	4.21x	3.77x	4.38x	12.85x	9.97x	10.81x	12.36x	12.74x	9.01x	6.86x	5.64x	5.23x	

Source: Philadelphia and Reading annual reports; author's calculations. Dollar figures, other than per share data, are in thousands. Per share figures, including share prices, are in 1954 share count equivalents; the data is adjusted for stock splits and stock dividends to reflect the value of one share purchased in 1954. Earnings are adjusted to exclude special items.

price. Acme became the world's largest bootmaker. But it too fell into decline. And in late 2001, Berkshire subsidiary H.H. Brown decided to buy the Acme Boot inventory and trademarks for just $700,000.[144]

It is tempting to dismiss these two companies re-entering Buffett's life decades later as interesting coincidences. But Buffett's life is filled with such "coincidences," and they perhaps point to some kind of emotional attachment he formed with a company during his formative years. To Buffett followers, the implication of these two coincidental acquisitions—and his decision to discuss them in his letter—should by now be obvious: P&R was an important investment for Buffett, largely because it served as a blueprint for Berkshire Hathaway.

This blueprint came along at exactly the right time. Early in his career, Buffett was a completely passive investor in companies over which he had no influence. Later, with companies like Union Street Railway, he saw how activist shareholders could influence management teams to distribute cash and make other investor-friendly moves.

But with P&R, Buffett saw up close the power of total control—all the many levers an intelligent investor can pull not when he influences management, but when he becomes management. Nearly all the characteristics that became famous hallmarks of Berkshire Hathaway—the 19th-century industrial beginnings, the irreversible secular decline of the original business, the initial cheap valuation, the fight for full control, the partial liquidation of inventory to raise cash, the reallocation of capital towards new and better businesses, the clever management compensation, the behind-the-scenes tax minimization strategies, the reliance on personal friendships to source deals, and the fundamental integrity and trustworthiness of company leadership as the foundation of a sprawling conglomerate—had some antecedent or inspiration in the way Ben Graham and Micky Newman transformed and built P&R.

The Partnership Years

Warren Buffett ended 1955 with a net worth of $127,000. While still a Graham-Newman employee, he began plotting his next steps. Ben Graham told Buffett that he intended to retire, and the Dean of Wall Street offered his star pupil the opportunity to replace him, with Micky Newman as senior partner and Warren as the new junior partner. But the Nebraska native wanted to go back to Omaha, so he left Graham-Newman as the fund wound down in 1956.[145]

Upon his return, the 25-year-old Buffett thought he could get rich on compound interest and live off his net worth. Then seven people, including relatives, approached him asking for advice on how to invest their money. Buffett had no interest in returning to his old trade as a stockbroker but told them he would create a partnership that they could join, which led to the creation of Buffett Associates, Ltd. on May 5, 1956. Establishing this vehicle set Buffett down the path that eventually made him the wealthiest man in the world.

Economic backdrop

As Table 1 shows, the post-war boom continued, with economic growth in all but one year. There were two mild recessions during the 14 years Buffett ran his partnership, one starting in 1957 and one beginning in 1960, with each lasting less than a year.[xxvi] Inflation and interest rates were low for most of this period, although both began rising during the partnership's final years in the late 1960s.

Portfolio construction

In his 1961 letter to partners, Buffett laid out three broad categories of investments: generals, workouts, and controls. Generals were undervalued securities where Buffett had no say in corporate policies, nor a timetable for when the stock might reflect its intrinsic value. Buffett pointed out that the generals would behave like the Dow in the short term but outperform the

---

xxvi   A recession also began in December 1969, when Buffett was winding down the partnership's affairs.

Table 1: Market and economic data

	S&P 500	Real GDP	CPI	3-month Treasury bill yearly average
1956	7.4%	2.1%	1.5%	2.6%
1957	-10.5%	2.1%	3.3%	3.2%
1958	43.7%	-0.7%	2.7%	1.8%
1959	12.1%	6.9%	1.1%	3.4%
1960	0.3%	2.6%	1.5%	2.9%
1961	26.6%	2.6%	1.1%	2.4%
1962	-8.8%	6.1%	1.2%	2.8%
1963	22.6%	4.4%	1.2%	3.2%
1964	16.4%	5.8%	1.3%	3.5%
1965	12.4%	6.5%	1.6%	3.9%
1966	-10.0%	6.6%	3.0%	4.9%
1967	23.8%	2.7%	2.8%	4.3%
1968	10.8%	4.9%	4.3%	5.3%
1969	-8.2%	3.1%	5.5%	6.7%

Source: Federal Reserve Bank of Minneapolis; Bureau of Economic Analysis; NYU Stern, Historical Returns on Stocks, Bonds and Bills: 1928–2023; Federal Reserve Bank of St. Louis.

index over the long term. Buffett expected to have five or six positions in this category that were 5% to 10% of total assets each, with smaller positions in another ten to fifteen. Later on, in his 1964 letter, Buffett would break generals into two categories: private owner basis and relatively undervalued. Private owner generals were generally cheap stocks with no immediate catalyst, while relatively undervalued securities were cheap compared to those of a similar quality. Relatively undervalued securities were generally larger companies where Buffett did not think a private owner valuation was relevant.[146]

Workouts were securities whose performance depended on corporate actions, such as mergers, liquidations, reorganizations, and spin-offs. Buffett expected to have ten to fifteen of these in the portfolio and thought this category would be a reasonably stable source of earnings for the fund, outperforming the Dow when the market had a bad year and underperforming in a strong year. He anticipated these investments would earn him 10% to 20%, excluding any leverage. Buffett would take on debt, up to 25% of the partnership's net worth, to fund this category. While he didn't disclose his allocation every year, he put around 15% of the partnership in workouts in 1966 but increased that to a quarter of the portfolio in 1967 and 1968, when he was having trouble finding bargains.[147]

The final category was controls, where the partnership took a significant position to change corporate policy. Buffett said these investments might take several years to play out and would, like workouts, have minimal correlation to the Dow's gyrations. Buffett pointed out that generals could become controls if the stock price remained depressed. After seeing the success of Union Street Railway and Philadelphia and Reading, he realized the spectacular profits that can be generated from activism and applied the tactic with fervor, occasionally allocating 25% to 35% of his portfolio to a single control.[148]

The partnership investments

The first investment I discuss occurs in 1962, six years after the partnership began. As mentioned in the preface, the reason for this time jump is that Buffett and others have detailed some of the earlier partnership investments in sufficient depth. Buffett describes activist investments such as Sanborn Map and Dempster Mill in his letters, and I can't add any value to his words. In these partnership days, Buffett was very much an activist investor. And not just an activist investor, but a *control* investor. In contrast to Union Street Railway, where he owned a single-digit percentage of the company, Buffett used the partnership's capital to buy much larger stakes in these companies. For example, he owned 73% of Dempster and 23% of Sanborn (with two other significant and sympathetic holders—including Phil Carret whom we met in the Greif chapter—owning another 21% of the map company). Both were cheap stocks with excess working capital, where Buffett took control and changed corporate policies to close the price-to-value gap.[xxvii] In the case of Dempster Mill, Buffett also replaced management and hired Harry Bottle as president, who helped convert assets into cold hard cash for Buffett to buy securities with.[149] Undoubtedly, the most famous partnership investment (and one not explored in this book) was Berkshire Hathaway. Buffett bought the New Bedford-based textile firm in 1962 when it was a cheap net-net. As mentioned in the chapter on Union Street Railway, he eventually accumulated a controlling interest in

xxvii   For Buffett's comments on Sanborn Map, see the January 30, 1961 partnership letter. For more on Dempster Mill, see the letters dated: January 24, 1962; January 18, 1963; July 10, 1963; and the appendix to the January 18, 1964 letter. Other investments discussed in the partnership letters include: Commonwealth Trust Co. in the February 11, 1959 letter and Texas National Petroleum in the appendix to the January 18, 1964 letter. Berkshire Hathaway is mentioned in multiple letters, including the January 20, 1966 letter.

the company in the spring of 1965 after its president lied to him. Buffett fired management and would become the company's chairman and chief executive officer himself in 1970. And, of course, he transformed this cigar-butt into the world's greatest conglomerate and one of the largest companies in the world.[150]

Like the pre-partnership years, Buffett remained a balance sheet-focused investor when he ran the partnership. However, he began dipping his toe in the 'better business' pool, foreshadowing the investor he would become in the 1970s and onwards. The most famous example, which we will cover, is American Express in 1964.

Buffett would begin griping about the challenges of the investing environment towards the end of the partnership years. In late 1967, he wrote, "Mushrooming interest in investment performance (which has its ironical aspects since I was among a lonely few preaching the importance of this some years ago) has created a hyper-reactive pattern of market behavior against which my analytical techniques have limited value."[151]

By 1969, Buffett found that quantitative bargains had dried up and thought the market was becoming increasingly short-term oriented and too speculative. Finding this environment too difficult to thrive in, he chose to close the partnership and 'retire' at year's end rather than continue on.

British Columbia Power: 1962

"The idea that very smart people with investment skills should have hugely diversified portfolios is madness. It's a very conventional madness. And it's taught in all the business schools. But they're wrong."

—Charlie Munger[152]

One of the reasons Charlie Munger and Warren Buffett became billionaires is because of their willingness to shun traditional investment thinking. For instance, in contrast to most money managers who run widely diversified portfolios, both frequently took concentrated positions when they found mispriced opportunities. One of the wagers the duo bet big on was an arbitrage opportunity found in British Columbia Power's stock.

Munger had known Warren for about three years in 1962. The future Berkshire Hathaway vice chairman realized Buffett was an investing genius, and therefore spent time and energy nurturing the relationship. While Buffett closely guarded his investments, Munger openly shared his ideas with his friend. One of the stocks Munger persuaded Buffett to buy was British Columbia Power. Munger, who had just started running his own partnership in 1962, thought the opportunity was such an extraordinary risk-reward that he not only put his entire partnership into the company but also used a credit line from the Pacific Stock Exchange to leverage his position.[153] While Buffett certainly liked the stock as well, he didn't go as far as his impatient friend—the investment accounted for 11.2% of the Buffett Partnership at the end of 1962, its second-largest position behind Dempster Mill Manufacturing Company.[154]

The opportunity arose due to a dispute between BC Power and the provincial government of British Columbia. The quarrel began when the province expropriated BC Power's principal asset, the British Columbia Electric Company. This regulated electric and gas utility provided electricity to almost every British Columbian resident and produced all of its parent company's profits. Without it, BC Power had no meaningful assets and no reason to continue as a going concern. While the provincial government compensated

BC Power for the seizure, the holding company found the price inadequate and pursued litigation to extract fair value for its confiscated asset.

With the conflict between the enterprise and the province raging on, BC Power's stock was selling at a discount to the cash the company received from the government. Buffett and Munger saw this discrepancy and snapped the stock up. Not only were they nearly certain the deal would close, but they knew there was additional upside potential if BC Power could extract a few more nickels from the government's coffers.

The seizure of British Columbia Electric

W.A.C. Bennett, British Columbia's premier, had an audacious plan for the province's power grid. Bennett imagined using two of the province's major rivers, the Peace and Columbia, simultaneously to provide his citizens with a reliable source of hydroelectric power. The proposal, known as the Two Rivers Policy, would produce more electricity than British Columbia needed, allowing the province to sell the excess power to the United States.

As the province's primary electric and gas utility, British Columbia Electric Company was the logical purchaser of the power generated by the Peace River. The Peace River Power Development Company, a privately owned venture that the government would also take over, tried to secure a purchase commitment from the utility company. A contract with BC Electric would allow the Peace River Power Development Company to raise the necessary capital to build the dams to produce the power. BC Electric's resistance prevented the project from getting off the ground.[155]

W.A.C. Bennett grew tired of the company's obstinance. In August 1961, after rumors of a potential takeover had circulated within the province for months, Bennett introduced the Power Development Act into the legislature in order to confiscate BC Electric for C$111.0 million. The bill passed unanimously, allowing the government to seize control of the utility. The move was highly controversial, sparking an uproar within the business press, with some overly dramatic papers even labeling Bennett a dictator. In an unfortunate coincidence, the head of British Columbia Power and BC Electric, A.E. "Dal" Grauer, had passed away a few days earlier, and his funeral transpired on the very same day the government took over the company he had led.[156]

In addition to taking BC Electric, the bill offered to buy the rest of BC Power for C$68.6 million, with interest accruing on this amount until the offer expired at the end of July 1963. Combined with the C$111.0 million paid for BC Electric, this offer would result in a total payment for all of BC Power's operations of

C\$179.6 million—or the equivalent of C\$38.00 per share. Bennett justified this price by highlighting that the proposal was a premium to the C\$34.75 price the shares sold for the day before the expropriation.[157]

While the combined price of C\$38.00 per share was reasonable, the valuation for the constituent parts was peculiar. The C\$111.0 million price for BC Electric matched its paid-in capital but ignored the other C\$28.6 million of common book equity. And this amount sidestepped the debate over whether book value was even an appropriate methodology for the utility in the first place. The C\$68.6 million price for the rest of BC Power's assets was even odder since these remnant assets generated no income and were carried on the balance sheet at only C\$4.0 million. This was a clear overpayment for the holding company's assets, proposed to entice it into consenting to the BC Electric takeover.[158]

Predictably, BC Power did not stand idly by. After preliminary attempts to negotiate a higher price were thwarted, the company took action in the Supreme Court of British Columbia on November 13, 1961. BC Power sought rulings on the validity of the initial Act, the right to additional compensation, and the convertibility feature of debentures issued by BC Electric (more on this last point in the next section).[159]

While the parties awaited trial, the government took additional steps to further entrench the takeover. At the end of March 1962—nearly eight months after the original seizure—the British Columbia legislature passed two new statutes. The first was the province's amendment of the Power Development Act, which paid an additional C\$60.8 million to BC Power for BC Electric and eliminated the offer for the rest of the parent company's assets. Table 1 shows that the amendment didn't significantly alter the total compensation. But the new consideration was a more realistic number for BC Electric and solved for the peculiar offer for the remaining assets, which BC Power would now have to sell themselves.

The second key legislation was the British Columbia Hydro and Power Authority Act. This act merged the British Columbia Power Commission, a government-owned public utility that served smaller communities unserved by BC Electric, with BC Electric into a single corporation named the British Columbia Hydro and Power Authority. This maneuver cemented the two entities together, creating an additional complication if the Court later reversed the takeover.[160]

With the Amending Act payment in hand, BC Power had cash—less all liabilities—of C\$19.30 per share. The stock sold for less than this, closing at C\$16.75 the day after the payment and then fluctuated around this number over

Table 1: Change in compensation

Under the 1961 Act as originally acted		Under the Amending Act	
Received on August 4, 1961	C$110,985	Received on August 4, 1961	C$110,985
Entitled to receive	68,613	Received on March 31, 1962	60,848
Total	C$179,598	Total compensation	C$171,833
Per share	C$38.00	BCP's estimated value for its remaining assets	10,000
		Total	C$181,833
		Per share	C$38.10

Source: British Columbia Power, 1962 annual report. Figures in thousands other than per share data.

the coming months.[xxviii] At this price, the stock traded at a 13.2% discount to net cash, held around C$2.10 of additional assets, and possessed continued upside if litigation went the company's way. While court delays would postpone the final resolution, BC Power's interest income exceeded legal expenses, so there was no cash burn associated with the case.[161] Any postponement would impact the timing of cash flows and weaken the investment's annualized return, of course, but BC Power was not at risk of chewing through its cash balance and destroying value.

Buffett and Munger pounce

The two investors bought BC Power's stock around the time the province issued the Amending Act.[xxix] Workout opportunities, including arbitrage, were a key component of Buffett and Munger's strategy. Buffett laid out his thinking on these opportunities in Berkshire Hathaway's 1988 letter, writing:

> To evaluate arbitrage situations you must answer four questions: (1) How likely is it that the promised event will indeed occur? (2) How long will your money be tied up? (3) What chance is there that something

---

xxviii   The stock traded on the American Stock Exchange in US dollars and three Canadian exchanges in Canadian Dollars. It closed at USD$16.00 on the American Stock Exchange the day after the payment.

xxix   It's possible Buffett and Munger bought the stock prior to the Amending Act, but they most likely purchased it afterwards. The stock was trading below the original offer before the amendment, so the analysis wouldn't change in a material manner; the language would merely change from 'below net cash' to 'below the offer'. Because the stock moved in a tight range in the months following the Amending Act, the specific date of analysis does not matter.

still better will transpire—a competing takeover bid, for example? and (4) What will happen if the event does not take place because of anti-trust action, financing glitches, etc.?[162]

Answering Buffett's first question relies upon examining the chessboard rather than possessing legal expertise. Bennett had already taken the extraordinary step of stripping BC Power of its principal asset. The premier then merged BC Electric into the British Columbia and Hydro Power Authority to further entrench the takeover. Unwinding the transaction would be a nightmare; the government had already gone to extraordinary lengths to get this deal done.

On the other hand, the company was ostensibly contesting the takeover. But this was a necessary procedural step; BC Power's actions indicated they wanted additional compensation and had come to terms with losing its subsidiary. BC Power's chairman spent much of the 1961 annual report griping about the price, asserting that a third-party firm thought BC Electric was worth at least C$225.0 million and writing, "…it was the Directors' plain duty to seek better compensation for the taking of the common shares of the Electric Company."[163] Furthermore, BC Power distributed C$89.2 million—or C$18.70 per share—of the proceeds from the government to its shareholders as a reduction of capital in December, indicating that the company would liquidate once the case was resolved.[164]

Answering the second problem—how long will the money be tied up?—is a bit trickier. A November 1961 article cited court observers who speculated litigation could take up to five years, an alarming prospect for an investor wanting to make a quick return.[165] But this estimate seemed to be a worst-case scenario, made only a handful of days after the company pursued litigation in the Supreme Court. In the 1961 annual letter—issued in March 1962—BC Power stated that it expected the trial to commence within a few months.[166]

Both parties seemed interested in a quick resolution, but an investor couldn't predict timing with any sort of precision. However, progress was being made towards the end of 1962, as the parties were in the middle of presenting their arguments to the Supreme Court, which would conclude in late February of 1963.[167] At that point, it was up to the judge to decide, and it was doubtful he would allow a vital case such as this to remain unresolved for long. While there was the potential for appeals, the parties seemed incentivized to get a deal done after the initial ruling.

The third question, about handicapping the odds of something better happening, also lacked a simple answer. It seemed credible that an agreement could be reached, with the province offering a little more money and allowing

BC Power to save face. It was hard to have total conviction that the government would need to pay more, but with the stock trading below the net cash on its books, this would be gravy.

For the fourth and final question about what would happen if the deal fell apart, it was clear the downside was minimal. The price was only 9.4% above the market price the day before the takeover and below its 1961 high of C$39.00. Additionally, the shares sold between C$30.63 and C$37.50 in 1960, so the compensation wasn't at a substantial premium to the historical trading prices.[168] Further, as Table 2 lays out, the company had grown revenue and operating income over the past decade and would likely continue doing so. BC Power was a growing company selling a needed service. Plus, the valuation before the seizure was reasonable—at the 1961 high of $39, the stock sold for an undemanding 16.46x P/E and provided investors with a 3.7% dividend yield. As a utility company with stable demand and rising earnings, the company's intrinsic value would increase over time. If the deal broke in 1963, the company's profits would likely be higher than they were before the seizure, and the stock would probably trade north of the 1961 takeover price. The downside protection allowed Buffett and Munger to feel comfortable diving into the opportunity.

There was one last quirk that Buffett and Munger had to get comfortable with. BC Electric—the subsidiary—issued debentures that were convertible into BC Power's stock. The debenture holders could, at their discretion, convert their debt into BC Power stock. This structure made sense when BC Power owned all of BC Electric but broke down once the parent company no longer had an interest in the subsidiary. Converting the debt into BC Power's common stock would erase a now unrelated entity's obligations while forcing the parent company to issue stock.

The Court needed to answer whether the debentures were still convertible into BC Power's shares and whether holders of those shares would retroactively be entitled to the C$18.70 distribution the company paid in December 1961. Optically magnifying the threat, the Supreme Court of British Columbia required BC Power to keep C$20.2 million of cash on its balance sheet in case the Court ruled that the debenture holders were entitled to the prior distribution and all holders decided to convert into BC Power shares.[169]

Fortunately, the risk this would materially impair BC Power stockholders was nearly zero. First, the British Columbia government assumed the debt as part of the expropriation and was explicit that the liability was theirs. Second, the risk quickly diminished after the enactment of the Amending Act when the British Columbia Hydro and Power Authority called the debentures in May 1962. By the end of June 1962, C$37.6 million worth of bonds from the C$40 million

Table 2: British Columbia Power 10-year financials

	1951	1952	1953	1954	1955	1956	1957	1958	1959	1960
Gross revenues from operations	46,880	52,690	56,007	59,244	63,443	68,324	74,594	83,273	96,924	103,297
Operating income	8,182	9,534	10,807	12,026	14,654	16,427	19,944	23,479	26,179	30,374
Operating margin	17.5%	18.1%	19.3%	20.3%	23.1%	24.0%	26.7%	28.2%	27.0%	29.4%
EPS	0.98	1.34	1.47	1.62	2.05	2.34	2.33	1.95	2.48	2.37
Dividends per share	0.80	0.80	0.85	1.00	1.15	1.35	1.40	1.40	1.40	1.45

Source: British Columbia Power annual reports. Dollar figures in thousands of Canadian dollars other than per share numbers.

issuance had been redeemed, with the amount outstanding whittling down to around C$0.3 million when the judge finally ruled on the case in 1963.[170] While there was still the possibility that the Court would rule this redemption invalid, it would be a logistical nightmare to reverse the transaction. Despite the optics, it was a non-issue.

British Columbia Power's electrifying returns

Chief Justice Sherwood Lett announced his decision on July 29, 1963, ruling the seizure illegal and constitutionally invalid.[171] Lett also stated that the province should have paid C$192.8 million—not the C$171.8 million it actually spent—for BC Electric, justifying this number based on a P/E of 17.5x plus 2.5% special compensation for loss of income. However, Lett did not order the government to return BC Electric to BC Power, creating uncertainty regarding the next steps in the process.[172]

Seeking to resolve the issue quickly, BC Power immediately sent a telegram to Premier Bennett indicating their willingness to negotiate a fair price. In the interim, there was a hearing in the Court for two items on August 5. First was an application on behalf of the British Columbia Hydro and Power Authority and the British Columbia Attorney General for a stay of proceedings pending appeal. Second, BC Power requested that the receiver appointed in the Court be directed to return BC Electric to BC Power. Neither of these actions wound up mattering, as the hearings were adjourned on August 13 as negotiations between the company and the government began.

The two parties set parameters around the cost and agreed to let Chief Justice Lett decide the appropriate amount to be paid within the agreed-upon limits. On September 27, 1963, Lett decided that C$197.1 million was the proper compensation for BC Electric, C$25.3 million higher—or C$5.30 per share—than what BC Power had already received. The C$4.3 million difference between the C$197.1 million Lett decided, and the C$192.8 million in the ruling was simply due to interest. The government paid BC Power the same day as Lett's decision, concluding the case. Finally, the convertible risk proved irrelevant since the government agreed to pay BC Power for any debentures presented to the company as part of the settlement.

After receiving its final payment from the government, BC Power began liquidating itself.[173] The company made three liquidating distributions with the bulk in the first payment, as seen in Table 3.[174] Buffett and Munger did extraordinarily well.

Table 3: Returns for BC Power shareholders

	Canadian Dollars	U.S. Dollars
April 2, 1962 Stock Price	$16.75	$16.00
Dividend paid December 20, 1962	0.25	0.23
Liquidating distribution, paid January 2, 1964	25.00	23.14
Liquidating distribution, paid March 12, 1965	0.50	0.46
Liquidating distribution, paid April 29, 1969	0.06	0.06
Total Return	54.1%	49.3%

Source: British Columbia Power, 1962 annual report; author's calculations. Distributions and dividends were paid in Canadian dollars. The author then converted those figures into U.S. Dollars.[xxx]

The investment was a huge win for Charlie Munger, who had just started his investment partnership. British Columbia Power made him $450,000 and helped him produce a 30.1% return in 1962 and a 71.7% result in 1963. Despite not knowing exactly when the deal would close (and stating that he never even heard of risk arbitrage before he found this opportunity), Munger was comfortable taking on leverage to increase his position because he knew arbitrageurs would help set a floor on the stock. These other investors would bid the stock back up if it fell, so he wasn't at risk of being margin called.[175]

Both Munger and Buffett have always been incredibly opportunistic investors, deploying arbitrage as one of their money-making techniques. Workout investments, such as British Columbia Power, allowed them to produce returns uncorrelated to the general stock market. For example, in 1962, workouts helped Buffett generate a positive return for the year. These investments went up 14.6%, while his generals declined 1.0%. In 1963, workouts were up 30.6%, aided by the resolution of the BC Power case.[176]

Buffett's investment philosophy was the same whether he was evaluating workouts, generals, or control situations—he was seeking attractive risk-rewards with downside protection. The analytical process was merely tweaked to fit the investment. Buffett was flexible during his research process, focusing on

---

xxx   While the precise timing of Buffett's purchase is unknown, he definitely held the stock at the end of 1962 when it was selling for USD$18.38. The stock traded below USD$18 until December of that year, so his and Munger's purchase price was likely below USD$18.

dissecting the most critical issues impacting the investment. In the case of BC Power, business analysis took a backseat to handicapping how the takeover would play out.

Up next, the most profitable investment of the Buffett Partnership.

American Express: 1964

"It is of the utmost importance that the Company's representatives bear constantly in mind the good repute of our Travelers Cheques and take quick action to remedy any difficulties or troubles in the encashment of Cheques by patrons in their territory."

—American Express in 1921[177]

In 1949, 34-year-old Anthony 'Tino' De Angelis bought control of the publicly traded meat-packing firm Adolph Gobel. Tino had made his early money in the hog-cutting business, so Gobel was a logical purchase for the bustling businessman.

Tino proceeded to rapidly drive the company into a ditch. Not only did he lead it into bankruptcy in 1953, but the SEC asserted the company understated its losses, the government accused him of cheating schoolchildren through a federal food program, and foreign countries griped about the quality of the product he shipped.

But these speedbumps did not slow De Angelis down. He then organized Allied Crude Vegetable Oil Refining in 1955 to conquer the soybean oil business, choosing a location in Bayonne, New Jersey, to accommodate oceangoing steamers that could carry refined oil overseas. In theory, it was a classic mid-stream commodity business: De Angelis would buy unrefined soybean oil from the Midwest, ship it to Bayonne, refine it, and then sell the oil overseas. The export companies—who would be Allied's customers—accepted this proposition and provided De Angelis with millions in financing advanced against future oil deliveries.

Tino's enterprise was successful: By the late 1950s, Allied supplied more than 75% of the edible oils shipped overseas, with revenues of over $100 million annually. But the industry could never figure out how he earned a profit in what should have been an asset-heavy, low-margin business since Allied paid the highest prices for unrefined oil and had additional transportation costs compared to its Midwest competitors.[178]

The answer was that Tino De Angelis was what he had always been: a swindler, and this was his most ambitious swindle yet. The scheme he hit on was to use his salad oil refining business as a way to borrow as much money as possible, using his oil inventories as collateral, and use the proceeds to speculate in the commodities futures market. If these doubly levered speculations worked out, De Angelis would make a fortune while having to put up almost no money of his own. But that wasn't even the worst part: The worst part was that Tino added a *third* layer of leverage by borrowing against oil inventories that *did not even exist.*

But to do this, De Angelis needed a little help. Given his past, he was too risky a credit for banks to lend to outright, so the lenders wanted some protection. De Angelis therefore built his business through financing obtained through field warehousing. Under this arrangement, a commodity-owning borrower would give a third party (the field warehouser) control over its inventory, which would be placed in a designated area on the borrower's property that the warehouser controlled. The warehouser did not take possession of the inventory; instead, it leased the tanks from the borrower, isolated the inventory on the borrower's property, and hired people from the borrower to act as custodians. The field warehouser would ensure that the inventory existed and had value and would write out a receipt for the value of the inventory. The borrower would take the receipt to a bank to get a loan, allowing the bank to earn interest while the warehouser earned revenue through storage fees paid by the borrower. The warehouser guaranteed the value of the inventory and was responsible if the amount was less than the amount certified. In one sense, then, a field warehouser was a simple financial guarantor earning what it considered to be 'easy' insurance premiums for guaranteeing what it considered to be 'easy' risks, just as MBIA would do decades later.

Due to the success of its better-known Travelers Cheques and money order businesses, American Express's leadership thought entering field warehousing was a logical extension of its operations.[xxxi] The company's treasurer at the time thought offering this service would allow banks to make loans they otherwise wouldn't consider, which would augment American Express's vital relationship with the banks that sold its cheques and money orders. And so, in 1944 American Express incorporated the American Express Field Warehousing Corporation with $1 million of capital as a subsidiary of the parent. The entity was little more than an afterthought until 1957, when Tino De Angelis sought to become a client. Ignoring common sense, American Express took him on.[179]

---

xxxi   American Express used the British spelling of 'check'.

Shortly after becoming an Amex customer, De Angelis found himself indicted by the Justice Department for suborning perjury during the SEC's investigation in 1953. An ex-employee of Gobel asserted that De Angelis had instructed him to lie when he testified that the stated value of the company's inventories was accurate. Foreshadowing future events, Tino had even borrowed money against phantom inventories. The case collapsed when the employee changed his testimony. But Tino's skirmishes with authority piled up: After becoming a client of American Express, he would be fined and barred (and reinstated) from participating in certain programs by the Agriculture Department, mired in a quarrel with the IRS, and attacked as 'disreputable' by a senator.[180]

The ticking Tino time bomb aside, was field warehousing even worth the trouble for American Express? No. From 1944 to 1962, the warehousing subsidiary made money in ten years and lost it in nine, cumulatively producing a loss. The profit or loss never exceeded $101,000. Helped by Allied, its best year was 1959 when it earned a net profit of $98,871. In contrast, American Express's total net income that year was $8.4 million. By the late 1950s, American Express Field Warehousing had around 500 accounts, with two responsible for all profits: Freezer House Corp. and Allied Crude Vegetable Oil Refining Corporation, both enterprises controlled by De Angelis, with Allied as the more important of the two.[181]

The subsidiary became a source of tension within American Express, with some executives wanting to dispose of it. Some employees were aware that no one at the company knew enough about vegetable oils to value the inventory. Michael Casserly, assistant secretary of the field warehousing subsidiary, thought having an Allied employee as a custodian was a foolish idea. Casserly also knew that underground pipes connected the tanks, providing an opportunity for fraud.[182]

American Express also had plenty of specific warning signs that something was amiss. In June of 1960, the president of the field warehousing subsidiary, Donald Miller, received a call from an anonymous person who said Tino's operation was a fraud. This person, who identified himself as "Taylor," said he worked at Bayonne. Miller had several conversations with Taylor, who claimed that Allied's tanks were filled not with valuable oil but with useless water.

Taylor pointed to Tank 6006, which he asserted had a metal chamber that went from the top of the tank to the bottom, while the rest was full of water. When an Amex inspector tested the tank, he would unwittingly drop his sampling device directly into the oil-filled chamber, leading to a sham measurement.[183]

In response to the tip, Miller sent four men to inspect Allied. They found water in the first five tanks checked. The water in the tanks ranged from one foot to eight feet in the 24-foot tanks, when no more than six inches (as a result of condensation) were supposed to be in there. As the inspection continued, they found unusual amounts of water in five more tanks, for a total of ten of the 70 tanks at Bayonne.[184]

Picture 1: Allied Crude's tanks

Source: Charles F. Cummings New Jersey Information Center, Newark Public Library.

The tanks were connected through a series of pipes, and some of Allied's ex-employees, now working as American Express custodians, had the keys for the tank locks. The inspection took place over several days. Over this period, the men were likely moving oil from tank to tank to hide the true water level from American Express Field Warehousing inspectors. They even allowed Tino's employees to provide some of the tank readings. Despite this farce, American Express Field Warehousing concluded its inspection without taking action, comforted by their finding that there was still more than enough oil to cover the firm's outstanding receipts. Miller was so naive that he later said, "We thought Allied would be as interested as we were in finding out if the tanks contained water."

Tino appeared apoplectic over the search, threatening to take his business elsewhere. His cousin, in fact, provided American Express with a letter ending the warehouse contract. While American Express, in theory, had all the leverage in the relationship—Tino needed Amex more than Amex needed him—the fat fraudster didn't act that way: When Amex asked Tino for a balance sheet, he told them he couldn't show it to them since it was a competitive secret.[185]

In November, a man who identified himself as an associate of Taylor's made a call to Howard Clark, who had become president and chief executive officer of American Express in April of that year. He was routed to Clark's assistant, Hasbrouck Miller (unrelated to Donald). Taylor's supposed associate said Donald Miller's inspection was a joke and that Tino had fooled the inspectors. After talking to other Amex employees about conducting a search without Donald's knowledge, Hasbrouck concluded only Donald knew enough to perform a proper investigation. As a result, Hasbrouck called Donald, who took the extraordinary step of warning Tino about the calls.[186]

There was simply no interest within American Express in uncovering the fraud. And Bayonne's inventories kept growing. In 1962, they rose from 165 million pounds in March to almost half a billion in September. By November, the field warehousing subsidiary had issued receipts for more than 400 million pounds, essentially guaranteeing $40 million worth of borrowing power, which Allied used to obtain loans from the largest banks in the country.[187]

Finally, in early 1963, Clark decided the subsidiary was not worth American Express's time and chose to dispose of it since he didn't think it would be able to reach his target of $500,000 of profit per year. He decided to sell the business to Lawrence Warehousing Company for $1.1 million. However, Donald Miller persuaded him to keep his two largest clients, saying they had never had an issue with the Allied or Freezer House accounts, a clearly false assertion levied by an employee desperate to keep his job. He also stated, "The account has never falsely represented any fact or circumstances to us." So, in May 1963, Clark sold the legacy subsidiary and incorporated American Express Warehousing Ltd. to handle only Tino's business.[188] A month before the formation of this new subsidiary, inventories at Bayonne hit 850 million pounds, and the predecessor subsidiary had issued receipts for 804 million… *which was more soybean oil than the U.S. Census Bureau said existed in the entire country.*

Clark continued grappling with what to do, wavering on whether field warehousing for only two clients was worth the risk. He went out to Bayonne to meet with Tino in July. Clark's visit prompted him to ask the company's auditor and American Express employees to review the controls and systems of the warehouse division, as he was concerned about the risks and adequacy of controls in place. American Express's auditor, Haskins & Sells, recommended enhancing controls but stated, "In our opinion, on the basis of our review, the system of internal controls of American Express Warehousing is satisfactory." Tino had fooled them, too.[189]

Senior vice president N.F. Page said the probe demonstrated that there was enough oil on hand at Bayonne to exceed the warehouse receipts. Page also pointed out that Amex had $30 million of insurance. Although the last warehouse receipts covered $51.5 million of oil, he remarked, "It is inconceivable that $21.5 million of oil could disappear without our knowledge." Page wrote in a memo to the Amex president, "Our only risk is that of dishonest operations which we failed to detect and it is inconceivable that this could reach proportions greater than our insurance coverage." Other executives, such as George Pfifer, urged Clark to dispose of the business, thinking the risk was too high. Plus, they found Tino difficult to deal with. Some credit officers responsible for a loan to Allied were frustrated when Tino failed to respond to their demands for additional collateral.

Between August 30 and September 27, the American Express Warehousing receipts for soybean oil went from 752 million pounds to 937 million pounds.[190] American Express Warehousing issued almost $20 million of receipts during September 1963, bringing the total to $87.4 million.

Finally, Clark chose to get out of the business entirely. While the American Express CEO was concerned about the size of the account, the catalyst for his change of heart was that he thought some of his warehousing employees had been compromised. Donald Miller had owned shares in one of Tino's companies, which led to his resignation. Other Amex employees had also bought stock in Tino's companies and invested alongside him in his futures speculations.

Lawrence Warehousing, which bought the previous Amex field warehousing subsidiary, agreed to purchase the last two accounts, with the deal expected to close on December 1, 1963. American Express told Tino that it would no longer issue warehouse receipts since it was exiting the business, but would honor the old receipts. So, at the end of September, the warehousing subsidiary was only issuing receipts to replace previously issued ones. With a two-month gap until Lawrence took over, Tino was in a bind.

Tino solved his problem of not being able to receive additional warehouse receipts from American Express. He simply stole them. Tino began forging American Express Warehouse receipts on October 14.

Meanwhile, Tino's buying on the futures exchanges continued to explode. His buying pushed prices higher, which made it less likely that a big order—which he needed to be able to unwind his trading—would come through. Commodity market rumors spread that the Soviet Union, after disastrous crops in Russia and Ukraine, would soon be forced to buy vegetable oil from the United States. These rumors ignored the fact that the Soviet Union government had sold oil to Spain the month before, something it wouldn't have done if there had been a shortage.

On Friday, November 15, 1963, Tino informed his aides that they couldn't buy any more contracts as the company's brokers were worried about the Congressional opposition to selling commodities to Russia. Allied's brokers prevented the firm from buying more contracts, so Tino created dummy accounts. These accounts were supposed to post margin to a broker, but Allied got around this because a partner of the brokerage firm was away attending his father's funeral. Tino also raised cash by forging orders to release the oil, leading to American Express issuing receipts that Tino could use to raise cash. The Commodity Exchange Authority, aware that Allied's had been the vast majority of the buying on the Produce Exchange, sent an investigator to Bayonne to look at Allied's books. News of the Senate suspending debate over Russian wheat without a deal being reached led to short selling that drove commodity prices down.[191]

Tino realized the jig was up and contacted a lawyer to help place Allied into receivership. Allied declared bankruptcy on Tuesday, November 19. When American Express learned about it, the company was unworried, comforted by its belief that there was enough oil to cover its receipts. Clark thought the company was also protected by $30 million of insurance coverage. But this nonchalance ended quickly: By the end of the week, the inspectors looked at the tanks and couldn't find the soybean oil. Allied clients asserted that oil was missing, and it became clear that Tino had forged receipts. Bunge Corporation sued American Express's subsidiary, claiming it had lost more than $15 million of its oil. The New York Stock Exchange suspended two brokerage firms with exposure to De Angelis after Allied failed to meet its margin calls to them. What became known as the salad oil scandal was front page news.

Tank 6006, the one Taylor warned about, was supposed to hold $3,575,000 worth of soybean oil. Instead, saltwater poured out of it for 12 days. And sure enough, the special chamber, which did hold a few hundred pounds of soybean oil, fell to the bottom of the tank.[192]

Despite all this, American Express's stock didn't plummet immediately when news of the fraud broke. The stock closed at $62.19 the Friday before Allied's bankruptcy and dropped to $60.81 the following Thursday. President John F.

Kennedy's assassination on November 22, 1963, rattled the entire market, with the Dow Jones Industrial index falling 2.9% and American Express declining 4.6% to $58.00 that day. But unlike the Dow, American Express kept falling as reports of the missing oil leaked out. Its stock ended the month of November 26.5% below where it traded the day before Lee Harvey Oswald fired his shot. In contrast, the Dow was up 2.4% over the same period.

After the fact, it emerged that people in the warehousing business had known that something was up, with one president of another warehousing company that didn't operate at Bayonne later stating, "We heard about funny business at Bayonne for years. At the workingman level you often heard talk about it. All of the men who worked there were getting extremely high salaries. But we couldn't prove anything, so we minded our own business." These revelations came too late for American Express: Inspectors could now only find 134 million pounds of oil at Bayonne. Between the 878 million pounds of oil American Express issued receipts for with a stated value of approximately $82 million and the 395 million pounds worth of forged receipts worth $39 million, American Express had vouched for nearly 1.3 billion pounds of oil. Plus, Bunge had accused American Express Warehousing of losing 161 million pounds of oil worth around $15 million, bringing the total attributable to American Express to around $135 million. Including the other companies Tino defrauded, there was a total shortage of 1,854,000,000 pounds of oil valued at $175 million.

The banks and export companies, who were legally only creditors of American Express's field warehousing subsidiary, looked to American Express (the parent company) for payoffs. Not only did the company have insurance and a large balance sheet, but it also couldn't afford to tarnish its relationships with the banks or compromise its brand name. Throughout its history, American Express had relied on being trusted, allowing it to create enormous value across several business lines over the previous 113 years.[193]

As if the situation wasn't stressful enough, American Express shareholders did not possess limited liability. Due to its history in the express business, where a lack of disclosure was a competitive advantage, the company had never incorporated. This meant that creditors could go after individual shareholders if the company couldn't pay its debts.[194]

On December 23, the Department of Justice indicted Tino.[xxxii,195] Receipt holders were stunned when American Express put its field warehousing subsidiary into

---

xxxii Tino was sentenced to twenty years in prison but released on parole after seven for the salad oil scandal. He would continue on as a scammer and returned to prison for meat-related frauds.

bankruptcy on December 30, 1963. The subsidiary had slightly more than $130,000 in assets. American Express said this was only a procedural step, executed to flush out all receipt-holding creditors through the bankruptcy process. $210 million of claims arose.[196] American Express's consolidated equity at the end of 1963 was only $78.7 million.[197] The future of the entire company seemed to be in doubt. By the end of the year, American Express stock had fallen to $38.63, down nearly 40% since November 15, erasing over $100 million from the company's market capitalization.

What became known as 'the salad oil scandal' was a textbook case of management incompetence and stupidity, and investors abandoned the company in droves. The 33-year-old Buffett had kept his eye on the scandal since it broke, but he waited months to start buying. And he started building his investment—the best of the Partnership—during a particularly trying time for him and his family, as his father Howard lay hospital-ridden in the final weeks of his life in April 1964. To the extent he was known at all at the time, Buffett was known for his ability to find quantitative bargains among the semi-anonymous flotsam and jetsam of American capitalism, but American Express was an extremely well-known company.

Moreover, Buffett proceeded to write a remarkable letter to Clark in which he rather breezily absolved Amex management of any responsibility for the scandal, encouraged it to use shareholder money (which included Buffett's) to pay creditors harmed by the scandal, and more or less encouraged Clark to forget the whole thing. Finally, and most importantly, Buffett continued adding to his American Express position long after the scandal had diminished in importance. By the time he sold his position years later, American Express had become the most important individual contributor to the results of the Buffett Partnership and arguably the biggest turning point in Buffett's career.

To see how this all came about, we have to go back more than a century.

Cash is the curse of the traveling class

In 1836, the U.S. federal government dissolved the Second Bank of the United States, ending the only national interbank messenger system. This created a problem for privately owned banks: Then, as now, they constantly transacted business with other banks, but unlike today, these transactions required cash and securities to physically travel from one bank to another. Without the government-sponsored interbank messenger system, banks would now have to handle these types of transactions themselves—a difficult, dangerous, and expensive proposition for any one bank to take on alone.

Special courier services called express companies emerged to solve this problem. Banks would hire the express companies, whose employees would accompany the shipments to ensure the banks' cash, securities, or gold arrived safely at their destination. Over time, express companies increased their business by combining bank shipments with other items requiring rapid delivery, such as packages, perishables, and fragile items. The added volume brought added efficiency, which was shared with customers, allowing the major express companies to drop the discount rate on deliveries (essentially the express's commission percentage) from 10% to around 1%. Because express companies charged for financial instruments by value and packages by weight, banks remained their most valuable customers.

Demand for these services grew as the population dispersed. Railroads became the critical infrastructure connecting the country. Express companies used the railroads to transport their goods, with the railroads charging either a flat monthly fee or a percentage of the gross receipts. Many leaned towards the gross-receipt formula since it aligned incentives between the two, with the railroads benefiting when the express business grew. Further, the contracts required the express companies to keep their rates above bulk-freight rates so they wouldn't directly compete with railroads. Expresses fought for exclusivity over the rail lines, which became a feature of nearly all express contracts by the 1870s.[198]

The American Express Company was formed in 1850 when William Fargo, Henry Wells, and John Butterfield merged their three separate express companies into one. The combination ended fierce competition between Wells and Butterfield and set the newly formed enterprise up to dominate the New York express business.[xxxiii]

When the trio merged, they structured the company as an unincorporated joint-stock association with a lifetime of only ten years. Unlike a limited liability corporation, this meant that shareholders were personally liable for the company's debts and could be assessed for what the company could not pay itself. American Express's founders chose this form because stock associations had fewer obligations to stockholders: They didn't vote on directors, had higher requirements to demand a vote, and weren't entitled to financial statements. The express companies viewed the lack of disclosure as a significant competitive advantage, as neither potential competitors nor railroads knew how profitable their business was.[199]

---

xxxiii William Fargo would later put forth a resolution for American Express to extend his territory to California. After the vote died, Wells and Fargo formed Wells Fargo & Company in 1852, which became one of the dominant express companies (like American Express). Wells Fargo, of course, morphed into the famous bank.

The economics were helped by the cartel nature of the express business: The companies cooperated, their networks seldom overlapped territories, and they fixed prices. The biggest threat was that the railroads would extract a greater share of revenues if they realized how profitable the business was. The largest express companies had leverage, however, as they had a larger territory than any individual railroad. Their networks required multiple railroads, steamships, and stagecoaches to get the job done. Any individual railroad was too small to pose a severe threat, and an express could often circumvent a hostile line if needed. With exclusivity and railroads receiving an attractive payment, the risk of competitive entry was minimal, allowing the express companies to mint profits.

By the end of the 1850s, American Express service ran on 6,000 miles of railroad track from New York to the Midwest and into Canada, and profits rolled in. At the same time, the company began developing what we would today call its brand image: The company used a watchdog as one of its early brand symbols in the 1850s and circulated an image of a canine guarding a lockbox in its promotional materials (see Picture 2), demonstrating that it knew what its job was.[200]

Picture 2: American Express branding

Source: American Express

After its first decade, American Express recapitalized the company after a phony auction of its assets, retaining the unlimited-liability joint-stock association structure, and giving it a life of 30 years subject to renewal by a vote of directors.[201]

While the express business continued booming, a new type of product emerged to solve the same problem of how to allow cash to travel safely from one place to another. This was the money order, a type of check that could be purchased at one office, sent long distances in place of cash, and then cashed at another office, with the two offices later settling the transaction between themselves. While American Express did not create the first money order itself, the company did improve upon it. The U.S. Post Office started offering postal money orders in 1864 to prevent postmen from stealing cash out of letters, encroaching upon the express companies' monopoly on sending small sums. However, the postal order had a variety of issues: It required English literacy, could only be cashed at a designated post office, and the value of the order could be changed. Marcellus Berry thought American Express could do better and badgered president James Fargo to let him create a competing money order, with the Amex leader finally relenting in 1881. Berry's money order, rolled out in 1882, listed all of the 5-cent increments from $1 to $10—$1.00, $1.05, $1.10, and so forth all the way up to $10.00. This allowed the clerk issuing the money order to physically cut a protective margin out of the money order to indicate a designated sum, similar to the way an old-fashioned ticket puncher cuts a physical hole in a train ticket. Once the protective margin was cut to, say, $5.00, neither the money order customer nor anyone else could tamper with the money order by raising its value because all increments in excess of $5.00 no longer appeared on the money order.

When a customer bought an order, the express clerk wrote the name of the payee and the amount on two stubs, giving the buyer one and keeping the other for the company's records. Later that decade, American Express would amend the money order by raising the limit from $10 to $50. With the new money order, the agent could only cut to a round number, which served as the maximum, and the agent wrote the exact amount on the order itself.[202]

The business required a network of offices where money orders could be bought and cashed. American Express had over 4,000 offices, but these locations were only in 19 states. Amex needed the other express companies to join their office networks to its own, which they did. These express companies honored American Express's orders, and American Express honored theirs. American Express benefited from being first, allowing it to dominate the money order business, with only the Post Office ever posing any credible threat.

Picture 3: The Money Order

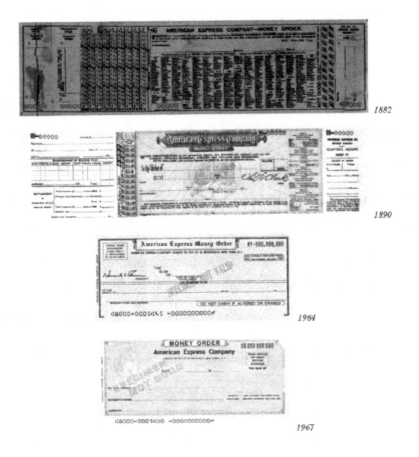

1882

1890

1964

1967

Source: American Express, 1967 Annual Report.

American Express did not initially expect to profit from the product, thinking it would only help promote the express business. But that expectation proved to be wrong. While the company made some money from the sales charge levied when a customer purchased a money order, it primarily benefited from investing the float created by outstanding money orders that had been paid for at their origin office but not yet cashed at their destination office. Plus, the money order business had an added benefit that helped later on: Immigrants sent the money order abroad, which forced American Express to create a network of banking relationships throughout Europe.[203]

The money order was an important product, but it required a predetermined amount and a predetermined payee at the other end, so it was not a true substitute for 'walking-around money' that could be used just like cash by those who did not want to walk around with actual cash. The innovation that addressed this was the travelers cheque, which became the next great business for American Express. This business started after company president James Fargo went to Europe with a letter of credit from an American bank. Letters of credit were the most common way for travelers to finance their trips abroad. This letter showed a sum that the traveler had on deposit in a bank in the United States and could use to draw cash at overseas banks. The banks would compare the signature to a sample in their files and write down the amount the traveler drew down on the letter. The letter benefited both parties: No one but the traveler could cash it, while the bank had safety through the signature system.

However, the letter of credit was a huge pain in the ass to use. During Fargo's trip, the European bank enraged the American Express president by keeping him waiting a long time for his cash. When Fargo returned to the United States, he asked Berry to figure out how to make it easier to carry money abroad, which led to the creation of the travelers cheque, which was really the only product American Express ever invented.

Like the letter of credit, the security of the check depended on the double signature: the first at the time of the cheque's purchase and the second when cashed. However, it contrasted with the letter of credit since the cheque came in small amounts—such as $10, $20, $50, or $100—allowing travelers to pay for individual items without being stuck with unwanted currencies. American Express offered some additional benefits for the consumer, too: It promised to reimburse customers for lost checks and had a fixed foreign exchange rate.[xxxiv] When American Express rolled out the travelers cheque in 1892, European banks quickly accepted it because of the relationships the company had built through the money order business.[204]

While customers paid a 1% service charge on each sale (with the bank keeping two-thirds for acting as sales agents), the real money was in the float, just like the money order business. In contrast to money orders, which were typically cashed within a few days, travelers cheques were cashed

---

xxxiv The conversion numbers were based on the average exchange rates over the prior two years (exchange rates were generally more stable when the cheque was introduced). American Express guaranteed they were convertible at the amounts printed on the cheque. This feature also prevented travelers from being taken advantage of by exchange dealers since the rates were fixed on the cheque.

Picture 4: The Travelers Cheque

Source: American Express, 1967 Annual Report.

45 days after issuance on average, with some taking years for consumers to use. The float was seasonal, peaking in the summer months as people enjoyed their vacations. Even though other express companies would enter the market, American Express's travelers cheque dominated, gaining the reputation as 'blue paper money.' The business also benefited from a travel boom the company had not foreseen, as middle-class Americans began to partake in overseas travel.[205]

The company's reputation rose during the bank holiday in 1933 when American Express persuaded the Treasury Department to allow the company's offices to remain open so that people could cash their cheques and money orders. American Express gained a leg up on its competition, and its main travelers cheque competitor—the American Banker Association travelers cheque—folded shortly after, granting American Express a near-monopoly in that business during the 1930s.[206]

The travel boom following World War II benefited the travelers cheque business enormously. In 1945, the war's final year, the company sold $522 million worth of cheques. The number passed $1 billion in the early 1950s, and the average float outstanding hit a quarter billion dollars.[207]

Closer to home, the end of the war heralded the rise of the Man in the Grey Flannel Suit generation, aka the Mad Men generation: a generation of corporate executives who traveled for business and entertained clients constantly at restaurants, nightclubs, and theaters. These executives faced a new version of essentially the same problem as travelers cheque holders and money order customers and express customers before them: They were able and willing to spend far more money than it was comfortable and convenient to physically carry as cash. This time around, innovation came to the rescue in the form of the charge card.

Formed in 1950, Diners' Club initiated the first universal restaurant charge card that prominent New York restaurants would accept. Cardholders charged for a meal, and the restaurant collected from the Club less a 5%–10% discount (which restaurants were willing to accept since cardholders typically spent more than those paying with cash on hand). Diners' Club paid the restaurant and had to collect from cardholders. In the 1950s, credit cards took off in the United States. There were cards for specific companies as well as universal travel and entertainment charge cards.[208]

American Express debated the merits of creating a card. But by the 1950s, the company's executives realized that people were using the cards for travel-related services, posing a risk for the travelers cheque. Furthermore, the money order business was becoming less important, with the rise of personal checking accounts stealing business away from money orders. The company finally decided it would be better for American Express to protect itself by making its own card rather than lose all that business.[209]

American Express debated entering the business by acquiring Diners' Club. After that deal fell through, American Express decided to go forward by launching its own American Express Credit Card in 1958. The American Express Credit Card was, in reality, a charge card, not a credit card. The latter had a revolving line of credit whose balance could be carried over from month to month. While technically still an extension of credit, the charge card required all outstanding balances to be paid in full each month.[xxxv,210]

Before launching, American Express reached a deal with the American Hotel Association, providing Amex with 150,000 cardholders and 4,500 participating hotels. American Express then bought 40,000 members from the Gourmet card.[211] And when rumors spread that American Express was thinking of starting a card, people wanted in. In contrast to the banks, who literally had to mass-mail cards to people when they rolled out their offerings (a practice made illegal in 1970), people flocked to American Express.[212] The brand, whose image had evolved from a guard dog to 'the guardian of Rome,' the centurion, had now become a status symbol.

By the October 1, 1958 launch date, American Express issued more than a quarter million cards, with the firm way behind on applications and more coming in each day. The company used credit bureaus to review applications, with the bureaus verifying employment, income, credit history, and bank information to analyze risk. When Howard Clark had researched the card division two years prior to the card's founding, he thought they could get to 196,000 holders five years after starting operations—they had surpassed that before opening. (As a sign of the company's prestige, American Express charged cardholders $6 per card annually—one dollar more than Diners' Club).

With the cardholder side of the equation solved, American Express needed to get more restaurants and hotels on board as merchants. Some came to American Express unsolicited due to the value of the brand name, and by opening day, American Express had 17,500 establishments signed up.[213]

The company struggled with core operational items due to the explosive demand. The accounting was complicated, and collection from customers proved challenging. The company initially did a lousy job evaluating credit risks, leading to abuse or slow payment. Since the company was committed to paying the merchants who accepted the card, these issues led to the business losing money: $4 million in the first two years and an estimated total of around $14 million by 1962 (the accounting was so poor that it was hard to get precise figures).[214]

Travel and entertainment cards were still a fresh concept. People were not used to paying off their debts within 30 days. American Express assured establishments they would pay within ten days, but cardholders often took three or even six months to pay—the reverse of the cherished float that had made American

---

xxxv   American Express later partnered with banks to offer revolving credit but did not debut a card with its own revolving line of credit until 1987.

Picture 5: American Express Credit Card

Source: American Express

Express such a profitable company. Howard Clark even considered exiting the card business and resurrected the idea of merging with Diners' Club. But American Express's lawyers decided it wouldn't pass antitrust vetting.[215]

The company lucked out. They hired George Waters to run the division, who attacked the card business's problems. He cleaned up the accounting and enforced stricter credit policies, taking late payers off the membership rolls and raising the standards to get a card in the first place. He also lifted the card fee. The demand for the card was so great that membership continued to rise even as price and membership standards rose. Waters also raised the discount rate charged to establishments and continued increasing the number of service establishments that took the card, allowing American Express to turn a profit in its card business in 1962.[216]

While there were competitors such as Diners' Club, Carte Blanche (the Hilton Hotels Corporation offering), and bank cards, American Express flourished. The company's superior resources, international connections from the travelers cheque operations, and brand name helped catapult it to the top of the field in the 1960s. People didn't see a need to hold more than one travel and entertainment card, and that card became American Express. The travel and entertainment cards stood apart with their annual fee, something the banks didn't impose until much later, fearful they would lose share amongst each other.

The bank cards were largely unprofitable through the 1960s, while American Express reached profitability in 1962.[217]

At the end of 1963, American Express had ten divisions: Travelers cheques, money orders and utility bids, travel, credit card, overseas commercial banking, military base banking facilities, foreign remittances, international freight, Wells Fargo & Company (an armored service company, not the bank), and Hertz American Express International (a 49% owned investment). Field warehousing was in bankruptcy, and American Express was, of course, exiting that business.[218]

The company didn't provide details on the financials of each division, but two segments truly mattered: travelers cheques and the charge card.[219] American Express had about a two-thirds share of the travelers cheque market, with the company selling around $2.6 billion worth in 1963. Only 20% of U.S. travel dollars were spent on travelers cheques, so the company thought there was room for growth. Competition had been increasing, with First National City Bank (which later changed its name to Citicorp and then Citibank) and Bank of America stepping up advertising in recent years, but American Express was proving resilient.[220]

The company charged a 4–7% commission to the participants (such as restaurants) to cover American Express's cost of billing members.[221] American Express's card was a premium product with a higher income-generating clientele. The card had just turned profitable in 1962, and the business demonstrated ample momentum in 1963: Billings were up 28%, cardholders grew 14.4%, and average cardholder expenditure was up 15% to $251.[222]

As Table 1 shows, the company was growing fast. Revenue rose 11.0% annually over the past decade, net income at 10.1%, and the credit card business had turned profitable and was gaining momentum. The banking subsidiary comprised nearly half of the company's assets, which likely weighed down returns on equity, obfuscating the capital-light nature of the other businesses. The company had spent a century building up its brand name, allowing it to capitalize on the integrity the American Express name bestowed. Amex knew exactly what it was about: In advertisements, the company called itself 'The Company for People Who Travel' and asserted, "Cash is the curse of the traveling class!"[223] But the salad oil scandal suddenly threatened all this.

The Partnership's best investment

We don't have much of a record of what exactly was going through Warren Buffett's mind when he invested in American Express. But based on some

Table 1: Ten-year financial summary

	1954	1955	1956	1957	1958	1959	1960	1961	1962	1963	CAGR
Revenue	37,144	42,219	47,936	53,821	59,045	61,117	74,709	77,378	86,771	100,418	11.0%
EBIT	5,008	6,273	7,302	8,119	8,505	9,609	11,496	11,194	11,951	15,979	12.7%
Net income	4,685	5,431	6,344	6,871	7,586	8,437	9,007	9,204	10,131	11,264	10.1%
Net income per share	1.05	1.22	1.42	1.54	1.70	1.89	2.02	2.06	2.27	2.52	10.1%
Dividends declared per share	0.60	0.64	0.83	0.95	1.00	1.05	1.20	1.20	1.25	1.40	10.8%
Total assets	620,963	629,326	700,136	667,635	680,115	732,703	787,844	876,546	915,179	1,020,206	6.1%
Travelers Cheques and Travelers Letters of Credit outstanding	259,637	282,832	304,436	320,297	337,510	358,703	365,526	386,389	421,063	470,127	6.7%
Customers deposits and credit balances	222,829	243,054	266,758	243,049	215,640	223,842	286,080	303,538	337,238	366,491	7.0%
Shareholders' equity	41,655	44,296	47,178	49,867	52,996	56,399	60,102	63,805	68,356	78,696	7.1%
Return on equity	11.5%	12.6%	13.9%	14.2%	14.7%	15.4%	15.5%	14.9%	15.3%	15.3%	
Revenue growth rate	5.0%	13.7%	13.5%	12.3%	9.7%	3.5%	22.2%	3.6%	12.1%	15.7%	
Travelers Cheques and Travelers Letters of Credit outstanding growth rate	5.3%	8.9%	7.6%	5.2%	5.4%	6.3%	1.9%	5.7%	9.0%	11.7%	
Customers' deposits and credit balances growth rate	19.5%	9.1%	9.8%	-8.9%	-11.3%	3.8%	27.8%	6.1%	11.1%	8.7%	
Number of offices at year end:											
Domestic offices	77	85	91	96	96	96	99	108	105	115	4.4%
Overseas commercial offices	75	84	87	90	94	102	99	98	105	110	4.6%
Overseas offices at military bases	197	203	208	213	183	186	181	173	179	177	0.2%
Total	349	372	386	399	373	384	379	379	389	402	2.3%
American Express correspondents	4,267	4,351	4,399	4,478	4,465	4,541	4,551	4,631	5,902	5,921	3.4%
Other American Express selling outlets	63,294	64,457	66,436	64,271	66,280	67,736	67,614	69,338	70,471	75,378	2.0%
American Express Credit Card service establishments	-	-	-	-	32,183	41,455	46,982	50,676	81,989	85,580	n/a

Source: American Express Annual Reports

nuggets, and even more importantly, based on the investor he became, we can make some very good educated guesses. What we don't have to guess about is this: Buffett did not simply exercise some primal instinct "to be fearful when others are greedy and to be greedy only when others are fearful" in a situation with significant uncertainty.[224] On the contrary, he did a lot of work, and he eventually gained a lot of certainty.

At first, however, there was indeed a definite sense of uncertainty and panic in the air regarding the true size of the liabilities related to the salad oil scandal. This risk was compounded by the fact that American Express shareholders faced the theoretical possibility of being personally assessed to cover those claims the company could not pay itself. Buffett saw the panic but did not immediately buy the stock. He later remarked:

> So every trust department in the United States panicked. I remember the Continental Bank held over 5% of the company, and all of a sudden not only do they see that the trust accounts were going to have stock worth zero, but they could get assessed. The stock just poured out, of course, and the market got slightly inefficient for a short period of time.[225]

In theory, the company could have just walked away after putting the subsidiary into bankruptcy. But there was *some* risk creditors could pierce the corporate veil. It was in the interest of both parties to settle the issue without a protracted fight. The banks held the loans, and American Express's relationship with them was critical. If American Express walked away from these liabilities, the banks could refuse to accept the travelers cheque, which would kill American Express. But Amex had leverage, too: The travelers cheques brought in commissions and deposits, so the banks didn't want to crush American Express.

Clark had put out a statement on November 27, eight days after Allied declared bankruptcy: "If our subsidiary should be held liable for amounts in excess of its insurance coverage and other assets, American Express Company feels morally bound to do everything it can, consistent with its overall responsibilities, to see that such excess liabilities are satisfied."[226] He had shown his hand—the issue of whether American Express Warehousing, Ltd. was an independent subsidiary or not was irrelevant.

But American Express needed time. There was a question of whether American Express was responsible at all. Receipt holders weren't interested in attacking the company directly. While they certainly wanted their money, they still wanted to maintain a good relationship with American Express.

The first formal meeting of creditors occurred on January 28, 1964, less than a month after the field warehousing subsidiary declared bankruptcy. American

Express indicated it was interested in settling. The company finally put forth a payment plan on April 12, 1964, in a convoluted 25-page document. American Express proposed to pay $35 million if the IRS ruled that the company could write off the payments for tax purposes and the courts ruled that shareholders couldn't block the payments. Amex also offered another $10 million that would be paid in three installments, a guarantee of at least $10 million from insurance, and the sale of actual oil at Bayonne might add another $5 million. Shareholders revolted against Clark at the shareholders' meeting later that month, and a group of them went to court to block the settlement.[227]

That same month, *Fortune* published a lengthy article on American Express. The article detailed how the initial number of $135 million in receipts was not real: $15 million stemmed from a claim that did not involve warehouse receipts at all and was likely going to be challenged, at least $35 million were forgeries for which American Express was not responsible, some were duplicates, and some indicated the total value of the collateral and not the amount actually lent by the banks. The article concluded that the after-tax figure would be between $10 million and $35 million once insurance proceeds and the rejection of certain claims were accounted for.[228]

Notwithstanding the shareholder lawsuit and the phony claims, the creditors had shown a willingness to negotiate. While there was some consternation over the terms of the offer, they did not sue. The offer was enough to make a lawsuit unappealing.[229] By April 1964, there was some sense of certainty regarding the ceiling on the salad oil liabilities. Through the bankruptcy process, which Buffett could follow, the liability became whittled down, ring-fenced, and easy to handicap.

Until now, Buffett had made most of his money as a balance sheet-oriented investor. If he had been following his normal practice, he would have compared American Express's new liabilities to its balance sheet assets to determine its new value. But this time around, and perhaps for the first time in his career, he realized that American Express's most important asset by far did not appear on its balance sheet—it existed in people's minds.

The company's four historical cash cows—express, money order, travelers cheques, and charge card—all depended on safeguarding cash before it arrived at its destination. In the express business, the composition of money did not change; it was transferred from one place to another. The location of the cash had to physically change. The money order business and travelers cheque businesses *did* change the composition of cash. A customer handed money to an agent in exchange for a piece of paper that he used elsewhere. The card was a slight twist, as it served both the merchants and cardholders. Merchants received assurances they would get paid, and cardholders could pay for items without the hassle of carrying cash. These four businesses solved the problem in different ways, but they were all based on the same premise: When a customer consents to place his cash into a state of temporary limbo, whether physical or virtual, that cash requires a bodyguard until it reaches its final destination. American Express was that bodyguard.

American Express solved the cash-carrying problem in different ways, from literally transporting and safeguarding it from one destination to another, to simplifying the process of using one's own money in the money order, travelers cheques, and charge card businesses. The company built a currency transfer network in the express business, and then created a currency substitute network within the money order, travelers cheque, and charge card businesses. In a way, American Express was a liquidity provider, lowering the cost to transact and thereby expanding the number of transactions that would have happened otherwise.

How did field warehousing fit into all this? The short answer is that it didn't. American Express claimed it got into the business to help the banks. But that rationale doesn't stand up to scrutiny given the repeated headaches the business produced. It seems more likely that American Express thought it could make some easy money with little capital investment. And once the subsidiary was formed, middle managers needed to fight to keep their jobs and made idiotic decisions.

In contrast to the other businesses that depended on the high-quality American Express name, the company had a concentration of risk in field warehousing, and it imploded. Lawrence Warehousing, the biggest field warehouse company in the country, guarded only $100,000 of inventory on average at its locations.[230] The charge card business had a dispersion of risk—any one customer couldn't blow up the company. The company also benefited from significant competitive advantages in its travelers cheque and charge card businesses that simply did not exist in the thin-margin field warehousing business.

This, of course, raised an all-important question for Buffett: The size of the salad oil liabilities aside, was the scandal impairing the value of American Express's most important asset by far, namely its reputation as cash's best bodyguard? To answer this, he performed scuttlebutt, visiting restaurants and other establishments to see if the salad oil scandal impaired the American Express brand. He also deployed Henry Brandt to execute some of the gumshoe work. Brandt, a stockbroker friend at Wood, Struthers & Winthrop, frequently performed research for Buffett. Brandt produced a foot-high worth of material on the company after researching bank tellers, bank officers, restaurants, hotels, and credit card holders.[231] They all reported the same thing: It was business as usual.

Actually, it was even better than that. That same April 1964 *Fortune* article added some morsels on the operating business that would have thrilled an investor: December 1963 travelers cheque sales for American Express rose 28% compared to December 1962, higher than the 9% growth for the year. Plus, the charge card business's billings rose 44% year-over-year for the month of December.[232] So not only were the liabilities from Allied's bankruptcy becoming defined, but the core business was not showing any signs of stress from the scandal.

That left valuation. At his $40 per share purchase price, and in contrast to most of the stocks discussed in this book, American Express did not sell for an obvious bargain price. With a $178.4 million market capitalization and $124.1 million enterprise value, the stock sold for 15.8x 1963 earnings, 7.8x EV/1963 EBIT, and 2.3x P/TB. It didn't look that cheap, and this valuation didn't include an adjustment for the cost of the salad oil settlement.[xxxvi]

However, the company was rapidly growing revenue and earnings, with both rising at a double-digit rate over the past decade. A simple discounted cash flow valuation shows how little growth was needed to make the stock cheap. Assuming the company grew its 1963 earnings at a 10% rate for just five years, assuming no terminal growth, and discounting the cash flows back at a 10% discount rate results in a valuation of $169.0 million for the company and $223.3 million for its equity ($50.06 per share).[xxxvii] Assuming the terminal growth rate after five years was instead 5% (with the same 10% growth rate in the interim years), the business would be worth $292.9 million and the equity would be worth $347.2 million ($77.83 per share). The eventual $40.6 million cost for the salad oil scandal—which an analyst could approximate by the time Buffett started buying—would subtract $9.10 per share from these figures, resulting in a simple range of $40.96 to $68.73 per share. As we will see shortly, that 10% growth rate assumption over the next five years proved way too low.

Buffett classified Amex as a 'relatively undervalued' general rather than a 'private owner' one. He first broke generals into 'Relatively Undervalued' and 'Private Owner' in January 1965, after his initial purchase of American Express. Buffett noted that this category comprised securities where the private owner concept was not meaningful, often due to the large size of the securities within this group, and said that 'relatively undervalued' generals were cheap compared to

---

xxxvi   Adding the eventual after-tax cost of the salad oil scandal to enterprise value and subtracting it from tangible book would result in an EV/EBIT of 10.3x and P/TB of 4.7x.
xxxvii The company had $54.4 million of net cash and financial assets/liabilities, which is why the equity value is higher than the enterprise value.

securities of the same quality.[233] In contrast to the S&P's 18.9x multiple in April 1964, American Express was cheap.[234] And Buffett knew American Express was much better than the average large American corporation, later saying:

> Look, the name American Express is one of the greatest franchises in the world. Even with terrible management it was bound to make money. American Express was last in the travelers cheque market and had to compete with the two largest banks in the country. Yet after a short time it had over 80% of the business, and no one has been able to shake this position.[xxxviii,235]

After buying 70,000 shares at around $40 a share for $2.8 million—1.6% of the company—Buffett wrote to American Express's CEO, Howard Clark, in June 1964:

> This purchase was made after extensive investigation among Travelers Cheque users, bank tellers, bank officers, credit card establishments, card holders and competitors in these various lines of endeavor. All confirmed that American Express's competitive vigor and preeminent trade position had not been damaged by the salad oil problem.

Buffett saw that Clark's move to cut a deal with the salad oil victims was not just protecting the brand but enhancing it. When Buffett wrote to the beleaguered CEO, he did not berate Clark for a foolish decision. He wanted the company to move past the scandal, generously labeling the scandal an 'Act of God.' Shirking its responsibilities by placing the warehouse subsidiary into bankruptcy and washing its hands of it—something the company could do—would have compromised this integrity and impaired the value of the franchise. By contrast, going out of its way to honor its subsidiary's debts was an investment in growing the value of that franchise.

In his letter to Clark, Buffett suggested a midyear letter detailing the growth of the other lines of business. He also offered to testify in the shareholders' suit that he would not have bought his stock if he thought the parent would ignore the claims against the subsidiary. Buffett thought the long-term value of American Express would be substantially reduced if it did. He knew that the brand value—the integrity attached to the American Express name—was much more valuable than the cost it would pay to settle the scandal.[236]

---

xxxviii Most sources indicated Amex's share was around two-thirds, not over 80% as Buffett notes. Additionally, in contrast to Buffett's comment that Amex was last in the travelers cheque market, American Express invented the cheque.

The investment was approximately 14.3% of the Partnership's assets when he wrote to Howard Clark in June 1964. But Buffett kept buying the stock as the salad oil scandal receded from the limelight. By November, he owned approximately 90,000 shares, up from the 70,000 in June. Buffett kept buying the stock into 1966, more than tripling his stake in the company: He scooped up more than 5% of American Express's shares, up from the 1.6% stake when he wrote to Howard Clark in 1964.[237]

The position became such a significant percentage of the portfolio that Buffett amended his 'Ground Rules' to partners in November 1965, adding a seventh rule:

> We diversify substantially less than most investment operations. We might invest up to 40% of our net worth in a single security under conditions coupling an extremely high probability that our facts and reasoning are correct with a very low probability that anything could drastically change the underlying value of the investment.[238]

American Express was the Partnership's largest investment at the end of 1965 and 1966, and it crushed the market in each of 1964, 1965, and 1966.[239]

The salad oil scandal was considered over by the end of 1964 despite negotiations still ongoing; the major claims wouldn't settle until 1967, with some minor suits outside the main case lasting until the 1970s.[xxxix,240] Table 2 shows that revenue and income exploded as the Partnership added to its stake. The travelers cheque business was slowing down, with the growth rate in the single digits as Buffett finished buying, but the charge card business was a machine: The number of cards outstanding increased by 20% in 1964, 29% in 1965, more than 19% in 1966, and 20% in 1967. Total billings increased 42% in 1964 and 62% in 1965 (and then they stopped disclosing it). And they had raised prices on the card: from $8 in 1961 to $10 in 1964 to $12 in 1966.[241]

While American Express started behind Diners' Club, Amex quickly surpassed them. In early 1960, Diners' Club had 1.1 million members, while American Express had more than 700,000. By 1970, American Express had twice the number of cardholders as Diners' Club and four times that of Carte Blanche, its other significant competitor.[242]

The incremental margins on the business were spectacular: Of the $119.2 million increase in the top line from 1963 to 1967, $33.2 million fell to the EBIT line,

---

xxxix The scandal wound up costing American Express $40.6 million, which included expenses related to the matter and not just the settlement amount. 1967 net income before extraordinary items was $22.6 million, so the settlement amounted to less than two years' income by this point.

Table 2: Summary financial and valuation metrics after Buffett's purchase

	1963	1964	1965	1966	1967
Revenue	100,418	122,282	156,273	187,950	219,612
EBIT	15,979	20,099	36,864	45,599	49,218
Net income before extraordinary items	11,264	12,587	15,343	19,240	22,622
Net income after extraordinary items	11,264	12,587	15,343	19,240	27,463
Return on equity	15.3%	15.3%	16.7%	18.6%	22.3%
EBIT margin	15.9%	16.4%	23.6%	24.3%	22.4%
Net income before extraordinary items margin	11.2%	10.3%	9.8%	10.2%	10.3%
Revenue growth rate	15.7%	21.8%	27.8%	20.3%	16.8%
EBIT growth rate	33.7%	25.8%	83.4%	23.7%	7.9%
Net income before extraordinary items growth rate	11.2%	11.7%	21.9%	25.4%	17.6%
Net income after extraordinary items growth rate	11.2%	11.7%	21.9%	25.4%	42.7%
Total assets	1,020,206	1,166,246	1,350,293	1,552,165	1,756,664
Shareholders' equity	78,696	85,544	97,657	109,095	93,386
Travelers Cheques and Travelers Letters of Credit	470,127	525,667	572,458	605,717	646,826
Customers deposits and credit balances	366,491	387,697	429,249	488,246	540,473
Total assets growth rate	11.5%	14.3%	15.8%	15.0%	13.2%
Total equity growth rate	15.1%	8.7%	14.2%	11.7%	-14.4%
Travelers Cheques and Travelers Letters of Credit growth rate	11.7%	11.8%	8.9%	5.8%	6.8%
Customers' Deposits and credit balances growth rate	8.7%	5.8%	10.7%	13.7%	10.7%
P/B					
High	3.5x	2.6x	3.6x	4.1x	9.6x
Low	2.0x	1.8x	2.3x	2.9x	4.5x
P/E					
High	24.7x	17.7x	22.6x	23.3x	39.7x
Low	14.1x	12.3x	14.8x	16.3x	18.7x
Market capitalization					
High	278,258	223,053	347,436	448,914	897,827
Low	158,925	154,464	227,731	314,121	423,974
Dividends per share	1.40	1.40	1.40	1.40	1.40
Stock Price					
High	62.38	50.00	74.38	94.50	189.00
Low	35.63	34.63	48.75	66.13	89.25

Source: American Express Annual Reports, *The New York Times*, and *Moody's Manuals*. Dollar figures in thousands, except per share numbers.[xl]

xl   The drop in equity in 1967 is due to the salad oil scandal payments. Valuation metrics are based on the current year earnings (e.g., P/E in the 1967 column is based on 1967 Net income before extraordinary items).

pushing margins from 15.9% in 1963 to 22.4% in 1967. The travelers cheque and charge card businesses were capital-light: The travelers cheque business bought securities financed by the float provided by customers, while the charge card business required minimal investment outside of some working capital (which existed because American Express had to pay merchants faster than it collected from cardholders). The size of the banking subsidiary encumbered historical returns on equity, hiding the strength of the travelers cheque business. But as revenue grew due to the charge card and cheque businesses, returns on equity exploded during Buffett's holding period.

Buffett's estimate and conviction in the company's intrinsic value kept increasing as the business continued to produce spectacular results. The price rose—with the stock increasing from $40 when he first bought it to trading between $66.13 and $94.50 in the last year he bought it—but so did his confidence in American Express. The $40.96 to $68.73 valuation above—that depended on a 10% growth rate for five years and a terminal growth rate, discounted back at 10%—proved way too low: EBIT more than tripled from 1963 to 1967, resulting in a 32.5% annual growth rate. The enterprise value Buffett first bought the stock at in 1964 wound up being 2.5x 1967 EBIT (3.3x if adding the settlement for the salad oil scandal to enterprise value).

Analysts estimated that the card contributed about 29% of Amex's 1967 net income and around a third of sales, resulting in margins for the card business of around 9%. The travelers cheque business was responsible for around 23% of revenue but nearly half of net income, resulting in net profit margins of over 20%.[243] These two businesses produced around three-quarters of the company's net income.

The stock never got particularly expensive as Buffett accumulated, either, peaking at a P/E ratio of 23.3x P/E in 1966, the final year he bought the stock. Once the valuation became rich in 1967—hitting 39.7x—he started selling. By this point, Buffett was growing concerned about the overall market environment due to the evaporation of statistical bargains and the public's refreshed interest in stocks, and would soon start thinking of winding down the Partnership.[244]

Buffett and Amex: fellow travelers

Buying American Express allowed Buffett to obliterate the market. American Express's stock price was up 29.9% in 1964 versus the Dow's 18.7%, 39.2% in 1965 versus the Dow's 14.2%, 32.4% in 1966 versus the Dow's negative 15.6%, and 88.6% in 1967 against the Dow's 19.0%. At the end of 1967, the stock more than quadrupled compared to when Buffett first bought it. With dividends adding another couple percent each year, this helped catapult the Partnership to up 27.8% in 1964, 47.2% in 1965, 20.4% in 1966, and 35.9% in 1967. All told, Buffett made $15 million off his $13 million investment, roughly a third of the Partnership's overall gain from 1964–1967.[245]

Buffett's timing was excellent. American Express acquired The Fund American Companies and Equitable Securities Corporation in 1968. With the acquisition, the quirky financial services company went from a business with a dominant franchise to a diversified company, with around half its earnings coming from the more competitive insurance field.[246] While the stock hit $235.50 in 1968, it fell in the subsequent years, ending 1971 at $195.38 and 1972 at $135.75.[xli]

American Express faced rising competition in its travelers cheque business in the 1960s, predominantly from First National City Bank and Bank of America. Amex still held about half the market, but this was down from peak levels and seemed likely to continue to decline.[247]

The banks stepped up their offerings in the credit card field as well. Bank of America and Chase Manhattan, the two largest banks in the country, had rolled out their credit card (with revolving credit) the same year American Express launched its charge card. The individual banks struggled to build a national network and chose to band together and cooperate in solving this problem. So in 1966, Bank of America began licensing its BankAmericard across the United States, and several other banks formed Interbank in response.[xlii,248]

Although he sold the Partnership's entire stake, this was not the end of the road for Buffett and this unique financial services company. Like other companies in this book, Buffett returned to American Express. While he knew the business was high quality, he was frustrated management kept looking to diversify away from its core business. In 1985, Buffett attended an American Express board meeting where they discussed selling the Fireman's Fund insurance business to a group that included Buffett. He advised them to get rid of it even if he didn't buy it and to focus on the one great business they had built. Buffett also expressed concern when GEICO (Berkshire Hathaway owned about half of GEICO at this time) bought American Express's stock, specifically worrying about CEO Jimmy Robinson.[249]

He finally invested in American Express again in 1991 when the company was struggling. Buffett bought a $300 million convertible preferred and then bought additional shares in the open market in 1994.[250] By this point, American Express's

---

xli   Stock prices are adjusted to 1964 equivalents so that the prices can be compared to Buffett's $40 purchase price. The company split its stock three-for-one in 1968.

xlii   The bank-sponsored entities, Interbank and BankAmericard, were the predecessors to Mastercard and Visa, respectively.

market capitalization was $14.6 billion.[251] Whenever Buffett buys back in decades later, there is a tendency to label his earlier sell decisions a mistake. But they rarely are: American Express's market capitalization compounded—using the low market capitalization in 1967, the year he started selling—at 14.0% through 1994. The company had diversified away from its core business, weighing down the return due to poor capital allocation. Dividends would have added some additional return, but Berkshire's book value had compounded by more than 20% over the same period.[252]

American Express was the greatest investment of the partnership years. It was Buffett's largest money maker by dollar amount and a sign of where he was evolving—the focus on the qualitative. In late 1967, Buffett wrote:

> Interestingly enough, although I consider myself to be primarily in the quantitative school (and as I write this no one has come back from recess—I may be the only one left in the class), the really sensational ideas I have had over the years have been heavily weighted toward the qualitative side where I have had a "high-probability insight." This is what causes the cash register to really sing. However, it is an infrequent occurrence, as insights usually are, and, of course, no insight is required on the quantitative side—the figures should hit you over the head with a baseball bat. So the really big money tends to be made by investors who are right on qualitative decisions but, at least in my opinion, the more sure money tends to be made on the obvious quantitative decisions.[253]

This was undoubtedly written with American Express at the front of Buffett's mind. With the statistical bargains that made him rich drying up, he started to spend more time on the qualitative, and Buffett's research techniques evolved to fit the problem.

Amex was also just a fascinating business to study. The thinking behind investing in companies with barriers to entry ('moats') is not only that such a barrier allows for the analyst to forecast cash flows with a higher degree of certainty than for mediocre businesses but also that the incumbent competitive advantage can lead to the formation of new business lines that capitalize on the initial competitive advantage. American Express is a prime example of this. That initial moat of the express business helped make evolving and developing additional business lines easier. The relationship with the banks from the express business made getting into money orders, traveler cheques, and eventually the credit card, easier. The original express business lowered the cost of acquiring banks in these other fields. By the time American Express introduced the credit card, consumers were clamoring for the American Express card. This not only lowered the cost to acquire customers but gave American Express the ability to charge more than its competitors.

Studebaker: 1965

"How much good does that do you to know that it's worth between 30 and 110? Well, it does you some good if it's selling below 30 or above 110."

—*Warren Buffett*[254]

Although Abraham Lincoln did not have a pleasant experience while at Ford's Theater, his journey there was undoubtedly comfortable. Traveling with his wife (I said comfortable, not peaceful) from the White House to watch *Our American Cousin*, the 16th president rode in a horse-drawn Studebaker carriage that April evening. Honest Abe didn't know it at the time, but the maker of that barouche would one day transform itself into a company worthy of attracting Warren Buffett's capital.

While John Wilkes Booth had no involvement in its demise, Studebaker's carriage business would also perish. The South Bend-based enterprise evolved as transportation became dependent on motors and not hooves, and the company developed into one of the leading car manufacturers in the United States.

Successful enough to be included in the Dow in 1916, Studebaker enjoyed a nine-year stay in the index before being displaced by automotive competitor General Motors. Seeing that scale was increasingly important in the automotive industry, Studebaker tried expanding its product line through acquisition, with an ill-timed purchase in 1928, right before the economy nosedived. Competition, poor decision-making, and the Great Depression all took a toll, leading to the company declaring bankruptcy in 1933.

Despite emerging from receivership two years later, Studebaker never could quite regain its competitive footing. The automobile industry was consolidating towards a three-player market, with Chrysler, Ford, and General Motors dominating the trade. The Big Three's advantages compounded over time, with economies of scale leading to lower unit costs and enhanced leverage over dealers. Additionally, the larger size allowed the trio to each maintain an extensive portfolio across multiple price points, decreasing their dependence on any single product. The independents, such as Studebaker, did not enjoy these benefits.

In a desperate last gasp to save its car business, Studebaker merged with another independent car manufacturer, Packard, in 1954. The merger was a resounding failure. The company, facing reality, began a diversification push that would eventually be successful enough to draw Buffett's attention. Studebaker downsized its automobile operations, moving all car production to Canada in 1963 and closing its famous South Bend plant as losses mounted. By 1965, the company had successfully diversified away from the legacy car business, with all earnings coming from non-automobile sources.[255]

However, Studebaker did not provide much detail on the individual segments. The company indicated that the diversified divisions were doing well, stating that these businesses produced over $11 million of pre-tax income combined in its 1963 annual report. Yet, the financials were lacking, with Studebaker providing investors with mere morsels of information on each division.[256]

But with a single-digit price-to-earnings multiple and large tax loss carryforward, the stock looked interesting. Plus, management had demonstrated a commitment to the bottom line. Sandy Gottesman, the founder of First Manhattan, saw this valuation, did some work on the company, and talked about it with his friend Warren Buffett on one of their frequent phone calls.[xliii]

The cheap consolidated financials were not enough for Buffett. With ten divisions and thin details on each one, he had to zero in on a couple of segments. As part of his research, he would journey to a Kansas City rail yard to count tank cars to try and estimate demand for STP motor oil additive, the segment that he and Gottesman figured out was the most important.[xliv] Through this research, Buffett uncovered that demand for STP was skyrocketing. So the two bought the stock in their respective funds in 1965, paying between $18 and $20 per share.[257]

Studebaker in 1965

The consolidated summary financials didn't give the analyst much. As Table 1 shows, assets and equity shrunk, while sales and income bounced around all

---

xliii   Gottesman was a Berkshire Hathaway director from 2004 until his passing in 2022.

xliv   There is some conflict over precisely who went to count railcars and where. Most sources describing the investment say Buffett himself went to Kansas City, but Sandy Gottesman's account differs, stating that Warren dispatched someone to "near Chicago." Sources closer to 1965 suggest it was Buffett who went to Kansas City while the Gottesman interview took place 50 years after the event—I lean towards believing it was Buffett who made the trek.

over the place. Assets and income fell from 1962 to 1963 due to write-downs associated with Studebaker shutting down the South Bend plant, with the company moving all automotive production to a plant in Canada that could maintain profitability with a smaller level of volume.[258] Since that closure didn't occur until late in the year, it didn't materially impact revenue until 1964, when sales fell but the company returned to profitability. This 1964 data indicated that Studebaker was turning itself into a sustainably profitable enterprise.

Table 1: Studebaker five-year summary financials

	1960	1961	1962	1963	1964
Operating results					
Net sales	323,227	298,476	365,452	403,314	261,756
Net income (loss)	709	(3,133)	490	(16,927)	8,065
Year-end position					
Current assets	105,617	124,552	145,039	110,003	81,461
Current liabilities	38,270	50,054	60,090	76,697	40,497
Working capital	67,347	74,498	84,949	33,306	40,964
Property, plant and equipment—net	48,947	43,565	73,420	55,876	37,880
Total assets	163,744	174,318	226,536	171,182	136,654
Long-term debt	25,815	20,128	47,810	50,043	27,248
Common equity	79,454	99,693	114,030	33,024	42,486
Shareholders' equity	98,954	103,666	117,801	36,725	46,108

Source: Studebaker annual reports. Dollar figures in thousands.

It was hard to tell which segments were relevant since the company didn't offer detailed disclosure on the individual segments. But an investor had to start somewhere. Newspaper articles and past annual reports provided crumbs to the starved securities analyst, with old articles about Studebaker's acquisition providing revenue and profit figures for some of the acquired enterprises. Understanding what the businesses did and what information was available would help piece the puzzle together. The ten segments were:

• Clarke: Acquired in 1960, this mechanized floor finishing and maintenance equipment manufacturer produced $9.1 million of sales and $0.9 million of pre-tax earnings in the year prior to Studebaker's purchase.[259]

• CTL (Cincinnati Testing Laboratories): Acquired in 1959, CTL was a plastics research and manufacturing organization. The division produced parts used in several United States missile and space programs. CTL made the nose cone that brought the United States' first round-trip space travelers, monkeys Able and Baker, back to Earth.[260]

- Franklin: Acquired in 1962 for $40 million, Franklin produced major appliances such as refrigerators, home freezers, dishwashers, and dryers. This enterprise sold its products to mass retail operations as 'private label' goods, meaning the merchandise was marketed under the name of the customer. In the last fiscal year prior to Studebaker's acquisition, Franklin produced $70 million and $7.2 million of pre-tax profits.[261]

- Gravely: Acquired in 1960, this tractor manufacturer generated sales of approximately $11 million and earnings before tax of around $2.1 million in 1959.[262]

- International: Established in 1962, the division handled the export efforts of Studebaker's other segments.[263]

- Onan: Acquired in 1960, Onan was the world's leading manufacturer of gasoline and engine-driven electric generating plants. The plants provided customers with power when commercial service was unavailable. In 1959, sales were $14.9 million and pre-tax earnings were $1.9 million. Studebaker's annual reports disclosed that sales grew 22% in 1962 and 6% in 1963.[264]

- Schaefer: Acquired in 1962, Schaefer was a top-ranking manufacturer of frozen food, ice cream, and dairy cabinets. Its first product was a mechanically cooled ice cream cabinet, an innovative idea at the time as ice cream used to be stored in wooden boxes and cooled with ice and salt. This business benefitted from a regulatory change in the 1950s, requiring ice cream to be held at much lower temperatures than had been previously used. Schaefer had more than $10 million of sales in 1961. While the 1962 annual report made no mention of sales growth, the 1963 report noted sales increased 12% in 1963.[265]

- STP: Acquired in 1961, STP (Scientifically Treated Petroleum) produced oil treatment that helped protect against engine wear and reduced oil consumption. In its fiscal year prior to Studebaker's purchase, STP made $1.3 million of pre-tax income. The division would produce $6 million of sales in 1961. STP became the leading oil additive in the U.S. in 1964.[266]

- Studebaker Automotive Division: This division comprised the last remnants of the formerly thriving car business.[267]

- StudeGrip: Formed in 1965, this segment manufactured and sold metal tire studs.[268]

Greasing valuation

This segment overview provides few clues about which divisions really mattered. But two key elements made the stock enticing and worth diving deeper into. First, the company's board and management had showcased their commitment to paying down debt and building a profitable enterprise. The firm had successfully diversified away from its legacy car business, with the painful decision to close the South Bend factory helping it return to profitability. And management indicated it would only continue car production in Canada if there were suitable profits to be made, writing in its 1964 annual report, "We have announced to our dealers that we will continue Canadian production only if a satisfactory return on investment can be realized."[269] Management communicated—and, more importantly, demonstrated—a commitment to value creation.

Second, the company was trading at an optically cheap valuation. At $18 a share, Studebaker's market capitalization stood at $51.9 million, 1.39x tangible book.[xlv] With 1964 net income of $8.1 million in 1964, the company's P/E ratio was 6.43x. Studebaker had an enterprise value of $57.1 million, only 5.19x the $11 million of pre-tax earnings the diversified divisions earned in 1963. Plus, the company had about $30 million of tax loss carryforwards at the end of 1964 that would keep years of income from Uncle Sam.

But the valuation work was complicated by the company's poor disclosure. The company had sold assets and distribution rights related to Mercedes-Benz in early 1965, which had contributed several million dollars to its 'other income' line in the years prior. It was unclear whether the $11 million figure for the non-automotive segments included this number or not.[270]

So Buffett had to do more detailed work to uncover which segments mattered. Franklin would be the first to gravitate to since, not only did Studebaker pay $40 million for the company, but this refrigerator manufacturer generated $70 million of revenue and $7.2 million of pre-tax profits in its last fiscal year prior to the purchase. At first blush, it seemed likely to be the largest source of the company's value.

This would be wrong. While it wouldn't be apparent from the annual reports, Franklin was, in fact, struggling. *The New York Times* often published articles whenever Studebaker made an acquisition, providing pre-tax profit figures for five of the companies purchased. The numbers were, of course, a few years old in 1965, coming from the year prior to Studebaker's acquisition, but they

---

xlv   Both figures assume the conversion of the company's First Preferred Stock.

were the best available. Totaling $13.4 million, the sum was higher than the $11 million figure for diversified divisions mentioned in the 1963 annual report. As the most significant component of the $13.4 million, a decline in Franklin's fortunes would be the most likely culprit for the loss of income.

STP would not have immediately stood out as the essential piece of the company based on the financials. During his research, Buffett likely called management and others surrounding the company, gaining information to supplement the deficient annual reports. As noted earlier, STP earned $1.3 million of pre-tax profits in its fiscal year ending February 28, 1961, and would produce $6 million of revenue for Studebaker during calendar 1961. After a torrid 36% revenue growth rate in 1962, volume grew 15% in 1963. But with around $10 million of sales in 1963 at this point, it didn't seem all that interesting when total Studebaker sales were $261.8 million in 1964.[271]

But growth was about to accelerate again. Buffett pieced this together when he journeyed to Kansas City to count railcars:

> In one case in 1965 Buffett says he spent the better part of a month counting tank cars in a Kansas City railroad yard. He was not, however, considering buying railroad stocks. He was interested in the old Studebaker Corp. because of STP, a highly successful gasoline additive. The company wouldn't tell him how the product was doing. But he knew that the basic ingredient came from Union Carbide, and he knew how much it took to produce one can of STP. Hence the tank-car counting. When shipments rose, he bought Studebaker stock, which subsequently went from 18 to 30.[272]

And while Buffett would not have known precise figures then, he would have figured out that STP's business was exploding. In 1968, when STP went public, the motor oil producer revealed sales had risen 44.5% in 1965. And it was a highly profitable business, too, with 1965 pre-tax margins at 36.8%. STP would generate $3.5 million of net income in 1965—at $18 a share, the Studebaker investor was paying 14.67x P/E for STP alone, a discount to the market multiple. Given its superior growth characteristics, STP alone was worth more than what Buffett paid for Studebaker's stock.[273]

On top of STP, Studebaker had some other interesting assets, such as Gravely and Onan. The profit figures were stale, but Gravely and Onan put up $2.1 million and $1.9 million of pre-tax profits during 1959, respectively. And they had grown since then: Gravely put up sales 2% under its record 1962 in 1963, while Onan's revenue grew 22% in 1962 and 6% in 1963.[274]

Valuing the company on a sum-of-the-parts basis, as an analyst might do today, illustrates how cheap this stock really was. Placing a 21.0x multiple on STP's 1965 net income (giving it a little credit for its growth potential) and an 8.0x multiple on Gravely and Onan's respective 1959 pre-tax earnings (giving no credit to any growth since) results in valuations of $74.3 million for STP, $16.8 million for Gravely, and $15.6 million for Onan. This appraisal leaves out the other segments, such as Franklin and Clarke, that were undoubtedly worth something (Studebaker sold Franklin in 1967 for around $20 million, less than half of the conglomerate's purchase price).[275] Once Buffett developed confidence in the value of STP, drilling down on the other segments became less important: The motor oil producer already protected his downside.

And then there was the large tax loss carryforward. With the top corporate tax rate at 48%, the asset would shield Studebaker from over $14 million of cash taxes. Assuming the company generated $10.8 million of pre-tax income—the combined value of STP's 1965 number and the Gravely and Onan 1959 numbers—and assuming no growth, the asset would be worth around $12.0 million, or $4.17 a share, at a 10% discount rate. The value of this asset would increase as income grew and decline if it fell—the quicker and faster profits rose, the more valuable it became due to the time value of money.

Piecing these disparate assets together in Table 2—and ignoring *all* of Studebaker's other segments—shows the stock was worth more than two times Buffett's $18 purchase price.[xlvi]

Table 2: Studebaker sum-of-the-parts valuation

	Value	Per share
STP	74,272	25.77
Gravely	16,800	5.83
Onan	15,560	5.40
Net present value of tax asset	12,031	4.17
Net debt, preferred, and investments	(5,188)	(1.80)
Value	$113,476	$39.37

Source: Studebaker annual reports and author's calculations. Dollar figures in thousands, other than per share figures.

xlvi   There would have been some minor value leakage due to stock options.

Tender offer spurs stock surge

On February 7, 1966, Hawaiian entrepreneur George W. Murphy made a tender offer for 17.6% of the company at $30 per share, $3.25 above that day's closing price.[276] Gottesman picked up the paper on his way home that evening—the morning edition came out at night back then— and called Buffett after seeing Murphy's advertisement regarding the offer. Buffett told Gottesman to buy all the stock he could the next day at the market's open. Gottesman said:

> So then, the question was, what would we do? A couple days later, I got a call from somebody I knew out in California, he was trying to put a deal together. So he offered us 44 bucks for the stock. We had cleaned up around 35. And they were wild and wooly days back then so I said, "Okay, we'll do it. We'll sell it to you." I thought it was a very rich price. He didn't have the money and he didn't have the client and maybe in the next couple hours, he called up Warren and said, "I have this terrific company for sale" and of course Warren said, "I'm the seller." So anyhow, we had put the trade up on the New York Stock Exchange and he was obligated so it went through finally.[277]

Murphy's tender offer created a frenzy. The Los Angeles brokerage firm Kleiner Bell had begun buying shares in January 1966 but started aggressively building its stake once Murphy's proposal became public. The brokerage firm purchased stock from First Manhattan at $32 per share from an undisclosed seller, which could very well have been Buffett.[xlvii] Allied Products, another company Kleiner Bell had invested in, was rumored to be considering making a tender offer for Studebaker. Kleiner would threaten a proxy contest later that year but eventually settled for some board seats.[278]

After the stock's post-tender offer rise, George Murphy pulled his offer and remarked that, "anybody who pays $40 a share for Studebaker doesn't know what he's doing."[279] The businessman from the Aloha State, as the valuation work in this chapter suggests, was quickly proven wrong. The stock took off, rising to a high of $40.50 by the end of February and $44.50 by the end of March.[280]

Studebaker exited the car business completely in 1966, demonstrating its commitment to the bottom line.[281] The company merged with Worthington in 1967, with shareholders receiving one share of the combined company's stock for each Studebaker share held. Studebaker-Worthington stock sold for $63.13 at the end of 1967, more than three times Buffett's purchase price two years prior.[282]

---

xlvii   The $32 price differs from the $44 price Gottesman mentions above. It's possible Gottesman's recollection is incorrect, that the $32 sale wasn't Buffett, or that Buffett and Gottesman sold to multiple sellers and got different prices for different blocks.

The combined company took a portion of STP public in 1968, keeping 87.5% of the company for itself. The stock was offered at $25 per share but popped to $35 the day of the IPO, with the market bidding the equity up to almost $200 million—nearly four times what Buffett had paid for *all* of Studebaker three years earlier and more than two-and-a-half times the valuation for STP found above in Table 2.[283]

At $18 a share, the stock offered investors a massive margin of safety. Buffett needed to do some creative detective work to get comfortable with just one segment. Once that conviction was gained, the rest was gravy—his downside was protected. Buffett was unsatisfied merely knowing the cheap consolidated valuation: He went out in the world to perform proprietary research to develop confidence in his margin of safety. Doing such detailed research on all divisions wasn't feasible or necessary. Knowing every little detail did not help generate spectacular returns in this case. Knowing the essential details did. But the lack of information also explains his sale decision: The lack of information made the investment much harder to underwrite when the stock shot up, so Buffett and Gottesman sold.

Studebaker was a superb example of Ben Graham's margin of safety concept in action. The stock was trading at a massive discount to intrinsic value, although no analyst could figure out exactly what it was worth. The next chapter explores Hochschild Kohn, a company Sandy Gottesman also brought to Warren Buffett's attention. Unlike Studebaker, however, this Baltimore retailer is an example of Buffett failing to properly apply the margin of safety concept, leading to a rare misstep for the great investor.

Hochschild, Kohn & Co.: 1966

"Buying Hochschild Kohn was like the story of a man who buys a yacht. The two happy days are the day he buys it and the day he sells it."

—Charlie Munger[284]

Howard and Lexington streets were once the center of ferocious competition between Baltimore's four leading downtown department stores. Hochschild Kohn's, Hutzler's, Hecht's, and Stewart's were practically neighbors—all standing within a block of one another. The retailers each offered similar merchandise—including jewelry, suits, shoes, silverware, furniture, and bedding—and shoppers would enjoy flitting between the four stores on their trips to the city center. They were social hubs, too, offering patrons food and drink at their in-store restaurants, where hungry shoppers could sit down to sandwiches and desserts in between browsing or making purchases.

Although Baltimore's shopping center thrived throughout the first half of the century, it had begun to lose some of its luster by the early 1960s. One of the reasons for this was the growing number of city residents who relocated to the suburbs. In response to this steady migration, the Baltimore firms built additional stores to be closer to their customers. Unfortunately, several discount stores and other rival chains met them there. Thus, not only did Hochschild Kohn suffer from the loss of traffic to its premier location at Howard and Lexington, but its newer stores found themselves locked into battle with formidable competition.

Amid this foggy outlook for the four Baltimore retailers, the leaders of the family-owned-and-managed Hochschild Kohn began looking for an exit strategy. As one of its senior executives later put it, "We decided that we were not the kind of store that could pay stockholders a lot of money. We got together and agreed that the store had to be sold."[285] For help facilitating the sale, company president Martin Kohn called his niece's husband, Sandy Gottesman, to sound out buyers. Gottesman was familiar with the company; his mother-in-law owned a portion of Hochschild Kohn's preferred stock and his wife owned less than 0.5% of the stock. Plus, the First Manhattan founder had previously helped the company issue debt. Kohn indicated that his family was willing to sell at a discounted price, prompting Gottesman to call his bargain-hunting friend Warren Buffett.

Buffett was struggling to find compelling investment ideas at this point in his career. With the Dow rising each of the last three years, finding bargains had become a lot more challenging. Buffett thought the Baltimore retailer was worth a look, prompting him to call Charlie Munger for help analyzing the deal, thinking that Munger's legal background and sharp business mind could be useful in studying the opportunity.[286] Intrigued by the prospect of buying this private business, the two investors set off to Maryland to investigate. After meeting the Kohn family and visiting the downtown store, they offered $12 million for Hochschild Kohn, a discount to tangible book. The Kohns accepted, and an agreement was reached in January 1966—the same month Buffett wrote in his letter to partners, "I do not have a great flood of good ideas as I go into 1966."[287]

In addition to buying the company at what he thought was a reasonable price, Buffett held the Kohns in high esteem, writing, "Even if the price had been cheaper but the management had been run-of-the-mill, we would not have bought the business."[288] Louis Kohn II, who took over as president after his father retired from the position and ascended to the chairmanship, would become a close friend of Buffett's after the acquisition. Buffett thought so highly of the younger Kohn that Louis earned an invite to Buffett's exclusive meeting of 'Grahamites' in 1969, a gathering where a group of Ben Graham disciples chatted about investing.[289]

Gottesman joined in on the deal, too, and the three investors formed Diversified Retailing Company, Inc. to acquire Hochschild Kohn. The Buffett Partnership, which had significantly more capital than the other partners, owned 80% of Diversified Retailing, while Gottesman and Munger each owned 10% through their respective investment funds. This structure allowed the trio to buy the Baltimore retailer, raise additional capital, and acquire other companies. The Hochschild Kohn investment, the first Buffett Partnership purchase of an entire company, accounted for approximately 10% of the partnership's assets in 1966. While the Maryland-based company wasn't Buffett's largest position— the partnership's stake in American Express was three times larger than the investment in Hochschild Kohn in 1966—it was still a significant slice of his portfolio.[290]

The acquisition was not without drama. Buffett and Munger went to the Maryland National Bank and asked for a loan to help fund the purchase. The lending officer was stunned when the pair asked for $6 million to help buy

Hochschild Kohn, thinking it was too large for the small firm. Despite these reservations, the lender acquiesced and partnered with another bank to provide short-term financing to fund the acquisition.[291] Unfortunately for the three future billionaires, the banker's skepticism proved justified.

Buffett and Munger have repeatedly harped on what an error this acquisition was. Buffett thought the purchase was such a bad decision that he included it in his 1989 letter under the heading "Mistakes of the First Twenty-five Years (A Condensed Version)." He wrote:

> Shortly after purchasing Berkshire, I acquired a Baltimore department store, Hochschild Kohn, buying through a company called Diversified Retailing that later merged with Berkshire. I bought at a substantial discount from book value, the people were first-class, and the deal included some extras—unrecorded real estate values and a significant LIFO inventory cushion. How could I miss? So-o-o—three years later I was lucky to sell the business for about what I had paid. After ending our corporate marriage to Hochschild Kohn, I had memories like those of the husband in the country song, 'My Wife Ran Away With My Best Friend and I Still Miss Him a Lot.[292]

But there's another side to the story. The third member of the trio, Sandy Gottesman, has given a more nuanced perspective, stating, "It goes down in history as an enormous mistake. And I don't think it was as big a mistake as represented… it's grown way out of proportion."[293] While arguing that one's flaws really aren't that bad is seldom a winning strategy with a spouse, the historical record should, in this case, lend a sympathetic ear to nuance.

The purchase was undoubtedly an error. During a period when Buffett nearly tripled his investors' money in the Buffett Partnership—a return dragged down by his ownership of Hochschild Kohn—he was only able to eke out a meager return from the Baltimore retailer. And the decision-making process was flawed. The three misjudged the firm's future economics and bought a mediocre business at a cheap—but not great—price. They should have tossed the investment in the 'too-hard' pile. But Gottesman's view has some truth to it as well. Hochschild Kohn was producing good results, seemingly successfully staving off competition; it was reasonable to think this would continue. And they did not lose money on the purchase—most investors would envy having their wall of shame adorned with investments that generated a modest profit.

Hochschild Kohn had a long history at Howard and Lexington when the three investors started looking at the company, having flourished at the same location for nearly 70 years. That sort of staying power is exactly what a long-term investor is looking for. To see how the company developed—and eventually stumbled—let's take a look at its history.

The rise of Hochschild, Kohn, & Co.

The department store's journey began when 21-year-old Max Hochschild opened his first shop in 1877. After the dry goods store outgrew its ten-foot-wide storefront, the precocious entrepreneur expanded his enterprise in 1883 by opening a larger location called Hochschild's One-Price House a few blocks away on the Gay Street retail corridor, about a mile from the city's downtown core. Meanwhile, two of Max's friends, Louis and Benno Kohn, operated a nearby clothing shop that their father had established. As both businesses grew, they each sought a new location to accommodate their growing volume.

Coincidentally, the two parties separately settled on the same site in downtown Baltimore. Rather than competing against one another, they opted to form a partnership and built the Hochschild Kohn department store at the intersection of Howard and Lexington streets. Opening in 1897, this five-story building would blossom into one of Baltimore's largest department stores, forming the foundation of the company that Buffett would eventually acquire. Over the years, the company would enlarge this store by adding additional stories and buying adjacent buildings to fulfill its swelling demand.

Despite the expansion, tensions arose in the partnership as Max advocated for a larger location, thinking the store was still too cramped for its given volume. Consequently, in 1923, the company announced plans to move to a bigger building a few blocks away. However, Benno and Louis Kohn had second thoughts, nervous about committing to such a significant expenditure. Frustrated at their reluctance to move forward with the relocation, Max decided to retire and sell his stake in the company in 1926. Various members of the Kohn family and the corporation itself purchased Max's shares, leaving the Kohns in control of the business.[294]

Max's exit was well-timed, as the Great Depression hit shortly after his sale. Hochschild Kohn struggled along with the rest of American industry, experiencing a 40% drop in sales from 1930 to 1934 and suffering four consecutive years of losses starting in 1932.[xlviii,295] After World War II, Hochschild Kohn began building branch stores in the suburbs to be closer to its customers.

---

xlviii   Hochschild Kohn's fiscal year ended in January—1930, for example, refers to the year ending January 31, 1931. Many retailers have fiscal calendars ending in January or February to better account for the impact of the holiday season.

The first two, located a handful of miles from the Howard and Lexington location, were smaller shops that lacked the breadth of merchandise offered by the larger emporium.

Hochschild Kohn eventually opened full-line branches at the Eastpoint Shopping Center in 1956 and the Harundale Mall in 1958.[296] When Buffett invested in the company in 1966, Hochschild Kohn owned the main downtown store, the four branch locations, and a small furniture twig.[xlix] The 410,000-square-foot store at Howard and Lexington was still the company's most important, accounting for more than 40% of 1965 revenue, while no other store was responsible for more than 20% of sales.[297]

Picture 1: Hochschild Kohn

Source: *The Baltimore Sun.*

Baltimore department store rivalries

At downtown Baltimore's peak, residents would ride the streetcar to the shopping district. While there, they would drop by the big four department stores. When the citizens started moving to the suburbs, the quartet in the city

---

xlix   A twig was a smaller branch store carrying a specific line of merchandise.

center, discounters, and other department store chains all opened locations to be closer to their customers.[l] All these stores—the discounters, national department store chains, and the Baltimore stores—fought for the same customer set. But the focus of competition shifted depending on the location.

At Howard and Lexington, Hochschild Kohn brawled with Hutzler's, Stewart's, and Hecht's.[li] The primary economic advantage of these department stores was a highly trafficked location. The four stores were each multi-story emporiums, offering substantially similar merchandise to one another, and they split the downtown market roughly equally. While there were some lesser rivals, too, such as Brager-Gutman and five-and-dime stores, the big four comprised the bulk of the business in the city center.[lii]

There were, of course, some differences between the stores; each had particular merchandising strengths and weaknesses. For example, a former Hochschild Kohn executive asserted that their store was particularly strong in toys, housewares, and cosmetics relative to Hutzler's but weaker in ready-to-wear clothing. And customers, of course, had their individual preferences in terms of which store to patronize. Generally, Baltimoreans considered Hochschild Kohn's a no-frills shop where average folks could buy goods at reasonable prices.[298]

On a company level, Hutzler's and Hochschild Kohn were very similar firms. Both had five stores, with Hochschild Kohn's also having the small furniture twig. The two had comparable income and asset levels as well as similar ownership structures; each was family-owned until Hochschild Kohn's sale to Diversified Retailing. The two companies also had familial ties in the early days after Max Hochschild's daughter married into the Hutzler family in 1911.[299] In contrast, Stewart's and Hecht's were part of much bigger, publicly traded companies. Stewart's was a part of Associated Dry Goods, which had assets and sales ten times that of either Hutzler's or Hochschild Kohn. Hecht's owner, the

---

l	The discounters were also chain operators. The line between department store chains and discounters became increasingly blurred as the legacy department stores frequently adopted the methods of its competitors. But department store chains usually offered broader price points than the discounters.
li	Hecht's and the May Company merged in 1959. The Howard and Lexington store, which was owned by the May Company at the time of the merger, was renamed Hecht-May, and eventually The Hecht Co.
lii	Companies such as E.J. Korvette's, Topps, Two Guys, and others, had smaller locations with low priced goods (known as five-and-dimes) within walking distance of Howard and Lexington, but these were all small stores that were not serious competitors to the big four. Their larger stores outside of downtown Baltimore competed more directly with Hochschild Kohn's branch stores, however.

May Company, was even larger, producing revenue twenty times that of the two smaller competitors.[300]

Despite these distinctions, the downtown stores found it difficult to meaningfully differentiate themselves. Buffett and Munger came to refer to this type of business as "standing on tiptoe at a parade."[301] If a competitor put in a new elevator or upgraded window displays, everyone else followed suit. Building a sustainable and meaningful advantage over the others was almost impossible.

Meanwhile, the branch locations competed head-on with the discounters and other department store chains. But these stores were still very close to the downtown city center. Hochschild Kohn's four branch stores were all within about ten miles of Howard and Lexington, making it a short drive from the shopping district. A customer that may have ventured downtown now had plenty of other options as the Baltimore department stores, discounters, and other chain competition all built locations outside of the city center.

These competitors possessed significant cost advantages over Hochschild Kohn. While Hochschild Kohn relied on gross margins in the mid-to-high 30s, discounters and national department store chains typically survived in the low-to-mid 20s. These competitors benefited from lower labor costs and economies of scale.[302] In contrast to the discounters, Hochschild Kohn prided itself on its hands-on service with trained professional staff. But this intimate support was costly. Further, the increased size of the competitors allowed them to procure unit cost advantages due to higher volume purchases. For example, manufacturers would offer shirts more cheaply to Macy's than to Hochschild Kohn because Macy's bought significantly more volume.[303]

Cost was the primary consideration for shoppers. While customers on the margins might choose to shop at Hochschild Kohn due to the service quality, the lowest price tended to win. And if that wasn't enough, banks began issuing credit cards, further impairing the company's value proposition and cutting into its charge account business.[304]

However, neither the migration to the suburbs nor competition was new when Buffett bought Hochschild Kohn. The discounters, for example, had been around for decades and started to accelerate after World War II. And by mid-century, most department stores were chains. But it looked like Hochschild Kohn was successfully fending these adversaries off in 1966.[305]

What was Buffett thinking?

Even against this worrying backdrop, Hochschild Kohn produced record sales and pre-tax profits in 1965.[liii] As Table 1 shows, revenue rose every year over the previous decade other than 1962, and operating income had more than doubled during this period. Like all department stores, profit margins were low. And the company was earning a respectable—but certainly not great—return on capital.[306]

In its 1962 annual report, the company stated, "Baltimore has had a veritable discount invasion, and Hochschild Kohn decided to be competitive on all prices of identical merchandise. The main attraction of these stores is price, and I think our sales record proves this decision a right one."[307] Hochschild Kohn noted its competition and seemed to be responding well, growing sales and increasing operating income.

Diving into the store-level analysis, the downtown premises at Howard and Lexington streets remained Hochschild Kohn's most important, responsible for 44.2% of revenue. As noted earlier, none of the other stores produced more than 20% of revenue.[liv] And all stores had grown since 1960. The downtown location increased sales at 1.9% annually over this period, while Belvedere and Edmonson had slightly lower growth rates at 1.4% each. Eastpoint and Harundale—the two largest branches—grew much faster, at 7.9% and 9.2%, respectively.

Hochschild Kohn provided third-party data detailing the Baltimore Metropolitan and downtown markets, which is reproduced in Table 2. The data shows that the additional competition was impairing the downtown market—while the total Metropolitan market grew 21.5% since 1960, downtown declined 0.8% over this period. However, Hochschild Kohn's share gains downtown allowed it to increase revenue there and maintain its share of total metropolitan Baltimore sales. Additionally, as Table 3 demonstrates, Hochschild Kohn stabilized its share outside the city center since 1962. It looked like the company was once again competing effectively.

However, the share data is less encouraging than it initially appears. The data ignored the vicious discount and other department store competition—it only included Brager-Gutman, Hochschild Kohn, Hutzler's, Stewart's, and

---

liii   Negotiations between Hochschild Kohn and the Buffett, Munger, and Gottesman trio occurred during January 1966, the last month of Hochschild Kohn's fiscal year. While Buffett would not have known the exact fiscal 1965 figures, he would have almost certainly been provided quality estimates by the time he was analyzing the company.

liv   Harundale produced 17.7%, Eastpoint 17.6%, Edmondson 9.7%, and Belvedere 10.3%. The Furniture Twig accounted for only 0.4% of revenue.

Table 1: Hochschild, Kohn ten-year summary financials

Fiscal Year	1956	1957	1958	1959	1960	1961	1962	1963	1964	1965
Revenue	27,100	28,721	29,692	32,367	33,685	35,359	34,550	36,113	39,026	40,932
Gross profit	9,915	10,503	10,821	11,737	12,109	12,766	12,336	12,904	14,146	14,894
EBIT	674	499	475	557	1,025	1,378	1,086	1,405	1,984	2,198
EBITDA	1,158	1,024	967	1,042	1,574	1,910	1,549	1,836	2,462	2,714
Net income	396	749	495	525	448	620	514	867	1,209	1,190
Revenue growth	10.4%	6.0%	3.4%	9.0%	4.1%	5.0%	-2.3%	4.5%	8.1%	4.9%
Gross margin	36.6%	36.6%	36.4%	36.3%	35.9%	36.1%	35.7%	35.7%	36.2%	36.4%
EBIT margin	2.5%	1.7%	1.6%	1.7%	3.0%	3.9%	3.1%	3.9%	5.1%	5.4%
EBITDA margin	4.3%	3.6%	3.3%	3.2%	4.7%	5.4%	4.5%	5.1%	6.3%	6.6%
Profit margin	1.5%	2.6%	1.7%	1.6%	1.3%	1.8%	1.5%	2.4%	3.1%	2.9%
Net working capital	7,637	7,771	8,548	8,790	9,557	9,723	9,812	10,001	10,029	9,970
Property, plant, and equipment	6,418	6,175	5,921	6,196	6,755	6,316	6,224	6,152	6,754	6,663
Total invested capital	14,055	13,946	14,469	14,986	16,312	16,039	16,036	16,153	16,783	16,634
Pre-tax ROIC	5.2%	3.6%	3.3%	3.8%	6.6%	8.5%	6.8%	8.7%	12.0%	13.2%
After-tax ROIC	2.8%	2.2%	1.6%	1.8%	3.1%	4.0%	3.3%	5.0%	7.0%	6.8%

Source: Hochschild Kohn financial statements and author's calculations. Dollar figures in thousands.

Table 2: Baltimore department store sales data

Year	Department store sales in Metropolitan Baltimore	Total Hochschild Kohn sales	Hochschild Kohn's share of Metropolitan Baltimore	Department store sales in Downtown Baltimore	Total downtown Hochschild Kohn sales	Hochschild Kohn's share of Downtown Baltimore
1960	135,950	33,685	24.8%	72,516	16,429	22.7%
1961	141,258	34,928	24.7%	71,326	16,739	23.5%
1962	143,527	34,745	24.2%	67,536	16,622	24.6%
1963	148,249	36,150	24.4%	69,152	17,184	24.8%
1964	158,034	39,026	24.7%	72,340	18,017	24.9%
1965	165,116	41,000	24.8%	71,946	18,144	25.2%
Cumulative $ change since 1960	29,166	7,315		(570)	1,715	
Cumulative % change since 1960	21.5%	21.7%		-0.8%	10.4%	

Source: Hochschild Kohn financial statements. Dollar figures in thousands; Hochschild Kohn Downtown sales include Reisterstown Road Plaza from 1963–1965.[liv]

liv   The sales figures for Tables 2 and 3 differ from Table 1 as these two tables are for the calendar year, while Table 1 uses the fiscal year data.

Table 3: Metropolitan Baltimore department store sales excluding the downtown market

Year	Deparment Sales Excludng Downtown	Hochschild Kohn Sales Excludng Downtown	Hochschild Kohn Share Excludng Downtown
1960	63,434	17,256	27.2%
1961	69,932	18,189	26.0%
1962	75,991	18,123	23.8%
1963	79,097	18,966	24.0%
1964	85,694	21,009	24.5%
1965	93,170	22,856	24.5%
Cumulative $ change since 1960	29,736	5,600	
Cumulative % change since 1960	46.9%	32.5%	

Source: Hochschild Kohn financial statements. Dollar figures in thousands.

Hecht's.[308] The data was simply incomplete and understated the impact of the competitive threats.

This financial data correlated with Baltimore's population trends. The city started shedding residents during the 1950s, dropping from 949,708 in 1950 to 939,024 in 1960, a mere 1.1% decline. Metropolitan Baltimore's population, on the other hand, grew by nearly 25% over this period.[309] This almost imperceptible loss in the city was easy to dismiss, with sales in downtown Baltimore falling by less than 1% since 1960 and Hochschild Kohn growing its revenue there through market share gains. While the data clearly shows that the market's growth was coming from outside Howard and Lexington, it was not clear that the city center was in danger of materially declining. Based on this data, it was reasonable for Buffett to assume that the downtown location would stay roughly flat while the other stores would continue growing.

The competitive analysis, of course, influenced the price Buffett was willing to pay for the business. In a letter to partners discussing Hochschild Kohn a few months after the acquisition, he wrote, "The quantitative and qualitative aspects of the business are evaluated and weighed against price, both on an absolute basis and relative to other investment opportunities. HK (learn to call it that—I didn't find out how to pronounce it until the deal was concluded) stacks up fine in all respects."[310]

He would never pay multiples of tangible book for a business with pedestrian growth prospects earning a middling return on capital. At 0.77x P/TB, the $12 million price was attractive on an asset basis—but not exceptionally so. But Buffett thought there was some additional value in two items the reported balance sheet didn't properly account for. First was a LIFO reserve—inventory values would be $0.8 million higher if the company used FIFO accounting rather than LIFO, which would increase tangible book by 5.3%.[lvi] Second, Buffett thought the real estate was worth more than what Hochschild Kohn was carrying it at on its balance sheet. These two pieces would have added another layer of asset value in Buffett's mind, protecting him if the business faltered.

Like the balance sheet appraisal, the earnings valuation was also attractive—but again, not remarkably so. Buffett bought the business for a 5.73x EV/1965 EBIT multiple, a 10.08x P/E multiple, and a 9.7% after-tax free cash flow yield; a fine but not screamingly cheap price. While the EV/EBIT and P/E multiples were lower than all comparable companies' (see Table 4), Hochschild Kohn deserved to sell for a cheaper multiple. It was a smaller company in an industry where scale mattered. The companies in this peer group all grew faster and most had superior returns on tangible common equity. Their valuation premiums were warranted.

What went wrong?

While Buffett, Munger, and Gottesman bought Hochschild Kohn at what seemed to be an attractive price, it was not the blatant bargain most of the other companies analyzed in this book were. Buffett was still trying to figure out the better business and was struggling to find good ideas when he bought the company. He strayed from his valuation discipline to make this investment, lured in by the illusory value of the balance sheet. And this caused him to make an error.

While Hochschild Kohn's revenue grew in both 1966 and 1967—Buffett's first two years of ownership—operating income was stagnant. Invested capital rose 9.4% over these two years while operating income only grew 2.4%. The company had to spend much more just to run in place.[311]

---

lvi   Under LIFO (last in, first out) accounting, the costs of the most recent inventory purchased are expensed first. This means that when prices rise the value on the balance sheet is lower than if the company used FIFO (first in, first out) or average-cost accounting. FIFO usually reflects the actual movement of inventory, meaning the inventory values on the balance sheet could be understated under LIFO accounting.

Table 4: Comparable company analysis

| | Market Capitalization | Enterprise Value | P/TB | EV/EBIT | | P/E | | Five-year revenue CAGR | Five-year average return on tangible common equity |
				Last FY	Five-year average	Last FY	Five-year average		
Hochschild Kohn	12,000	12,589	0.77x	5.73x	7.82x	10.08x	13.63x	4.0%	6.7%
Allied Stores	244,400	555,218	1.12x	11.00x	15.48x	10.98x	15.23x	7.0%	7.9%
Associated Dry Goods	377,802	376,604	2.32x	10.62x	15.47x	16.95x	26.14x	12.7%	11.7%
EJ Korvette	120,191	148,014	2.01x	10.65x	14.44x	12.05x	17.55x	35.5%	20.4%
Federated Department Stores	1,331,671	1,338,729	2.93x	10.13x	12.54x	18.88x	25.40x	11.1%	15.0%
Gimbel Brothers	226,197	289,324	1.50x	7.55x	9.90x	12.42x	17.38x	6.6%	10.3%
JC Penney	1,540,491	1,436,886	3.53x	9.43x	11.55x	20.25x	25.16x	9.3%	16.9%
Macy's	221,865	285,773	1.81x	7.78x	10.21x	14.38x	19.87x	6.7%	9.7%
Marshall Field	237,864	238,882	1.91x	8.33x	10.79x	16.04x	21.66x	5.5%	9.9%
The May Department Stores Company	745,522	895,122	2.10x	10.76x	14.10x	16.26x	22.48x	4.9%	11.6%
Montgomery Ward	416,760	491,743	0.65x	16.90x	16.51x	18.13x	21.49x	7.0%	3.1%
S.S. Kresge	434,012	399,495	1.89x	11.50x	17.69x	19.59x	31.68x	15.3%	6.5%
Sears	9,093,823	10,276,552	4.17x	16.67x	20.25x	28.68x	34.01x	9.1%	14.9%
Woolworth's	862,408	778,152	1.41x	11.86x	14.79x	12.31x	15.75x	6.9%	10.1%
Mean—excluding Hochschild Kohn	1,219,462	1,346,961	2.10x	11.01x	14.13x	16.69x	22.60x	10.6%	11.6%
Median—excluding Hochschild Kohn	416,760	491,743	1.91x	10.65x	14.44x	16.26x	21.66x	7.0%	10.3%
High—excluding Hochschild Kohn	9,093,823	10,276,552	4.17x	16.90x	20.25x	28.68x	34.01x	35.5%	20.4%
Low—excluding Hochschild Kohn	120,191	148,014	0.65x	7.55x	9.90x	10.98x	15.23x	4.9%	3.1%

Source: *Moody's Manuals* and Hochschild Kohn annual reports. Dollar figures in thousands. Stock prices are as of January 29, 1966. Fiscal 1965 data is used for all companies even though results for most companies wouldn't have been reported until a couple of months after Buffett's.[lvi]

lvi   As noted previously, the May Department Stores Company owned Hecht's, and Associated Dry Goods owned Stewart's. Hutzler's was privately owned and therefore does not appear anywhere on this table. However, the Baltimore stores themselves would not have been meaningful contributors to the revenue or earnings for May or Associated Dry Goods.

After these two challenging years, bad luck struck Hochschild Kohn. Riots broke out across the United States after Martin Luther King, Jr.'s assassination on April 4, 1968. While the mayhem did not lead to property destruction in Baltimore, the unrest changed the city. Middle-income families fled the urban core and left it largely to lower-income residents, further harming the shopping district's traffic and real estate values.[312] The city of Baltimore continued to shed citizens, with the population falling 3.5% from 1960 to 1970—likely at least partly attributable to the riots.[313]

The business's struggles led Buffett to sell Hochschild Kohn to Supermarkets General in December 1969. Diversified Retailing received a package of cash and debt that Buffett valued at $11 million. Based on the $12 million purchase price, this was an 8.3% loss for Diversified Retailing—but Hochschild Kohn paid out $3.5 million worth of dividends within the two years after Buffett's purchase.[lviii] Adding the dividends to the present value of the package received from Supermarkets General would result in a 20.6% return over nearly four years. That return is abysmal, but not a complete disaster. Opportunity cost is real, of course—especially when the Buffett Partnership produced a 20.4% return in 1966, 35.9% in 1967, 58.8% in 1968, and 6.8% in 1969, all of which were weighed down by Hochschild Kohn—but the error Buffett and Munger would later dwell on still made them money.

Charlie Munger and Warren Buffett entirely disagree with my conclusion that this was not that egregious of an error. Taking a step back and thinking through the business's likely future should have been enough for them to pass on the retailer. Buying a company whose primary economic driver faced three remarkably similar competitors on the same block in a no-growth market was a recipe for poor financial performance.

Fortunately, Diversified Retailing diversified away from the department store, buying Associated Cotton Shops in 1967. Ownership of Hochschild Kohn allowed the holding company to use the Baltimore retailer's earnings and assets to raise additional debt. Diversified Retailing was eventually merged into Berkshire Hathaway in 1978.[314]

Following Buffett's sale, Hochschild Kohn began declining at an alarming clip. The downtown store closed in 1977 after experiencing rapidly falling sales in each of the four years prior to shutting down.[315] The building lay dormant for years—disproving Buffett's thinking that Hochschild Kohn's real estate had substantial value—and eventually burned down in a fire in 1983.[316] Finally,

---

lviii   It's possible Hochschild Kohn paid additional dividends to Diversified Retailing prior to the sale to Supermarkets General.

in 1984, Supermarkets General sold four of the strongest Hochschild Kohn stores to Hutzler's, with the Hochschild Kohn name dying when the rest of the locations closed in 1986.[317]

The downtown department stores had a deep emotional connection to their communities. Hochschild Kohn's Toy Town parade was a staple of the Baltimore Christmas season. People even cried when neighboring Hutzler's closed its doors. But all these stores shut down; the emotional attachments simply did not translate into sustainably attractive economics.

What did Buffett learn from Hochschild Kohn?

Buffett's primary mistake with Hochschild Kohn was buying into a business with no sustainable competitive advantage at a 'kind of cheap' price. Hochschild Kohn's outlook clouded once this geographic advantage of being close to the streetcars diminished. Buffett said he thought that he was buying a second-tier department store at a third-class price, which was a foolish needle to try and thread.

He later remarked:

> Retailing is like shooting at a moving target. In the past, people didn't like to go excessive distances from the streetcars to buy things. People would flock to those retailers that were nearby. In 1966 we bought the Hochschild Kohn department store in Baltimore. We learned quickly that it wasn't going to be a winner, long-term, in a very short period of time. We had an antiquated distribution system. We did everything else right. We put in escalators. We gave people more credit. We had a great guy running it, and we still couldn't win. So we sold it around 1970. That store isn't there anymore. It isn't good enough that there were smart people running it.[318]

In the 1989 letter where he labels Hochschild Kohn a mistake, Buffett ends the section stating, "It's far better to buy a wonderful company at a fair price than a fair company at a wonderful price."[319] The issue with Hochschild Kohn was that it was not a wonderful company, nor was it purchased at a wonderful price. It was a middling business in 1966 whose competitive position would continue to decline. The price wasn't cheap enough and the business wasn't good enough.

While it was reasonable to forecast that the company would continue doing well given its recent performance in 1966, the alternative argument that this was a business destined to decline was more persuasive. Value investing requires properly calibrating the probability distribution of the range of future outcomes. Developing conviction in Hochschild Kohn's future economics was simply too hard. The high-level multiples—0.77x P/TB, 10.08x P/E—charmed Buffett, but this valuation was only really attractive if Hochschild Kohn could continue growing earnings. With the population's shift to the suburbs and the competitive backdrop, this was not a bet he should have been willing to make.

Munger and Buffett would point to the decline and closure of the Howard and Lexington store almost eight years after their sale as additional evidence of their error. But Hochschild Kohn still had the branch locations that survived for a couple of decades following Diversified Retailing's disposal of the company. Further, they did err in thinking that the real estate provided protection. They shouldn't have counted on the real estate value, as the only scenario in which it would become pertinent was one where the store's economics were eroding. In a world where the hard asset value mattered, the Baltimore city center would also be in decline, depressing the value of any real estate owned by the company.

The other major mistake Buffett made was not exercising capital allocation control. Later, when heading Berkshire Hathaway, he wrote that one of the main advantages of controlling a company was that he could dictate how to allocate capital.[320] Buffett did not properly utilize this benefit here. While the company planned to open two new stores before Diversified Retailing's purchase, he put his foot down on one but relented on the other. He should have stopped both expansions but didn't because he dreaded disappointing his employees.[321]

Shortly after the Hochschild Kohn acquisition, Buffett bought Disney's stock. In contrast to the Baltimore retailer, he did not purchase the House of Mouse at a discount to tangible book value. However, this business, too, was operating in a challenging industry. Despite the movie industry's inherent volatility, Disney was producing spectacular results. After *Mary Poppins* helped the company generate record results, its stock was selling for a very low price-to-earnings multiple. But Buffett couldn't count on the cheap earnings multiple to protect him. In this case, he had to think creatively to get comfortable pulling the trigger on this investment.

Walt Disney Productions: 1966

"Practically perfect people never permit sentiment to muddle their thinking."

—*Mary Poppins*

Warren Buffett's purchase of 5% of Disney's common stock is one of the most famous investments of his early career. Yet, at first glance, it was an abnormal investment for him to make at the time.

For one thing, the stock did not seem to offer investors much downside protection. Disney did not trade at a discount to tangible book; in fact, relative to its peers in the movie industry, it was actually quite expensive on this basis. The stock was selling for a cheap earnings multiple, but the movie industry was too unpredictable to rely on historical earnings. It takes a film studio two to three years to produce a film, completely uncertain of how it will ultimately fare at the box office. Disney's low price-earnings ratio in 1966 was based on the record profits of *Mary Poppins*, the fourth highest grossing film of all time at that point, so investors were justifiably concerned that Disney could not replicate its success. Finally, while Disney was more than just a studio—the company also owned Disneyland in California and was beginning to invest in the Florida park that would become Walt Disney World—these other assets were not simple to value either.[322]

Aside from the risk that Disney's films would begin flopping at the box office, the company's corporate governance was the biggest concern for an investor. There were three concerns regarding how the company was managed. The most obvious was key man risk. Walt Disney himself[lix], the company's founder and executive producer-in-charge of all production, was irreplaceable. While his brother Roy retained the titles of company president and chairman, Walt controlled the company. He was a creative genius; constantly pushing the boundaries of the entertainment industry, from producing *Snow White* to

lix   To try and minimize confusion, I will use Walt Disney's first name when referring to the person and Disney or Walt Disney Productions when referring to the company.

building the world's most incredible amusement park. Walt's loss would be debilitating.

The second corporate governance concern was that Walt would destroy capital in his risky endeavors. Walt cared about the creative aspect of his work much more than creating shareholder value, often confessing he did not care about profits.[323] Historically, his ventures worked out stupendously for shareholders, but there was always risk the next one would stumble.

Finally, there was a history of dubious self-dealing between Walt and Walt Disney Productions. Although Buffett has never spoken about this aspect of the investment publicly, a May 1966 article in *Fortune* detailed this risk at length, suggesting he was almost certainly aware of it. This conflict of interest arose in 1952, when Walt formed WED Enterprises to provide his family with income outside of the Disney corporation.[324] Walt Disney Productions consummated a contract with WED Enterprises to license Walt's name and execute a personal services contract shortly after the creation of WED. The agreement was so contentious that three Disney board members resigned over it, fearful of shareholder lawsuits (which did, in fact, arrive).[325]

In 1965, Walt Disney Productions paid $4 million to acquire WED Enterprises' architectural, design, and engineering department, along with the WED Enterprise name.[326] So Walt changed the name of his personal company to Retlaw (or Walter spelled backwards). After Walt Disney Productions bought the design portion of the business, Retlaw was left with three sources of income.

First, Walt possessed the right to produce one movie a year outside of Walt Disney Productions as well as the option to purchase up to a 25% stake in Disney's feature-length live-action films. Walt frequently exercised this right—Retlaw, for example, brought in over a million dollars of profit in 1965 on *Mary Poppins* alone.

The second revenue stream came from licensing Walt's name, earning the entity $292,349 in 1965. Walt Disney Productions had the right to use the Walt Disney name in its corporate title and on films and TV shows in which Walt personally participated. Otherwise, the name had to be licensed and Retlaw would have to be paid.

The third piece was ownership of a steam railroad and elevated monorail at Disneyland. This component grossed $2.5 million in 1965. Retlaw remitted 20% of this to Walt Disney Productions as rent for the right-of-way, but kept the other 80%.

Walt was charging the public company all sorts of fees, taking value for himself that should have accrued to Walt Disney Productions. It was hard for an outside shareholder to stop these shenanigans—though some tried—as Walt and his family owned nearly 40% of the company, with Walt and his wife holding around 16.5%. Walt justified the name agreement by saying it was a typical Hollywood arrangement and the company could count on having the rights to his name after he died; but this was a completely ridiculous notion. There is no getting around the fact that Walt's insider dealings with Disney were problematic.[327]

Finally, as if the valuation and corporate governance concerns were not enough, there was no particular reason to believe Disney's main business of filmmaking was a good one. The United States movie industry was in decline when Buffett made Disney an 8.5% position in his partnership, and no one was immune from the realities of Hollywood economics and its inherent volatility. To see why this was such a challenging industry, let's look back at the history of the movie business.[328]

Tinseltown

The motion picture industry has three key branches: production, distribution, and exhibition. The production process includes acquiring the story rights, developing a script, casting, filming, and editing. These steps culminate in the creation of the negative film. Distributors sell, market, and deliver the film to the theaters. Finally, the exhibitor displays the movie to the audience and collects the admission fees from theatergoers.

The cumulative collections are known as the box office receipts. The exhibitor remits an amount to the distributors, known as the film rental. The film rental, usually negotiated as a percentage, typically amounted to about a third of the box office receipts. After deducting its fees, the distributor remits the remainder to the producer.[329]

Distribution was the kingpin of the industry. Distributors were in charge of manufacturing the negative and sending the film to the theater; they benefited from risk-bearing economies of scale and network effects. The larger firms aggregated risk and could afford to have a flop at the box office because of the high volume of films distributed, while a miss could cripple a smaller firm. Further, producers wanted their creations to be shown as far and wide as possible, so they wanted to work with the biggest distributors. Exhibitors would want to limit the number of distributors they worked with; it would be too cumbersome to speak with more than a handful of players.[lx]

---

lx   As evidence of their strength, of the eight majors discussed in the next paragraph, only RKO became defunct. And only Disney ascended to 'major' status, which didn't happen until the 1980s.

The Golden Age of Hollywood began in the late 1920s, when eight major studios dominated all aspects of the business. These studios were known as the Big Five and Little Three. The Big Five—which included MGM, Warner Bros., 20th Century Fox, RKO, and Paramount—were completely vertically integrated; they produced films, handled distribution, and owned movie theaters. On the other hand, the Little Three—Universal, Columbia, and United Artists—did not own theaters. In fact, United Artists merely distributed movies and did not produce them. The other two produced and distributed movies. While the Little Three lacked the vertical integration of the Big Five, they had leverage over talent, independent producers such as Disney, and exhibitors not owned by the oligopoly.

Not only did the Big Five own theaters, but they also owned the most profitable ones, controlling most of the first-run theaters in the biggest cities, ensuring that their films were shown in the best venues.[lxi] Additionally, all the players engaged in monopolistic distribution tactics such as selling multiple movies in a single bundle and requiring a film's purchase without allowing exhibitors to view the product. During the Golden Age of Hollywood, the major movie studios were quite profitable, but their profitability was based on tactics deliberately designed to reduce competition. Understandably, the government was frustrated and eventually sued all eight companies within the oligopoly.[lxii]

Relief finally arrived for the independents in 1948 when a landmark Supreme Court ruling resulted in each of the major studios reaching consent decrees with the Department of Justice. The agreements, known as the Paramount Consent Decrees, required the Big Five to separate distribution from exhibition. Additionally, all players were barred from using certain prohibitive distribution practices that they had previously forced upon independent theaters.[330]

The Paramount Consent Decrees coincided with the rise of television. The percentage of U.S. homes with a TV increased from 0.4% in 1948 to 92.6% in

lxi   Hollywood operated on what was known as the run-zone-clearance system. The theaters in each zone, or geographic area, were given exclusivity to show the movie for an allotted time. The first run was the most valuable since this was the film's first showing and would therefore attract the most viewers. After a contracted amount of time, known as clearance, the film would be shown again in the same zone in the second-run theater. This process would continue through multiple runs. By controlling most of the first-run theaters in the biggest cities, the Big Five distributors therefore channeled most of the profit pool from exhibition to themselves.

lxii   There is some dispute among movie industry historians over whether the Little Three deserved to be included at all; the Big Five were clearly the bigger problem.

Figure 1: Average weekly attendance (millions)

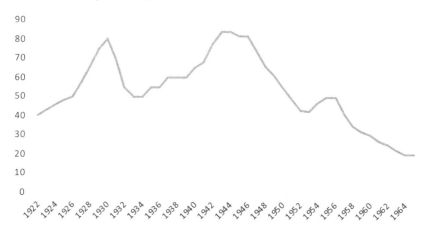

Source: Finler, J. W. (2003). *The Hollywood story: everything you ever wanted to know about the American movie business but didn't know where to look.*

Figure 2: Box office receipts (millions of dollars)

Source: Finler, J. W. (2003). *The Hollywood story: everything you ever wanted to know about the American movie business but didn't know where to look.*

1965.[331] As Figures 1 and 2 illustrate, TV's emergence as an entertainment option delivered a devastating blow to movie attendance and box office receipts. The U.S. box office declined by nearly 40% from 1948 to 1965, cushioned by rising ticket prices, while attendance fell by 70% over the same period.[332] The demand destruction led to a decline in both the number of theaters and feature films released by the majors in the United States.

The falling number of films meant that studios had to change their strategies. One Paramount executive said, "Today, people go to see a movie; they no longer go to the movies. We can't depend on habit anymore. We have to make 'I've got to see that' pictures."[333] In response to the changes in consumer behavior, studios spent more per film, raising the business risk of each one. A greater percentage of films lost money, and the studios became increasingly dependent on the biggest box office hits to drive profits.[334]

Despite all these changes, the majors—a group that continued to exclude Disney due to the low number of films it released—still dominated distribution. While independent producers increased their percentage of total films released after the Paramount consent decrees, they were still dependent on the majors to distribute the product. In addition, the independents relied upon the majors for financing, as the legacy players had the tangible assets needed to raise capital.[335] Now down to seven after RKO failed due to Howard Hughes' mismanagement, the majors distributed 44 of 1965's 50 highest-grossing films.[336]

The bottom line: The movie business was struggling in 1966, and there was no reason to believe a movie studio would fit Buffett's famous definition of "a good business." Disney was still considered a smaller player in the industry, with the majors still releasing the vast majority of box office hits. Given these concerns, how did Buffett build the comfort he needed to take such a significant stake? Well, Disney was not just any studio, and to see why let's look at the company's history.

The ascent of the House of Mouse

Walt established his first animation business in 1921 when he founded Laugh-O-Gram Studio, based in his hometown of Kansas City. The small studio produced animated and live-action cartoons but struggled financially, declaring bankruptcy two years after its inception. After Laugh-O-Gram's receivership, Walt moved to California and founded Disney Brothers Cartoon Studio with Roy in 1923. This entity later merged with two other predecessor companies to form the Walt Disney Productions company Buffett later invested in.[337]

While Walt possessed remarkable creative abilities, he was at the mercy of powerful distributors, and struggled to build a business as a small company battling against giants. Disney experienced success in the 1920s with *Oswald the Lucky Rabbit* and *Alice's Wonderland* short cartoons, but after a contract dispute his distributor Charles Mintz poached the company's animators and made Oswald cartoons himself. Walt had given up his rights to the rabbit in his distribution agreement, and therefore had no recourse to get his character back. The young animator persevered through this setback and developed Mickey Mouse shortly after. In 1928, Mickey made his public debut in *Steamboat Willie*, one of the first synchronized sound cartoons.[lxiii,338]

Walt's dedication to the craft of animation helped create a significant gap between the company and its competitors. The company spent about twice as much on its short cartoons as its competitors did (shorts were brief films played prior to the feature film) and acquired an initial monopoly on a Technicolor process that enhanced the quality of the cartoons. Further, Walt formed a school at the studio dedicated to artist development.[339] These investments resulted in a product vastly superior to competitors', as evidenced by Disney winning every single Oscar for animated shorts during the 1930s.

However, the company was still a minor character in the entertainment industry. Animation was still a novelty. Walt began pushing animation's boundaries in 1934 when he started production on *Snow White and the Seven Dwarfs*, the first feature-length animated film. Walt's initial estimate for the film's production cost was around $250,000. However, actual costs mushroomed and approached $1.5 million, an amount surpassing each of Disney's 1935 and 1936 revenues.[340] But the film was a booming success both with critics and at the box office, becoming the second highest-grossing film released in the 1930s, only trailing *Gone with the Wind*.[341]

Snow White's success helped Walt Disney Productions raise capital through a preferred stock offering in 1940. But the 1940s were not prosperous for Disney. Films such as *Pinocchio* and *Bambi* struggled commercially, partially due to the closure of foreign markets during World War II. During this difficult period, the studio discovered its library had enormous value, a finding that would later be critical to Buffett's investment thesis. The reissuance of *Snow White* helped the company power through this turbulent decade, contributing significantly to net income in 1944 and 1945.[342]

The 1950s spawned two critical turning points for the company. The first was the creation of Disney's own distribution arm. After a dispute with RKO over *The Living Desert*, Disney formed Buena Vista Film Distribution Co. in 1953.

lxiii   Mickey fanatics would correctly point out that the mouse first appeared in the silent cartoon *Plane Crazy*—however, the film initially failed to gain distribution. *Plane Crazy* was released again, with sound added, after the success of *Steamboat Willie*.

The creation of this subsidiary gave the company greater control over its movies and allowed Disney to reduce its distribution costs. Buena Vista severed the company's reliance on third-party distributors and enabled Disney to capture more of the economics its films produced.[343]

The second pivotal event of the 1950s was the construction of Disneyland. However, the famous Anaheim amusement park began as a source of contention between Walt and Roy. Roy had reservations about the project, so Walt worked on the park within his own personal company, the aforementioned WED Enterprises. Roy wasn't keen on the endeavor until Walt raised seed money from a bank to work on it.

Eventually, Walt needed partners to fund the park, which is when Disneyland came under the purview of Walt Disney Productions. This led to a complicated deal with ABC-Paramount in 1954. The arrangement involved ABC buying a TV program from Disney, investing in the park, and providing loan guarantees. ABC received a much-needed TV show, headlined by Walt himself, while Walt secured the capital required to construct the Anaheim park. ABC and Walt Disney Productions each owned 34.5% of Disneyland, a publisher of Disney books had a 13.8% stake, and Walt retained the rest. Roy told ABC that the park would cost between $2 and $5 million to open—it wound up costing $17 million.[344]

Despite costing substantially more than expected, the park opened in July 1955 and—after a rough opening day—was quickly successful. However, Walt's perfectionism eventually led to the ABC/Disney relationship deteriorating, as constant cost overruns frustrated the TV network. Walt Disney Productions eventually bought out all its partners, concluding with a $7.5 million payment for ABC's share in 1960.[345]

Disney was now an entertainment company, not simply a movie studio or a theme park business. Roy Disney stated, "Our diversified activities are related and tend to complement each other."[346] Image 1 shows Disney's strategy map from 1967, and illustrates how the different components fed into one another. Walt maintained a cohesive view of how the disparate parts fit together to build a stronger business.

Walt Disney Productions entering 1966

Disney was a unique gem in Hollywood, having built an exceptional brand associated with high-quality, family-friendly films. And the entertainment titan built a thriving theme park business, constructed through Walt's genius and creative financing. Finally, Walt was an early pioneer in monetizing

Image 1: Disney's strategic map

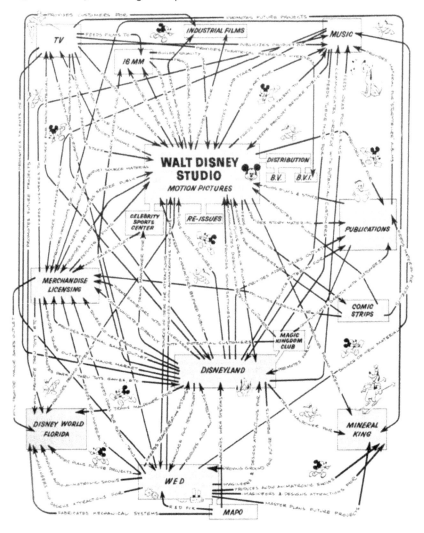

Source: Reforge Staff. (n.d.). "Disney's 60 year old growth map answers the Netflix question," www.reforge.com/blog/disney-growth-map.

existing intellectual property through ancillary products like merchandise and publications.

Table 1 lays out the company's summary financials for the ten-year period ending in 1965. Disney disclosed three segments: film, other, and Disneyland. The 'Film and Other' segments should be viewed jointly since the latter segment

Table 1: Walt Disney Productions summary financials

	1956	1957	1958	1959	1960	1961	1962	1963	1964	1965
Film segment revenue	22,052	24,385	29,117	35,317	27,928	46,253	48,402	49,179	46,136	60,894
Disneyland revenue	n/a	6,002	13,496	17,096	18,101	18,998	20,057	25,731	32,758	35,421
Other segment revenue	5,514	5,392	5,964	6,020	4,903	4,997	7,153	7,013	7,757	13,632
Revenue	**27,565**	**35,778**	**48,577**	**58,432**	**50,931**	**70,248**	**75,612**	**81,922**	**86,651**	**109,947**
Revenue growth	*11.9%*	*29.8%*	*35.8%*	*20.3%*	*-12.8%*	*37.9%*	*7.6%*	*8.3%*	*5.8%*	*26.9%*
Film segment operating income	7,884	9,335	11,882	11,054	1,963	15,018	16,700	16,838	15,061	25,637
Disneyland operating income	n/a	2,155	2,753	4,921	3,338	2,319	1,503	5,107	6,791	3,929
Other segment operating income	1,909	2,410	1,590	1,655	1,201	1,651	2,018	2,044	1,936	3,885
Segment operating income	**9,793**	**13,899**	**16,225**	**17,631**	**6,502**	**18,988**	**20,222**	**23,990**	**23,788**	**33,451**
Segment operating margin	*35.5%*	*38.8%*	*33.4%*	*30.2%*	*12.8%*	*27.0%*	*26.7%*	*29.3%*	*27.5%*	*30.4%*
Operating income	**4,953**	**8,114**	**8,486**	**8,707**	**(1,010)**	**11,362**	**11,830**	**13,844**	**13,554**	**22,211**
Operating margin	*18.0%*	*22.7%*	*17.5%*	*14.9%*	*-2.0%*	*16.2%*	*15.6%*	*16.9%*	*15.6%*	*20.2%*
Net income	**$4,465**	**$3,649**	**$3,865**	**$3,400**	**($1,342)**	**$4,465**	**$5,263**	**$6,574**	**$7,057**	**$11,379**
Profit margin	*16.2%*	*10.2%*	*8.0%*	*5.8%*	*-2.6%*	*6.4%*	*7.0%*	*8.0%*	*8.1%*	*10.3%*
Earnings per share	*$2.01*	*$2.44*	*$2.51*	*$2.15*	*($0.83)*	*$2.75*	*$3.14*	*$3.81*	*$3.96*	*$6.08*

Source: *Moody's Manuals*, Walt Disney Productions annual reports, and author's calculations. Dollar figures in thousands, except per share numbers.

included movie-related products such as publications, merchandising, music, and records. In 1965, these two segments produced 88.3% of Disney's segment operating income—which excluded corporate G&A expenses—and 67.8% of revenue. Disneyland, whose earnings were currently depressed due to substantial investment in the park, generated about a third of revenue but only 11.7% of 1965's segment operating income. The company also had net cash, making it a conservatively financed enterprise.

Disney had produced explosive financial growth in all segments over the previous ten years. But an investor would be concerned about the sustainability of the 1965 numbers, with the Film and Other segments' operating income both at a peak due to *Mary Poppins*. While the movie was still being rolled out globally, investors were concerned that it would be hard to replicate these spectacular numbers once it was no longer in theaters.

Film and Other segment

Disney seemed to have a magic touch, as the explosive growth shown in Table 2 illustrates. Disney nearly tripled film revenue since 1956 while U.S. box office receipts fell by a third. While this isn't a perfect comparison because Disney's film division included television revenue and growing foreign markets while the box office didn't, Disney was outclassing its peers and producing fantastic results.

The company, however, was still not considered a major due to the low number of films it released in 1966. While the seven majors averaged 22 annually from 1961 to 1965, Disney usually only released about six.[347] Despite its status, the company produced far superior margins relative to its film studio peers, as seen in Table 3.[lxiv]

Disney had gravitated away from solely using animation in its films as it had with *Snow White*. Rather, the company now layered animation onto live actors as it did in *Mary Poppins*. Disney's record of producing family-friendly films helped the company build a brand with consumers. Families sought out Disney movies, knowing the studio's films would be fun and appropriate for children.[348]

While *Mary Poppins*'s success led to record 1965 results, Disney had proven it could produce box office hits consistently. Segment income averaged over $15

---

lxiv   This analysis is imperfect, as it takes Disney's Film and Other segment but excludes corporate overhead and compares it to its peers whose numbers include corporate overhead. However, Disney would have had higher five-year average earnings than all players other than United Artists even if one were to take the punitive (and analytically incorrect) step of allocating all of the company's G&A to the Film and Other segments.

Table 2: Film and Other revenue

	1956	1957	1958	1959	1960	1961	1962	1963	1964	1965
Film revenue	$22,052	$24,385	$29,117	$35,317	$27,928	$46,253	$48,402	$49,179	$46,136	$60,894
Other revenue	$5,514	$5,392	$5,964	$6,020	$4,903	$4,997	$7,153	$7,013	$7,757	$13,632
Film and Other revenue	$27,565	$29,777	$35,081	$41,337	$32,830	$51,250	$55,555	$56,191	$53,893	$74,526
Film revenue year-over-year revenue growth	*11.9%*	*8.0%*	*17.8%*	*17.8%*	*-20.6%*	*56.1%*	*8.4%*	*1.1%*	*-4.1%*	*38.3%*
Amortization of theatrical and television publication costs	(11,327)	(12,284)	(13,726)	(19,402)	(14,619)	(19,226)	(15,586)	(16,146)	(14,520)	(12,705)
Distribution costs—print, advertising, etc.	(2,096)	(2,399)	(3,167)	(4,244)	(10,103)	(11,162)	(15,488)	(15,471)	(15,477)	(20,101)
Stories and pre-production costs abandoned	(745)	(368)	(342)	(617)	(1,243)	(847)	(627)	(723)	(1,077)	(2,451)
Costs applicable to other income	(3,605)	(2,982)	(4,374)	(4,365)	(3,702)	(3,346)	(5,135)	(4,968)	(5,821)	(9,747)
Total Film and Other expenses	(17,773)	(18,032)	(21,609)	(28,627)	(29,667)	(34,581)	(36,837)	(37,309)	(36,896)	(45,004)
Film and Other segment income	$9,793	$11,745	$13,472	$12,709	$3,164	$16,669	$18,718	$18,882	$16,997	$29,522
Film segment margins	*35.5%*	*39.4%*	*38.4%*	*30.7%*	*9.6%*	*32.5%*	*33.7%*	*33.6%*	*31.5%*	*39.6%*

Source: *Moody's Manuals*, Walt Disney Productions annual reports, and author's calculations. Dollar figures in thousands, except per share numbers.

Table 3: Peer summary financials

Company	FY 1965			5-Year Average			10-Year Average		
	Revenue	EBIT	Margin	Revenue	EBIT	Margin	Revenue	EBIT	Margin
Walt Disney Productions—Film and Other	$74,526	$29,522	39.6%	$58,283	$20,158	34.6%	$45,801	$15,167	33.1%
20th Century-Fox	154,361	10,432	6.8%	111,836	(9,830)	-8.8%	112,590	(5,057)	-4.5%
Columbia Pictures	140,626	7,101	5.0%	138,387	6,324	4.6%	123,196	4,835	3.9%
MGM	160,749	15,289	9.5%	147,697	5,755	3.9%	146,830	8,676	5.9%
Paramount Pictures	124,499	10,740	8.6%	114,176	4,404	3.9%	109,967	4,589	4.2%
United Artists	193,757	27,529	14.2%	147,631	13,496	9.1%	116,000	10,782	9.3%
Universal	79,796	12,345	15.5%	74,828	9,571	12.8%	69,194	7,681	11.1%
Warner Bros. Pictures	97,096	7,580	7.8%	87,191	6,607	7.6%	84,100	6,365	7.6%

Source: *Moody's Manuals*, Walt Disney Productions annual reports, and author's calculations.

million over the preceding decade and more than $20 million in the last five years. The company had one bad year—in 1960—when segment margins were only 9.6%. In every other year, the 'Film and Other' super-segment generated total profit margins in excess of 30%. In other words, Disney's filmmaking had relatively low downside volatility.

While Disney was certainly not immune from the realities of its chosen industry, it successfully occupied the family-oriented niche, building a brand that could be monetized. This brand value demonstrated itself by lowering search costs for customers who wanted to entertain their children at the movie theater. While the brand did not guarantee attendance forever, with its value rising and falling with each movie, the Disney label gave viewers assurances about the type of film they would be seeing.

Disneyland segment

During Buffett and Munger family visits to Disneyland, Warren and Charlie would skip out on *Dumbo the Flying Elephant* and *Snow White's Enchanted Wish*, choosing to spend their time trying to dissect the profitability of each ride.[349] While insufficient for a ride-by-ride analysis, the annual reports assisted their efforts in analyzing the park's economics. Disney began consolidating Disneyland's financials in June 1957, when the company acquired a majority stake. And as mentioned previously, Disney didn't acquire full ownership of the park until 1960.

Disneyland generated revenue by charging a general admission entrance fee and an additional amount for rides. In 1965, the park attracted 6.5 million attendees and generated about $5.45 of revenue for each one. Image 2 shows that Disneyland had stagnant attendance from 1959 to 1962 but started to grow again as the company added rides and learned how to better market the park. Table 4 presents Disneyland's financials, showing tremendous revenue growth. The capital investment, attendance, and financial figures illustrate that Walt was not sloppily throwing cash around; he had a ten-year track record of triumph at the park.

It was clear that this was a phenomenal business, producing nearly $4 million of income—in a down year—on around $20 million of net invested capital. And the company was going to spend another $20 million on the park in 1966—more than the entire cost of Disneyland on the day it opened.

How did Buffett get comfortable?

Disney was a great business after all, very much the exception to the general Hollywood rule. But the quality of the business did not solve the company's

Image 2: Disneyland attendance and capital investment

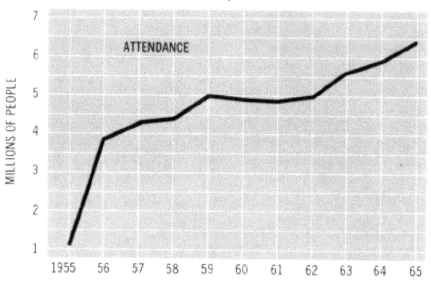

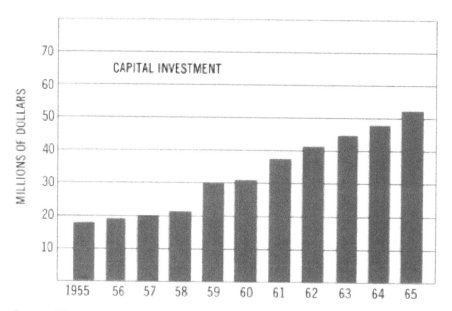

Source: Walt Disney Productions, *1965 Annual Report.*

Table 4: Disneyland summary financials

	1956	1957	1958	1959	1960	1961	1962	1963	1964	1965
Disneyland revenue	n/a	6,002	13,496	17,096	18,101	18,998	20,057	25,731	32,758	35,421
Disneyland year-over-year revenue growth			124.9%	26.7%	5.9%	5.0%	5.6%	28.3%	27.3%	8.1%
Disneyland segment income	n/a	2,155	2,753	4,921	3,338	2,319	1,503	5,107	6,791	3,929
Disneyland segment margins	*n/a*	*35.9%*	*20.4%*	*28.8%*	*18.4%*	*12.2%*	*7.5%*	*19.8%*	*20.7%*	*11.1%*

Source: Walt Disney Productions annual reports and author's calculations. Dollar figures in thousands.

corporate governance issues, which on the surface seemed disqualifying. As part of his research, Buffett decided to meet Mickey Mouse's creator, saying, "I went out to see Walt Disney (he'd never heard of me; I was 35 years old). We sat down and he told me the whole plan for the company—he couldn't have been a nicer guy."[350]

Walt's corporate governance sins must therefore be seen in this context. He grew up poor and he had experienced others stealing his work, as evidenced by the theft of Oswald. Walt was paranoid, and for good reason; Hollywood was full of examples of the originators of creative work being robbed of the windfalls from their labors. While this doesn't excuse the behavior, it is easy to see how Buffett could accept this risk. And this danger may have limited Buffett from making this a larger position. While an 8.5% bet is not small, Buffett frequently took much larger swings.

Understanding the origins of WED also helps frame the issue. While Roy encouraged Walt to form WED to protect his interests, Walt wanted an organization to incubate Disneyland. Walt felt constrained at the studio—now a publicly traded company with sprawling departments—and found his work at the smaller WED invigorating. He was so passionate about the park that he used his own funds to finance it by borrowing against his life insurance policy and sold a home he had built.[351] Walt wasn't an evil, cynical, opportunistic predator who set out to take advantage of shareholders, he was simply worried about being taken advantage of. Moreover, Walt Disney Productions was the entity that owned the films, the theme park, the Florida land, and all the other important assets, not WED.

Finally, the valuation was enticing enough to overlook these concerns. Buffett laid out his thinking:

> We bought 5% of the Walt Disney Company in 1966. It cost us $4 million dollars. $80 million bucks was the valuation of the whole thing. 300 and some acres in Anaheim. The Pirate's ride had just been put in. It cost $17 million bucks. The whole Company was selling for $80 million. *Mary Poppins* had just come out. *Mary Poppins* made about $30 million that year, and seven years later you're going to show it to kids the same age. It's like having an oil well where all the oil seeps back in. Now the [numbers today are] probably different, but in 1966 they had 220 pictures of one sort or another. They wrote them all down to zero—there were no residual values placed on the value of any Disney picture up through the '60s. So [you got all of this] for $80 million bucks, and you got Walt Disney to work for you. It was incredible. You didn't have to be a genius to know that the Walt Disney company was worth more than

$80 million. $17 million for the Pirate's Ride. It's unbelievable. But there it was. And the reason was, in 1966 people said, "Well, *Mary Poppins* is terrific this year, but they're not going to have another *Mary Poppins* next year, so the earnings will be down." I don't care if the earnings are down like that. You know you've still got *Mary Poppins* to throw out in seven more years, assuming kids squawk a little. I mean there's no better system than to have something where, essentially, you get a new crop every seven years and you get to charge more each time.[lxv,352]

Buffett builds the valuation through the assets, including those marked to zero on the balance sheet. He starts with the land in Anaheim, which cost $5 million.[353] Then, he marvels at the pirate's ride; expressing a kind of disbelief at the fact the world's greatest entertainment genius, who was also the world's greatest theme park designer, chose to spend $17 million on a ride—and that the stock market was valuing this whole company at a little under five times this single attraction. He then talks about *Mary Poppins*, briefly mentioning its earnings but then moving to how it could be released again in the future. Later, Buffett says:

I wanted to go see *Mary Poppins*, to see if she'd be recycled, and she was showing at the Loews Theater on 45th and Broadway in New York, and here I am with a briefcase at 2:00 in the afternoon heading in to see *Mary Poppins*. I almost felt like I had to rent a kid.[354]

His research focused on the persistence of *Mary Poppins* and the timeless value of Disney films. Importantly, using the film library was not a theoretical thought—Disney had repeatedly dug into the vault to generate income in the past, including *Cinderella* which earned over $2.5 million of rentals in calendar 1965.[355] Roy Disney called the film library "the floor under our company." At the end of 1965, Disney owned hundreds of shorts, 21 animated features, 47 live-action animated features, and various other films and TV shows. The total negative cost of this library was $205 million, only $9 million of which remained on the balance sheet.[356] But it was clearly worth a lot more than the carrying value.

---

lxv   Buffett has indicated elsewhere he bought the stock at $53 a share in the first half of 1966, implying a market capitalization of $99 million. The stock didn't fall to the $80 million valuation until the back half of the year. He has most frequently cited the $80 million figure and wrote that he bought the stock when the market valuation was "less than $90 million" in Berkshire Hathaway's 1995 annual report. Additionally, he bought Disney within Berkshire at an average price of $43.24. It's possible he initially bought at $53 and bought more as the stock fell. The investment thesis does not change whether he paid $53 or $43.

Buffett, in a separate conversation, commented that the written-off films were worth as much as the $80 million market capitalization.[357] While the major studios had monetized at least some of their film libraries, finding quality comparable transactions was challenging. The best available at the time was a deal between NBC and Universal for just the TV rights to their movie library. While the deal transformed into a more extensive arrangement between NBC and Universal, this wouldn't have been known at the time.[358]

Using the per-film value of this deal applied to Disney's 21 animated features and 47 live-action animated features results in an absurdly conservative $40.8 million valuation. First, this was only a TV deal, not a total library sale. Second, it would not account for the shorts and TV shows Disney had. Third, Disney's library was almost certainly more valuable than Universal's on a film-by-film basis. While Disney was a much smaller studio than Universal, with fewer films released each year, it produced more top movies than Universal.

Simply adding these three items up—the film library valuation using the Universal deal of $40.8 million, the cost for the Pirates ride at $17 million, and the $5 million for the land in Anaheim—results in a valuation of $62.8 million. On top of this, the company had $8.5 million of net current asset value, and *Mary Poppins* was continuing to be debuted in international markets in 1966. Earnings would rise 8.9% to $12.4 million that year. Obviously, Buffett wouldn't have known the precise figure, but he would have known it was doing well globally. Adding the net current assets and one year's worth of earnings to the $62.8 million number puts the valuation at $83.7 million, north of the $80 million market capitalization Buffett bought the stock at.

Buffett used back-of-the-envelope math, piecing together a coherent downside valuation. His critical insight was not that Disney was worth a specific number but that it was certainly worth more than the market cap he bought the stock at. And he thought about this creatively, anchoring volatile future income stream to more solid and already-proven asset values.

But Buffett continues:

> It was a joke. If he'd privately gone to some huge venture capitalist, or some major American corporation, if he'd been a private company, and said "I want you to buy into this. This is a deal," they would have bought in based on a valuation of $300 or $400 million dollars. The very fact that it was just sitting there in the market every day convinced [people that $80 million was an appropriate valuation]. Essentially, they ignored it because it was so familiar. But that happens periodically on Wall Street.[359]

Now, Buffett's valuation range is quite broad, from more than $80 million to $400 million. But, looking at the company on a sum-of-the-parts basis, the way a modern analyst might do it, the high number is a reasonable valuation.

Film and Other valuation

As Table 5 illustrates, Disney traded at a discount to every comparable company on five-year average EBIT numbers.[lxvii] Applying the median multiple and peak multiple to Disney's Film and Other segment operating income results in a range of $246.9 million to $452.1 million.[360] The high case was bolstered by Paramount, which was in the middle of being taken over by Gulf + Western.

Disneyland valuation

Disneyland had no comparable companies; there was truly nothing like it. Walt was obsessed with the park, constantly brainstorming how to make it better, and wasn't shy about spending capital.

However, like the movie business, it was difficult to develop a calibrated estimate of future cash flows. While almost certainly better than the average business, it was difficult to know what multiple to apply to which earnings. But one only needed to get broad strokes rather than precision to develop the investment case. For the base case, using the market multiple on 1965 Disneyland earnings—adjusted for tax—results in a $28.9 million valuation. And for the high case, a 21.0x multiple will be applied to peak 1964 earnings,[lxviii] again accounting for Uncle Sam's share.[361] This calculation results in a range of $28.9 million to $74.3 million for Disneyland, a wide range for a business whose future economics were very difficult to discern.

Sum-of-the-parts valuation

There are a couple of minor pieces needed to finalize the valuation. First, an adjustment for G&A expenses.[lxix] Second, the film library valuation—using the number derived above from the Universal valuation in the base case and doubling that for the high case, which would approximate Buffett's remark that the library's value matched the company's equity value when he purchased

---

lxvii   This includes Universal, which MCA acquired in a non-arms length transaction that a court would later rule undervalued the company.

lxviii The implied multiple assuming a 10% discount rate and 5% growth rate.

lxix   G&A is deducted at the implied blended multiple for the operating businesses in both the base and high cases.

Table 5: Comparable company valuation

Company	Market capitalization	Enterprise value	EV/1965 revenue	EV/1965 EBIT	FY 1965 P/E	5-Year Average		
						EV/revenue	EV/EBIT	P/TB
Walt Disney Productions	$80,882	$77,890	0.71x	3.51x	7.11x	0.92x	5.35x	1.60x
20th Century-Fox	77,742	114,940	0.74x	11.02x	6.61x	1.03x	n/m	0.98x
Columbia Pictures	47,051	82,282	0.59x	11.59x	23.25x	0.59x	13.01x	1.12x
MGM	69,229	91,148	0.57x	5.96x	8.87x	0.62x	15.84x	0.86x
Paramount Pictures	102,061	98,779	0.79x	9.20x	16.35x	0.87x	22.43x	1.39x
United Artists	47,365	96,479	0.50x	3.50x	3.69x	0.65x	7.15x	0.80x
Universal[1]	63,119	59,187	0.74x	4.79x	9.35x	0.79x	6.18x	1.17x
Warner Bros. Pictures	64,628	58,622	0.60x	7.73x	13.86x	0.67x	8.87x	1.39x
Average[2]	69,010	84,916	0.66x	7.16x	11.13x	0.77x	11.26x	1.16x
Median	66,928	86,715	0.66x	6.85x	9.11x	0.73x	8.87x	1.14x
Average—excluding Disney[2]	67,314	85,920	0.65x	7.69x	11.71x	0.75x	12.25x	1.10x
Median—excluding Disney	64,628	91,148	0.60x	7.73x	9.35x	0.67x	10.94x	1.12x

Source: *Moody's Manuals* and company annual reports. (1) Universal was acquired by MCA earlier in the year; this valuation uses the $75 per share purchase price. (2) EBIT averages exclude companies with negative EBIT. Averages are based on each company's fiscal year. Universal changed its fiscal year end in 1961. Market capitalization and enterprise value calculations are based on August 31, 1966 stock prices. Dollar figures in thousands.

the stock. And finally, the Florida land value (at cost) and the net cash on the balance sheet.

As Table 6 shows, Buffett's $300–$400 million range was perfectly reasonable. While the base case falls short, movie stocks had traded higher earlier in the year and were a little cheap at the chosen valuation date. Furthermore, Disneyland would quickly prove to be worth well more than even the high-case valuation as earnings would explode a few years after Buffett bought the stock. Because of the volatility of the movie industry, a wide range was the best an analyst could do. And Buffett bought the stock way below this sum-of-the-parts analysis.

Table 6: Valuation

	Base	High
Film and Other segment	$246,879	$452,125
Disneyland	28,942	74,294
G&A	($92,678)	($176,881)
Total operating value	$183,143	$349,539
Film library valuation	40,800	81,600
Florida land	5,000	5,000
Net cash	2,992	2,992
Total value	$231,935	$439,131
Per share value	$97.93	$186.91
Upside from Buffett's purchase price	126.4%	332.2%

Source: Walt Disney Productions annual reports and author's calculations. Dollar figures in thousands other than per share numbers.

Why did Buffett sell Disney's stock?

After buying the stock in 1966 at around $43 per share, Buffett sold it for a 55% gain about a year later, at around $65–$70 per share.[lxx] The valuation work suggests the stock was worth much more than this sale price. So why did Buffett sell? First, one significant risk was realized when Walt Disney passed away in December 1966 at the age of 65. The stock rose after Walt's passing, continuing a trend that started before his death. Roy Disney attributed the rise to movie

---

lxx   Buffett had also purchased a small stake in Disney through Berkshire Hathaway. Berkshire owned 3,900 shares in 1966 compared to the approximate 94,000 shares the Buffett Partnership bought. Berkshire held its shares much longer, until at least 1969.

stocks being underpriced, but some investors speculated the company could be subject to a takeover.[362]

Disney without Walt was a different animal than Disney with Walt. It became much more difficult to confidently project that Disney would continue producing high-quality films with Walt gone. More than perhaps any other significant American corporation at the time, Disney was an extension of its founder. Walt's death almost surely played some role in Buffett's decision to sell, rationally so.

Second, the stock didn't have the same degree of downside protection once the stock price rose. The outcome distribution for the movie business was wide, a problem Buffett solved for by analyzing the company on an asset basis. Buffett was always more interested in how cheap Disney was than he was in its theoretical intrinsic value. When it stopped being cheap, it made sense for him to sell.

Disney released 1966 earnings shortly after Walt's death. Earnings improved, with operating income rising from $22.2 million in 1965 to $23.6 million in 1966, as *Mary Poppins* continued to be shown worldwide.[363] In the years following Walt's death, Disneyland's earnings exploded, with the segment's operating income growing from $3.9 million in 1965 to nearly $20 million in 1968.[364]

Now, did Buffett sell Disney stock too soon? After Disney bought Capital Cities/ABC, Buffett wrote about the deal in Berkshire Hathaway's 1995 chairman's letter, saying:

> Buffett Partnership Ltd. bought a significant amount of Disney stock at a split-adjusted price of $0.31 per share. That decision may appear brilliant, given that the stock now sells for $66. But your Chairman was up to the task of nullifying it: In 1967 I sold out at $0.48 per share.[365]

Despite Buffett's protestations to the contrary, he did not make a mistake selling Disney stock when he did—he was able to produce even better results over the years. He compounded Berkshire's book value at 23.9% from 1967 to 1995, while Disney's stock price compounded at about 18.5% (dividends would have increased this number a bit). Disney's market capitalization grew to $30.9 billion at the end of 1995, an astounding rise from the $80 million market cap when Buffett bought the stock. Berkshire Hathaway, on the other hand, grew from $18.3 million around the time he bought Disney in 1966 to $38.3 billion at year-end 1995. Despite Disney thriving after his 1967 sale, Warren was able to do even better.

Buffett has said:

If you've got a good enough business, if you have a monopoly newspaper, if you have a network television station—I'm talking of the past—you know, your idiot nephew could run it. And if you've got a really good business, it doesn't make any difference.[366]

Walt Disney Productions was certainly not a business this good—management mattered, especially in the movie business. However, through Walt and Roy's creativity and intellect, they were able to develop Disneyland into a great business.[lxxi]

In contrast to Ben Graham, who often shunned speaking with management, Buffett tenaciously analyzed the leaders of the companies he invested in. Walt helped show how a single manager can transform and elevate a company in a mediocre industry. Buffett has frequently made similar investments like this, such as his purchase of the Nebraska Furniture Mart in 1983, Borsheim's in 1989, and Helzberg's in 1995. These three companies operated in the tough retail business—Nebraska Furniture Mart in carpets; Borsheim's and Helzberg's in jewelry—but all were able to create competitive advantages through great managerial effort.

Buffett was starting to journey into the 'better business'. This was a gradual transition, rather than a swift, revolutionary shift. Disney is a linchpin investment of the partnership years. In the case of Disney, he used the asset value as a safety net if the business went awry, dipping his toes into the quality pool. He was able to find a way to use the logic of balance sheet analysis to gain comfort with a volatile cash flow stream. Rather than box himself in with strict criteria, he was light on his feet, opportunistically pouncing on value wherever he could find it.

---

lxxi   In a funny twist to Buffett's 'idiot nephew' comment, Walt would complain about Roy Disney's son, who worked at Disney and was also named Roy. This led Card Walker, who succeeded the elder Roy Disney as president in 1971, to label the younger Roy as the 'idiot nephew.' Nephew Roy would later help engineer a management change in 1984, bringing in Michael Eisner to replace Ron Miller (who was the husband of Walt's daughter). He would later launch a campaign to replace Eisner two decades later, which led to Eisner resigning as chairman in 2004 and then as CEO in 2005.

Conclusion

"We had a very good thing in the 1930s, then Ben had to go and write a book about it, and now everybody knows how to do it."

—Jerome Newman[367]

The less-famous Graham-Newman partner uttered the above quote in 1959, three years after Buffett created his first partnership and had already started trouncing the Dow. Buffett would continue crushing the market over the decade following the quote. And then the boy genius would close the partnership and 'retire.'

Of course, we now know the story doesn't stop there. Buffett took control of Berkshire Hathaway in 1965, becoming its chairman and chief executive officer in 1970, and turned it into one of the most valuable companies in the world. As a reward for his efforts, he became one of the richest people on the planet and briefly claimed the top spot in 2008.[368] So despite Jerome Newman's grumbling, there was still a lot of money to be made from value investing. Sometimes, people *really* overestimate the importance of writing books.

More ink has been spilled about Warren Buffett than any other investor. But I wrote this book because I thought there were significant gaps in the public's understanding of how he built his early fortune and how this period influenced his thinking throughout his career. Investing during these earlier years was harder than even Buffett and Munger have made it seem. A myth has formed that Buffett merely flipped through *Moody's Manuals* and scooped up crazy bargains. While financial markets have become more efficient since the 1950s and 1960s, it was always difficult to outperform the market, especially to the degree Buffett has.

The 'obvious' quantitative bargains often had some issues or were so thinly traded that Buffett had to perform significant legwork to accumulate stock, as we saw with Union Street Railway. Or they were cheap stocks that simply didn't do all that well. Companies such as Marshall-Wells and Greif Bros., which earned good returns for their shareholders, didn't stack up to the 29.5% rate Buffett put up during his partnership years.

As mentioned in the Preface, I think there were four reasons for Buffett's outperformance that I explore in greater depth here: activism, concentration, a fluid and creative research process, and a discerning filter. These factors are related: An investor taking an activist stance against a company only makes sense if the position is meaningful. Someone with influence—and, more importantly, control—*should* be more concentrated, with his or her actions presumably de-risking the situation. Analysts can only know so many companies; deploying creative research techniques to uncover information only makes sense if one can bet big. Buffett used these factors to assist in superior security selection, leading to his substantial outperformance.

Influence

Warren Buffett is a capital allocation snob. He knew power needed to be taken out of the hands of the incompetents and given to those who knew what they were doing. Buffett knows that capital allocation is important. He also knows that most people, left to their own devices, are mediocre at best and terrible at worst. Finally, he knows that he is very good at allocating capital.

Early in his career, Buffett used 'hard power,' building sizable stakes in companies to seize control. His early big winners frequently came from ideas where he or someone close to him exerted power and influence. Philadelphia and Reading succeeded because of a significant change in capital allocation. Then, during the partnership, Buffett would take control of Sanborn Map and Dempster Mill, change capital allocation, and generate enormous profits for himself.

As Buffett evolved, he began to use soft power. While American Express wasn't an activist idea in the conventional sense, Buffett wrote the president in the middle of the Salad Oil scandal, gently encouraging a midyear letter to shareholders detailing the continued strength of the company's competitive position. Additionally, Buffett encouraged Amex to fulfill the claims against its subsidiary arising from the scandal, thinking the enterprise would damage its reputation and become less valuable if it tried to skirt its responsibilities.[369]

Another more famous example is his tutelage of *The Washington Post*'s CEO Kay Graham. After acquiring the newspaper publisher's stock in 1973, Buffett helped teach Graham about business and capital allocation, which paid dividends as the investment produced billions for Berkshire. Today, his reputation means people come to him seeking his advice, letting him apply soft skills to persuade managements to do the right thing.

Buffett's elitist view on capital allocation lets him sniff out who is good. On the surface, Walt Disney was not really a Buffett guy. But in a weird way, and despite claiming not to care about shareholder profits, Walt was a superb capital allocator. He had a comical habit of spending too much money. But his ideas worked out despite the bean counters thinking he was nuts. Walt would shower his best animators with attention and feedback, ignoring the less talented. Buffett is the same way with his businesses, putting money to work in the best companies and starving the struggling businesses.

Lastly—and in my view, most importantly—Berkshire Hathaway is the shining star example of how Buffett uses control to create value. People think Buffett *used* to be an activist investor, but he really just evolved. When Berkshire acquires a business, Warren Buffett controls its capital, something he repeatedly points out in his letters and at Berkshire's annual meetings. Full ownership allows him to circumvent the need to persuade managements and boards entirely.

Concentration

One of the key reasons for Buffett's success is that he invests with huge *cojones*. Buffett bets big. While people know he is a focused investor, folks underestimate how hard he worked to remain incredibly concentrated throughout his career. In his 1965 letter to partners, he wrote, "We probably have had only five or six situations in the nine-year history of the Partnership where we have exceeded 25%."[370] That means one 'big' idea every one and a half years or so.

A sampling of his big bets, starting with the pre-partnership years:

- At the end of 1951, four ideas accounted for almost 90% of his portfolio, with GEICO responsible for more than 50%.

- In 1954 P&R, his largest position, was around a third of his net worth.

And then during the partnership:[lxxii]

- Commonwealth Trust was the largest holding in 1958, between 10% and 20% of assets of the partnerships (recall, Buffett operated multiple partnerships before collapsing them into a single entity in 1962).

- Sanborn Map was 25% of assets at the beginning of 1959 and 35% at the start of 1960. It looked to contribute the vast majority of 1960 profits.[371]

lxxii   Readers should note that this section—especially the attribution portion of Sanborn Map and Dempster Mill—relies on my estimates based on *The Snowball*, Buffett's commentary, and the partnership letters. The data is imprecise and relies on my tying different sources and datapoints together. Further complicating matters is the fact that Buffett did not necessarily value control situations at market value.

- Dempster was more than a 20% position in 1961 through 1963 and contributed about 70% of the partnership's profits in 1962 and a third in 1963. British Columbia Power was also an 11% position at the end of 1962. These two positions were responsible for over a third of his portfolio at the end of 1962.

- Towards the end of 1964, he had around half his fund in three stocks (American Express, Texas Gulf, and Pure Oil). American Express got as high as 40% of his portfolio and would produce roughly a third of the partnership's profits from 1964 through 1967.[372]

- In 1966, American Express, Hochschild Kohn, and Berkshire Hathaway made up around 60% of the investment portfolio.

And Buffett didn't stop there. People often miss how concentrated he was even in his Berkshire and Blue Chip Stamps days:[lxxiii]

- Purchased National Indemnity in 1967, with the acquisition cost at more than a quarter of Berkshire's beginning of the year assets. In his 2004 chairman's letter, Buffett said, "Nevertheless, for almost all of the past 38 years, NICO [National Indemnity] has been a star performer. Indeed, had we not made this acquisition, Berkshire would be lucky to be worth half of what it is today."[373]

- Acquired Illinois National Bank & Trust in 1969, with the cost at over 40% of Berkshire's beginning of the year assets.

- Purchased See's Candy, with the purchase price worth nearly a quarter of Blue Chip Stamps' beginning of the year assets when acquired in 1972.

- Bought the *Buffalo Evening News* at a price equivalent to around 20% of Blue Chip Stamps' beginning of the year assets when acquired in 1977.

- Purchased Cap Cities/ABC's stock at a price equal to approximately 25% of Berkshire's beginning of the year assets when acquired in 1985.

- Invested about 10% of Berkshire's total assets in Coca-Cola stock when buying it in 1988 and 1989.

As Berkshire Hathaway has grown, it has become harder to find these opportunities. The sheer size of the company means there are only so many things that Berkshire can actually invest in to make a difference. Additionally, these larger companies tend not to be as heavily discounted as the smaller stuff Buffett invested in earlier in his career; the risk-reward isn't as attractive and,

---

lxxiii   Blue Chip Stamps was a trading stamps company whose stock Buffett had purchased through Berkshire. Blue Chip Stamps was merged into Berkshire in 1983.

therefore, less worthy of a big swing. But even Burlington Northern Santa Fe was acquired in 2010 at about 10% of beginning of the year assets.[lxxiv]

Gumshoe research

There is an incomplete narrative that Buffett's success is attributable to his unique genius. This doesn't do justice to the tremendous amount of old-fashioned shoe-leather research he performed. Much of his success came from performing proprietary investigative research to uncover unique insights about businesses.

When asked about how Buffett is different from other value investors, Alice Schroeder, the author of Buffett's seminal biography *The Snowball*, said:

> In terms of how that affects his investing behavior, number one, in his classic investments he expends a lot of energy checking out details and ferreting out nuggets of information, way beyond the balance sheet. He would go back and look at the company's history in depth for decades. He used to pay people to attend shareholder meetings and ask questions for him. He checked out the personal lives of people who ran companies he invested in. He wanted to know about their financial status, their personal habits, what motivated them. He behaves like an investigative journalist. All this stuff about flipping through *Moody's Manuals* picking stocks… it was a screen for him, but he didn't stop there.[374]

There are multiple examples of Buffett performing tenacious and creative research in this book:

- Skipped class to attend Marshall-Wells' annual meeting.

- Flew to Ohio to attend the annual meeting of Cleveland Worsted Mills after the dividend cut.

- Drove to New Bedford to meet Union Street Railway's president. He also purchased ads in a local paper to find stock.

- Met with employees to better understand Greif Bros. and would later meet the company's chairman driving back to Omaha after leaving Graham-Newman.

- As part of his research on American Express, he visited restaurants in Omaha to see if these establishments still took the company's cards and

---

lxxiv   Berkshire owned 22.5% of BNSF prior to the acquisition. Berkshire paid $100 per share for the rest of BNSF in cash and stock in February 2010, with this additional outlay accounting for 8.9% of Berkshire's December 31, 2009 assets.

Travelers Cheques. He also deployed an associate to research the company, culminating in the production of a foot-high stack of material.

- Traveled to Kansas City to count railcars to estimate demand for STP when analyzing Studebaker.

- Watched *Mary Poppins* in theaters and traveled to Anaheim to meet Walt Disney.

And then there are some stories not covered in this book:

- GEICO in 1950, when Buffett traveled to D.C. on a weekend to visit company headquarters because Ben Graham owned the stock. While there, he learned about insurance from the company's future CEO, Lorimer Davidson.

- National American Fire Insurance, where he sent an associate to drive around Nebraska to find and buy this stock, which was trading around 1.0x earnings.

At only 20 years old, he was visiting companies and attending annual meetings to figure out what was happening with the businesses he bought. He was not an office-based investor, merely reading documents to make decisions. Instead, he dedicated significant shoe leather to accumulate knowledge about companies.

Buffett has never thought much of his competitors in the investment research game. And he still doesn't. Today, there are a plethora of expert networks and services that allow investors to connect with ex-employees and customers of their target company to learn more about a business. But this work has frequently morphed into 'check-the-box' research, allowing investors to create a laundry list of due diligence work done on investments to pretend they did real work. Buffett was always rigorous about answering the right questions to make money.

His fluid analytical process allowed him to jump from investment to investment, always focused on finding value. From figuring out whether American Express's competitive position was impaired due to the Salad Oil scandal to handicapping the odds of the British Columbia Power deal closing, he focused on solving the right problem. The prevailing thinking on Buffett far too often tries to box him in by repeating cliches about finding great businesses and great management teams. But it ignores how flexible he was in the variety of opportunities he scooped up, as well as the different types of research he performed to uncover information.

Filter

One of the things this book does not do is explain all the investments Buffett looked at and rejected. Throughout my research, I looked at the same *Moody's Manuals* Warren Buffett did when he was investing in the partnership. There were *a lot* of cheap stocks. But not all of them did well of course. Buffett built a remarkable ability to sift through ideas and find the ones where he can accurately assess the odds. Over time, he built his circle of competence to the point where he can give sellers one of his famous five-minute decisions.

Warren Buffett and Charlie Munger often serve as Rorschach tests for investors: Folks hear what they want to hear, filtering the words and analyzing them in a way that conveniently re-affirms their own investment processes. People miss how incredibly opportunistic both were throughout their careers. They looked for mispriced bets—whether that was in the form of a business with a moat, a net-net, or a liquidation—and loaded up when they found them.

Buffett wrote, "Dollars are dollars whether they are derived from the operation of media properties or of steel mills."[375] He cares about cash flows and the price he pays for those cash flows. The focus on competitive advantage and moats stems from the idea that good businesses allow him to project their future cash flows with conviction. This confidence makes him comfortable allocating significant sums to a single opportunity. Plus, the truly great businesses often find additional levers to create value—whether through new product lines, increased efficiency, a surprising degree of pricing power, longer growth runways than anticipated, or through other means. Buffett's filter, built through decades of scanning investment opportunities, lets him sift through opportunities quickly and spend time on the ones that he thinks he can accurately evaluate.

Would Buffett be as successful today?

Yes. Back in 1999, Buffett said:

> If I was running $1 million today, or $10 million for that matter, I'd be fully invested. Anyone who says that size does not hurt investment performance is selling. The highest rates of return I've ever achieved were in the 1950s. I killed the Dow. You ought to see the numbers. But I was investing peanuts then. It's a huge structural advantage not to have a lot of money. I think I could make you 50% a year on $1 million. No, I know I could. I guarantee that.[376]

He has reiterated this view in recent years, including at the 2024 annual meeting.

While there are some disadvantages in today's market—such as rules like Reg FD eliminating selective disclosures and an increased number of security analyst competitors—I think the benefits of information dissemination balance these two factors out.

It's wrong to attach Buffett to any particular era. He's found ways to make money in every financial era he operated in; he was incredibly flexible in the opportunities he sought out but inflexible in demanding value. The themes mentioned above—differentiated research process, concentration, influence, and a rigorous filter—can be applied in any era and by any investor. He would still crush the market today.

A final note

Buffett is often deified, anointed with monikers such as 'The Oracle of Omaha' that grant him superhuman attributes. I think this does a disservice to the work required to produce his investment record. He was not struck by a thunderbolt giving him the skills to allocate capital; he built these skills through tenacious work. Buffett *was* blessed with a high IQ—north of 150—but this gift wasn't enough to produce the returns he did.[377]

He also had some humanizing stumbles, such as recommending Cleveland Worsted Mills to his friends and relatives just before the dividend cut and embarrassing himself in front of Louis Green after the Marshall-Wells meeting. These serve as reminders that Buffett, too, has erred and needed to grow and develop as an investor.

He started crafting his understanding of competitive analysis and moats in a world where the research on such subjects was quite poor. Ben Graham's classic books were relatively unsophisticated about dissecting businesses, and mostly encouraged using quantitative analysis to select securities. Young Warren Buffett spent a lot of time with bad businesses, observing how they can get worse, which later helped him learn how to identify companies with quality economics. These experiences helped him hone his filter and grow to truly appreciate quality, helping him develop into the world's greatest investor.

Acknowledgments

This book would not have been possible without Warren Buffett, who has led such an interesting life that I had to write about a portion of it. While he declined to be interviewed, he pointed me in the right direction on a couple questions I had and sent along a note of encouragement. I have to thank Charlie Munger, who graciously hosted me at his home for lunch two months prior to his passing. Charlie was even funnier and kinder in person. I was very lucky to have met him.

There were a number of people who helped me throughout the process of writing this book: Peter Kaufman who generously provided advice and invited me to meet Charlie; Henry Work who answered my questions on the cooperage industry; Matt Eichmann who helped on Greif's corporate history; Richmond Bates, Stan Madyda, John Barton, Jeff Hakner, Joe Thomas, and Amy Ferguson who helped on Union Street Railway; Bill Tieleman who spent an hour on the phone with me answering questions about the British Columbia Power litigation (and wrote an excellent thesis on the subject); Ira Galtman who assisted with American Express's corporate history, Michael Lisicky and Jacques Kelly who answered questions about Hochschild Kohn and the history of downtown Baltimore; Jerry Beck who provided me with a crash course in the history of animation; Tino Balio, Peter Lev, and Thomas Schatz for answering questions on the movie industry; and Shani Raja and Nadav Manham who helped improve my writing and radically changed my thinking on how to construct this book to make it much better. The folks at the New York Public Library and various libraries across the country also helped me hunt down various documents and point me to resources I would have never known about.

My friend Frederik Gieschen introduced me to the wonderful team at Harriman House. Working with Nick Fletcher, Chris Parker, and the rest of the team was an absolute pleasure. They provided excellent advice and were incredibly patient with my constant tinkering.

I've been lucky to meet some people throughout my career who have provided enormously helpful advice (on this book or otherwise): Marius Morar, Jim

Moore, Robert Joo-Hyung Lee, Jeffrey Piermont, Jag Sriram, Drew Marcus, Seth McCormick, Yehuda Lisker, Charlie Stone, Dev Chugh, Tim Cox, Vince Aita, Tilman Versch, Simon Kold, Tushar Shah, Steve Clearman, George Ho, Sanjay Shah, and Steven Keating.

I also wanted to especially thank Eric Stewart, Greg Demo, Hyung-kyoon (HK) Kim, Jonathan Bloom, and Soo Chuen Tan for their outsized influence on my career. Jonathan, Soo Chuen, and Eric each played a pivotal role in getting me into the investment management business and have continued to support me at every step along the way. Soo Chuen also wrote the excellent foreword. Each of these five has become a valued friend.

I also wanted to thank my family. While this note is written with our dogs first and foremost in mind, my dad was the one to drive me to the library to pick up *The Snowball* and *Buffett: The Making of an American Capitalist* for my first reads.

Last but certainly not least, I want to thank all my readers. While writing this book, I have met many of you either in person or through social media and I have been galvanized by your interest in this part of Buffett's career. I hope to meet even more of you in the future. Please feel free to contact me at Brett@BuffettsEarlyInvestments.com with any questions, disagreements, or compliments (compliments are heavily favored over disagreements, to be clear). I hope you enjoyed the book—I certainly enjoyed writing it!

Notes

1   Munger, C., & Combs, T. (2022, April 19). Charlie Munger in conversation with Todd Combs [video]. YouTube, www.youtube.com/watch?v=xy8ny BC9TQ0.

2   Berkshire Hathaway 2023 Chairman's Letter.

3   Lowenstein, R. (2008). *Buffett: The Making of an American Capitalist* (p. 35). Random House Trade Paperbacks; Graham, B. (2006). *The Intelligent Investor* (p. ix). Harper Business.

4   Milne, R., & Kahn, I. (1977). Benjamin Graham: The Father of Financial Analysis. The Financial Analysts Research Foundation; Graham, B. (2006). *The Intelligent Investor* (p. xii). Harper Business.

5   Schroeder, A. (2008). *The Snowball: Warren Buffett and the business of life* (p. 240). Bantam Dell; Warren Buffett letter to partners, January 18, 1965.

6   Davis, L. J. (1990, April 1). Buffett Takes Stock. *The New York Times*, 61. www. nytimes.com/1990/04/01/magazine/buffet-takes-stock.html.

7   *The Commercial and Financial Chronicle*, dated December 6, 1951; Schroeder, A. (2008). *The Snowball: Warren Buffett and the business of life* (pp. 134–138). Bantam Dell.

8   *The Commercial and Financial Chronicle*, dated December 6, 1951.

9   Schroeder, A. (2008). *The Snowball: Warren Buffett and the business of life* (pp. 190–193). Bantam Dell; Berkshire Hathaway 1988 Chairman's Letter.

10   Schroeder, A. (2008). *The Snowball: Warren Buffett and the business of life* (p. 208). Bantam Dell.

11   Schroeder, A. (2008). *The Snowball: Warren Buffett and the business of life* (pp. 131–132). Bantam Dell; Kilpatrick, A. (2020). *Of Permanent Value: The Story of Warren Buffett* (p. 76). AKPE.

12   Schroeder, A. (2008). *The Snowball: Warren Buffett and the business of life* (pp. 133–134, 852). Bantam Dell.

13   *Graham-Newman Annual Report* dated February 27, 1950; Author's estimates.

14   Fortune 500's List from 1955, retrieved from money.cnn.com/magazines/ fortune/fortune500_archive/full/1955/301.html.

15   Dodge, R. E. (1952). *History, Organization, Functions, and Evaluation of the Marshall-Wells Company and the Marshall-Wells Stores Program* (pp. 19–20). The Department of Business Administration and the Graduate School of the University of Oregon; S3614 Marshall-Wells Company Northeast Minnesota Historical Collections, University of Minnesota Duluth. Marshall-Wells

Timeline   docs.google.com/document/d/1VQ3OgIi1KnfiiQ5w9uXoXlHvAquJ WkjpkY7dHKvwidA/edit.

16   Dodge, R. E. (1952). *History, Organization, Functions, and Evaluation of the Marshall-Wells Company and the Marshall-Wells Stores Program* (p. 19). The Department of Business Administration and the Graduate School of the University of Oregon.

17   Vereen, B. (2010). *Surviving in spite of everything: A postwar history of the hardware industry* (p. 12). Dog Ear Publishing, LLC; Kantowicz, E. (1986). *True Value: John Cotter 70 years of hardware* (p. 137). Regnery Books.

18   Kantowicz, E. (1986). *True Value: John Cotter 70 years of hardware* (p. 137). Regnery Books; Dodge, R. E. (1952). *History, Organization, Functions, and Evaluation of the Marshall-Wells Company and the Marshall-Wells Stores Program* (pp. 22–23). The Department of Business Administration and the Graduate School of the University of Oregon.

19   Kantowicz, E. (1986). *True Value: John Cotter 70 years of hardware* (p. 137). Regnery Books.

20   Company history accessed from Marshall-Wells Company records, S3614, Northeast Minnesota Historical Collections, Archives and Special Collections, Martin Library, University of Minnesota Duluth; Wickland, J. A. (1952, December 7). Duluth Hardware Firm Says: "Our Frontier's the Far North." *Minneapolis Sunday Tribune*, 6; Dodge, R. E. (1952). *History, Organization, Functions, and Evaluation of the Marshall-Wells Company and the Marshall-Wells Stores Program* (pp. 23–24, 27). The Department of Business Administration and the Graduate School of the University of Oregon.

21   Dodge, R. E. (1952). *History, Organization, Functions, and Evaluation of the Marshall-Wells Company and the Marshall-Wells Stores Program* (pp. 30–31, 75, 110). The Department of Business Administration and the Graduate School of the University of Oregon.

22   Dodge, R. E. (1952). *History, Organization, Functions, and Evaluation of the Marshall-Wells Company and the Marshall-Wells Stores Program* (pp. 39, 126). The Department of Business Administration and the Graduate School of the University of Oregon.

23   Dodge, R. E. (1952). *History, Organization, Functions, and Evaluation of the Marshall-Wells Company and the Marshall-Wells Stores Program* (pp. 41–42, 137). The Department of Business Administration and the Graduate School of the University of Oregon; Wickland, J. A. (1952, December 7). Duluth Hardware Firm Says: "Our Frontier's the Far North." *Minneapolis Sunday Tribune*, 6.

24   King, A. W. (1952, June 1). A.M. Marshall Pioneer Builder. *Duluth News-Tribune*; *Moody's Manuals*.

25   Wickland, J. A. (1952, December 7). Duluth Hardware Firm Says: "Our Frontier's the Far North." *Minneapolis Sunday Tribune*, 6; Dodge, R. E. (1952). *History, Organization, Functions, and Evaluation of the Marshall-Wells Company and the Marshall-Wells Stores Program* (pp. 71–72). The Department of Business Administration and the Graduate School of the University of Oregon.

26   Grape, E. F. (1966). *Retailer-Owned Cooperative Wholesaling in the Hardware*

Trade (pp. 158). The Ohio State University; *1950 Moody's Manuals: Industrial Securities* p. 1796; Author's estimates.

27   Dodge, R. E. (1952). *History, Organization, Functions, and Evaluation of the Marshall-Wells Company and the Marshall-Wells Stores Program* (p. 10). The Department of Business Administration and the Graduate School of the University of Oregon.

28   J.M. Dain & Company Report on Marshall-Wells, dated April 30, 1951.

29   J.M. Dain & Company Report on Marshall-Wells, dated December 12, 1950.

30   Marshall-Wells, *1948 Annual Report*, page 6; Kantowicz, E. (1986). *True Value: John Cotter 70 years of hardware* (pp. 80–81). Regnery Books.

31   Wickland, J. A. (1952, December 7). Duluth Hardware Firm Says: "Our Frontier's the Far North." *Minneapolis Sunday Tribune*, 6.

32   Kilpatrick, A. (2020). *Of Permanent Value: The Story of Warren Buffett* (p. 76). AKPE.

33   Kantowicz, E. (1986). *True Value: John Cotter 70 years of hardware* (p. 83). Regnery Books.

34   Kantowicz, E. (1986). *True Value: John Cotter 70 years of hardware* (pp. 83–86, 128). Regnery Books.

35   Kantowicz, E. (1986). *True Value: John Cotter 70 years of hardware* (pp. 48–49). Regnery Books.

36   Grape, E. F. (1966). *Retailer-Owned Cooperative Wholesaling in the Hardware Trade* (pp. 29, 157–158). The Ohio State University; Kantowicz, E. (1986). *True Value: John Cotter 70 years of hardware* (pp. 51–52, 130–131, 184, 186, 188). Regnery Books.

37   Grape, E. F. (1966). *Retailer-Owned Cooperative Wholesaling in the Hardware Trade* (p. 30). The Ohio State University.

38   Kantowicz, E. (1986). *True Value: John Cotter 70 years of hardware* (pp. 128–129). Regnery Books; Grape, E. F. (1966). *Retailer-Owned Cooperative Wholesaling in the Hardware Trade* (p. 29). The Ohio State University; 20 Years of Trends in Hardware Retailing. *Hardware Retailer*, 59. July 1961.

39   Kantowicz, E. (1986). *True Value: John Cotter 70 years of hardware* (p. 138). Regnery Books; Marshall-Wells Company records, S3614, Northeast Minnesota Historical Collections, Archives and Special Collections, Martin Library, University of Minnesota Duluth.

40   Kantowicz, E. (1986). *True Value: John Cotter 70 years of hardware* (p. 139). Regnery Books; *Moody's Manuals*.

41   Kantowicz, E. (1986). *True Value: John Cotter 70 years of hardware* (pp. 139–140). Regnery Books; *Moody's Manuals*.

42   Kantowicz, E. (1986). *True Value: John Cotter 70 years of hardware* (p. 133). Regnery Books.

43   Kantowicz, E. (1986). *True Value: John Cotter 70 years of hardware* (pp. 139–140). Regnery Books; *Moody's Manuals*.

44   Marshall-Wells Co. *Capital Changes U.S.*

45   Walter J. Schloss Associates memo to limited partners, January 20, 1959, retrieved from the Schloss Family Business Papers, Rare Book & Manuscript Library, Columbia University Libraries.

46 Kilpatrick, A. (2020). *Of Permanent Value: The Story of Warren Buffett* (p. 76). AKPE; Schroeder, A. (2008). *The Snowball: Warren Buffett and the business of life* (p. 857). Bantam Dell; Buffett, W. E. (1984). "The Superinvestors of Graham-and-Doddsville". *Hermes*.

47 Grape, E. F. (1966). *Retailer-Owned Cooperative Wholesaling in the Hardware Trade* (pp. 173–174). The Ohio State University.

48 Kantowicz, E. (1986). *True Value: John Cotter 70 years of hardware* (pp. 8, 14). Regnery Books.

49 Buffett, W. (2012, March 26). Warren Buffett's $50 billion decision. *Forbes*. www.forbes.com/sites/randalllane/2012/03/26/warren-buffetts-50-billion-decision.

50 Lowe, J. (1996). *Benjamin Graham on Value Investing: Lessons from the Dean of Wall Street* (p. 162). Penguin Books.

51 Schroeder, A. (2008). *The Snowball: Warren Buffett and the business of life* (pp. 183. 828). Bantam Dell; Wyatt, E. (1998, May 30). Philip Carret, Money Manager, Dies at 101. *The New York Times*. www.nytimes.com/1998/05/30/business/philip-carret-money-manager-dies-at-101.html; Zweig, J. (1994, June 20). Buy 'em cheap and hold 'em. *Forbes, 172–173*.

52 The Greif Bros. Co. Advertisement. (1907, January), *Packages*, 11; *Containers and Packaging* (Spring 1951), 19; Coyne, F. (1940). *The Development of the Cooperage Industry in the United States 1620–1940* (p. 39). Lumber Buyers Publishing Company; Paine, Webber & Co. November 1, 1927 report on The Greif Bros. Cooperage Corporation.

53 Greif, Inc. Form 10-K, dated December 18, 2019.

54 Coyne, F. (1940). *The Development of the Cooperage Industry in the United States 1620–1940* (p. 33). Lumber Buyers Publishing Company.

55 Hankerson, F. (1947). *The cooperage handbook* (p. 23). Chemical Publishing Co., Inc. babel.hathitrust.org/cgi/pt?id=mdp.39015006133204&view=1up&seq=6&skin=2021; Wagner, J. B. (2015). *Cooperage: A treatise on modern shop practice and methods; From the tree to the finished article* (p. 153). Forgotten Books; Coyne, F. (1940). *The Development of the Cooperage Industry in the United States 1620–1940* (p. 43). Lumber Buyers Publishing Company.

56 Report of the Federal Trade Commission on Changes in Manufacturing 1935 to 1947 and 1950, 72–73; Email exchange with Henry Work, June 30, 2020.

57 Baldwin, W. (1982). Homely virtues. *Forbes*, 54–55; Paine, Webber & Co. Research Report on The Greif Bros. Cooperage Corporation, dated November 1, 1927; *Moody's Manuals*.

58 Report of the Federal Trade Commission on Changes in Manufacturing 1935 to 1947 and 1950, 73.

59 *Containers and Packaging* (Spring 1951), 19; Coyne, F. (1940). *The Development of the Cooperage Industry in the United States 1620–1940* (p. 39). Lumber Buyers Publishing Company.

60 The Greif Bros. Cooperage Corporation, *1950 Annual Report*.

61 *Moody's Manuals*.

62 The Greif Bros. Cooperage Corporation, *1956 Annual Report*.

63 Baldwin, W. (1982). Homely virtues. *Forbes*, 54–55.

64 Warren Buffett letter to Ben Graham, October 31, 1951, retrieved from the Ben Graham papers, University Archives, Rare Book & Manuscript Library, Columbia University Libraries.

65 The Greif Bros. Cooperage Corporation Annual Reports; *Moody's Manuals*; John R. Raible. (1948, March 4). *The New York Times*, 25.

66 The Greif Bros. Cooperage Corporation, *1950 Annual Report*.

67 The Greif Bros. Cooperage Corporation Annual Reports.

68 Schroeder, A. (2008). *The Snowball: Warren Buffett and the business of life* (pp. 183. 828). Bantam Dell; Buffett, W. (2012, March 26). Warren Buffett's $50 billion decision. *Forbes*. www.forbes.com/sites/randalllane/2012/03/26/warren-buffetts-50-billion-decision.

69 Schroeder, A. (2008). *The Snowball: Warren Buffett and the business of life* (p. 857). Bantam Dell; Buffett, W. E. (1984). 'The Superinvestors of Graham-and-Doddsville'. *Hermes*.

70 Wyatt, E. (1998, May 30). Philip Carret, Money Manager, Dies at 101. *The New York Times*. www.nytimes.com/1998/05/30/business/philip-carret-money-manager-dies-at-101.html.

71 Schroeder, A. (2008). *The Snowball: Warren Buffett and the business of life* (p. 168). Bantam Dell.

72 Schroeder, A. (2008). *The Snowball: Warren Buffett and the business of life* (pp. 168, 856). Bantam Dell.

73 Graham-Newman Annual Report dated February 29, 1952; Graham, B., & Dodd, D. (2004). *Security Analysis: The Classic 1951 Edition* (3rd ed.). McGraw Hill.

74 *Moody's Manuals*; Martin, S. (2015). *A Stich in Time* (p. 12). Western Reserve Historical Society; Hritsko, R. (1983). *A Case Study of the Cleveland Worsted Mills 1878–1957* (pp. 84, 135). University of Akron.

75 Hritsko, R. (1983). *A Case Study of the Cleveland Worsted Mills 1878–1957* (pp. 3, 7–12). University of Akron.

76 Hritsko, R. (1983). *A Case Study of the Cleveland Worsted Mills 1878–1957* (pp. 8–20). University of Akron.

77 Hritsko, R. (1983). *A Case Study of the Cleveland Worsted Mills 1878–1957* (pp. 59–60). University of Akron.

78 Hritsko, R. (1983). *A Case Study of the Cleveland Worsted Mills 1878–1957* (pp. 28, 59–60, 90–91). University of Akron.

79 Hritsko, R. (1983). *A Case Study of the Cleveland Worsted Mills 1878–1957* (pp. 93–99). University of Akron; Oliver Mead Stafford. (1929, August 18). *The New York Times*, N5.

80 Hritsko, R. (1983). *A Case Study of the Cleveland Worsted Mills 1878–1957* (pp. 4–5, 101, 117). University of Akron.

81 Hritsko, R. (1983). *A Case Study of the Cleveland Worsted Mills 1878–1957* (pp. 5, 121, 135). University of Akron.

82 Hritsko, R. (1983). *A Case Study of the Cleveland Worsted Mills 1878–1957* (pp. 124, 130–132, 134–135). University of Akron.

83 Schroeder, A. (2008). *The Snowball: Warren Buffett and the business of life* (p. 168). Bantam Dell.

84   Schroeder, A. (2008*). The Snowball: Warren Buffett and the business of life* (pp. 168–169). Bantam Dell.

85   Hritsko, R. (1983). *A Case Study of the Cleveland Worsted Mills 1878–1957* (pp. 136–140, 146). University of Akron.

86   Capital Changes U.S., Cleveland Worsted Mills Co.

87   Hritsko, R. (1983). *A Case Study of the Cleveland Worsted Mills 1878–1957* (pp. 5–6, 124, 131–132, 138, 140, 145). University of Akron.

88   Berkshire Hathaway 1989 Chairman's Letter.

89   *The Literary Digest*, October 14, 1899.

90   Schroeder, A. (2008). *The Snowball: Warren Buffett and the business of life* (pp. 194–196, 858). Bantam Dell.

91   Cummings, O.R. (1978). *Union Street Railway* (pp. 3–4, 7–8, 17–18, 23–24). Connecticut Valley Chapter, National Railway Historical Society.

92   Riess, S. A. (2013). *Sport in industrial America, 1850–1920* (2nd ed). Wiley.

93   Cummings, O.R. (1978). *Union Street Railway* (pp. 26–28). Connecticut Valley Chapter, National Railway Historical Society.

94   Dunbar, C. S. (2005). *Buses, trolleys & trams* (p. 46). Hamlin Publishing Company; Mason, E. (2018). *The Street Railway in Massachusetts: The rise and decline of an industry* (pp. 3–4, 5, 12). Forgotten Books.

95   Mason, E. (2018). *The Street Railway in Massachusetts: The rise and decline of an industry* (pp. 7–10, 21–26). Forgotten Books.

96   Mason, E. (2018). *The Street Railway in Massachusetts: The rise and decline of an industry* (pp. 13–14). Forgotten Books; Jackson, D. (1917). *Street Railway Fares* (pp. 2, 3, 11–15). McGraw-Hill.

97   Mason, E. (2018). *The Street Railway in Massachusetts: The rise and decline of an industry* (pp. 41, 48). Forgotten Books.

98   Mason, E. (2018). *The Street Railway in Massachusetts: The rise and decline of an industry* (pp. 14–16). Forgotten Books; Cummings, O.R. (1978). *Union Street Railway* (p. 59). Connecticut Valley Chapter, National Railway Historical Society.

99   *History of the NTD and transit in the United States*. History of the NTD and Transit in the United States | FTA. n.d.). Retrieved October 9, 2023, from www.transit.dot.gov/ntd/history-ntd-and-transit-united-states; Mason, E. (2018). *The Street Railway in Massachusetts: The rise and decline of an industry* (p. 7, 14, 16–17). Forgotten Books.

100   Cummings, O.R. (1978). *Union Street Railway* (pp. 4, 72). Connecticut Valley Chapter, National Railway Historical Society.

101   Cummings, O.R. (1978). *Union Street Railway* (p. 78). Connecticut Valley Chapter, National Railway Historical Society.

102   Cummings, O.R. (1978). *Union Street Railway* (pp. 59, 75). Connecticut Valley Chapter, National Railway Historical Society.

103   Cummings, O.R. (1978). *Union Street Railway* (pp. 82–83). Connecticut Valley Chapter, National Railway Historical Society.

104   Cummings, O.R. (1978). *Union Street Railway* (pp. 59, 84). Connecticut Valley Chapter, National Railway Historical Society.

105 Cummings, O.R. (1978). *Union Street Railway* (p. 85). Connecticut Valley Chapter, National Railway Historical Society.

106 Dewees, D. (1970). Decline of American Street Railways. *Transportation Quarterly*, 24 (pp. 577–578). babel.hathitrust.org/cgi/pt?id=mdp.39015021808848&view=1up&seq=1&skin=2021.

107 *Moody's transportation manual.* (1954).

108 Schroeder, A. (2008). *The Snowball: Warren Buffett and the business of life* (pp. 194–196). Bantam Dell.

109 Schroeder, A. (2008). *The Snowball: Warren Buffett and the business of life* (pp. 196–198, 859). Bantam Dell.

110 Schroeder, A. (2008). *The Snowball: Warren Buffett and the business of life* (p. 195). Bantam Dell.

111 Schroeder, A. (2008). *The Snowball: Warren Buffett and the business of life* (p. 195). Bantam Dell.

112 Schroeder, A. (2008). *The Snowball: Warren Buffett and the business of life* (p. 859). Bantam Dell.

113 Author's estimates.

114 United Street Railway Co. (New Bedford, Mass.) *Capital Changes U.S.*

115 *Moody's transportation manual.* (1963).

116 Berkshire Hathaway Annual Reports, 1955–1960.

117 Schroeder, A. (2008). *The Snowball: Warren Buffett and the business of life* (pp. 272–273). Bantam Dell.

118 Kunhardt, P. (Director). (2017). *Becoming Warren Buffett.*

119 Schurr, S., & Netschert, B. (1960). *Energy in the American Economy, 1850—1975* (p. 500). The John Hopkins Press; Summary of the Report of the Examiner in the Bankruptcy Proceedings of The Philadelphia and Reading Coal and Iron Company, by Nicholas G. Roosevelt (December 23, 1940), 27; Dublin, T., & Licht, W. (2005). *The Face of Decline: The Pennsylvania Anthracite Region in the Twentieth Century* (pp. 1, 17). Cornell University Press.

120 Bogen, J. (1927). *The Anthracite Railroads: A Study in American Railroad Enterprise* (pp. 41–75, 209). The Ronald Press Company; Summary of the Report of the Examiner in the Bankruptcy Proceedings of The Philadelphia and Reading Coal and Iron Company, by Nicholas G. Roosevelt (December 23, 1940), 5–6; Freese, B. (2016). *Coal: A Human History* (pp. 131–132). Basic Books; Dublin, T., & Licht, W. (2005). *The Face of Decline: The Pennsylvania Anthracite Region in the Twentieth Century* (pp. 16–20). Cornell University Press; Holton, J. (1989). *Reading Railroad: History of a Coal Age Empire: Vol. Volume 1: The Nineteenth Century* (p. 5). Garrigues House Pub.

121 Bogen, J. (1927). *The Anthracite Railroads: A Study in American Railroad Enterprise* (pp. 221–222, 227). The Ronald Press Company; Jones, E. (2013). *The Anthracite Coal Combination in the United States, With Some Account of the Early Development of the Anthracite Industry* (p. 187). HardPress Publishing.

122 Philadelphia and Reading, *1923 Annual Report, 6.*

123 Minerals Yearbook 1953, published by the United States Bureau of Mines; Bakerman, T. (1956). *Anthracite Coal: A Study in Advanced Industrial Decline*

(Energy in the American Economy) [A Dissertation in Economics] (pp. 2–3). University of Pennsylvania; Emory, E. (1921, March). How The Retail Coal Merchant Can Get More Anthracite. *The Retail Coleman*, 87–88.

124 Summary of the Report of the Examiner in the Bankruptcy Proceedings of The Philadelphia and Reading Coal and Iron Company, by Nicholas G. Roosevelt (December 23, 1940), 8–10.

125 Philadelphia and Reading, *1945 Annual Report*, 8–9.

126 Schroeder, A. (2008). *The Snowball: Warren Buffett and the business of life* (pp. 168, 186). Bantam Dell.

127 Schroeder, A. (2008). *The Snowball: Warren Buffett and the business of life* (p. 168). Bantam Dell.

128 Schroeder, A. (2008). *The Snowball: Warren Buffett and the business of life* (p. 186). Bantam Dell.

129 Philadelphia and Reading, *1954 Proxy Statement*, 2; Graham-Newman Annual Report dated March 1, 1954; Graham-Newman Annual Report dated February 28, 1955; Financial: Baltimore & Ohio. (1952, February 4). *Railway Age*, 98.

130 Rieser, C. (1959, August). The Egghead, the Upstart, and Old P. & R. *Fortune*, 84–88, 188–192; Coal Company Gets Off Hook. (1957, April 20). *Business Week*, 99–100, 105–108.

131 Lowe, J. (1996). *Benjamin Graham on Value Investing: Lessons from the Dean of Wall Street* (p. 183). Penguin Books.

132 Philadelphia and Reading, *1954 Annual Report*, 10.

133 Philadelphia and Reading, *1954 Annual Report*; Philadelphia and Reading, *1955 Annual Report*.

134 Rieser, C. (1959, August). The Egghead, the Upstart, and Old P. & R. *Fortune*, 84–88, 188–192; Coal Company Gets Off Hook. (1957, April 20). *Business Week*, 99–100, 105–108; Philadelphia and Reading, *1955 Annual Report*, 8.

135 Berkshire Hathaway 2001 Chairman's Letter.

136 Philadelphia and Reading, *1955 Annual Report*; Rieser, C. (1959, August). The Egghead, the Upstart, and Old P. & R. *Fortune*, 84–88, 188–192.

137 Lowe, J. (1996). *Benjamin Graham on Value Investing: Lessons from the Dean of Wall Street* (p. 182). Penguin Books.

138 Coal Company Gets Off Hook. (1957, April 20). *Business Week*, 99–100, 105–108.

139 Philadelphia and Reading, *1954 Annual Report*.

140 Rieser, C. (1959, August). The Egghead, the Upstart, and Old P. & R. *Fortune*, 84–88, 188–192; Raleigh, Jr., W. A. (1957, February). How Diversification Pays Off. *Coal Age*, 94–97; Coal Company Gets Off Hook. (1957, April 20). *Business Week*, 99–100, 105–108.

141 Finding The Right Combination. (1965, August 21). *Business Week*, 49–52; Rieser, C. (1959, August). The Egghead, the Upstart, and Old P. & R. *Fortune*, 84–88, 188–192; Philadelphia and Reading, *1960 Annual Report*; Philadelphia and Reading, *1961 Annual Report*; Philadelphia and Reading, *1965 Annual Report*.

142 Schroeder, A. (2008). *The Snowball: Warren Buffett and the business of life* (p. 283). Bantam Dell; Bedingfield, R. (1965, December 19). Personality: "Intelligent Investor" Pays Off. *The New York Times*, F3.

143 Rosenheim, D. (1985, April 11). Farley Buying Northwest for $1 billion. *Chicago Tribune*. www.chicagotribune.com/news/ct-xpm-1985-04-11-8501200890-story. html.

144 Berkshire Hathaway 2001 Chairman's Letter; Fruit of the Loom, Ltd. Form 10-K, dated April 15, 2002.

145 Buffett, W. (2012, March 26). Warren Buffett's $50 billion decision. *Forbes*. www. forbes.com/sites/randalllane/2012/03/26/warren-buffetts-50-billion-decision/

146 Warren Buffett letter to partners, January 24, 1962; Warren Buffett letter to partners, January 18, 1965.

147 Warren Buffett letter to partners, January 24, 1962; Warren Buffett letter to partners, January 25, 1967; Warren Buffett letter to partners, January 24, 1968; Warren Buffett letter to partners, January 22, 1969.

148 Warren Buffett's letters to partners and author's estimates.

149 Warren Buffett letter to partners, January 18, 1963; Schroeder, A. (2008). *The Snowball: Warren Buffett and the business of life* (p. 863). Bantam Dell.

150 Schroeder, A. (2008). *The Snowball: Warren Buffett and the business of life* (pp. 266–277). Bantam Dell.

151 Warren Buffett letter to partners, October, 9, 1967.

152 Berkshire Hathaway 2004 Annual Meeting, Morning Session, accessed via buffett.cnbc.com/video/2004/05/01/morning-session-2004-berkshire-hathaway-annual-meeting.html.

153 Schroeder, A. (2008). *The Snowball: Warren Buffett and the business of life* (pp. 254–255). Bantam Dell.

154 Kilpatrick, A. (2020). *Of Permanent Value: The Story of Warren Buffett* (p. 223). AKPE.

155 Mitchell, D. J. (1995). *W.A.C. Bennett and the rise of British Columbia* (pp. 289–292). Douglas & McIntyre.

156 Mitchell, D. J. (1995). *W.A.C. Bennett and the rise of British Columbia* (pp. 304, 306–309). Douglas & McIntyre.

157 Stock Tables (1961, August 1). *The New York Times*, 46; Bennett, W. A. C. (1961, September 20). Why I took over B.C. Electric. *The Monetary Times*, 20–22; Mitchell, D. J. (1995). *W.A.C. Bennett and the rise of British Columbia* (pp. 308–309). Douglas & McIntyre; *Moody's Manuals*; British Columbia Power, *1961 Annual Report*, 10.

158 British Columbia Power, *1960 Annual Report, 18 and 24–25*.

159 British Columbia Power, *1961 Annual Report*, 10.

160 British Columbia Power, *1962 Annual Report, 3–4;* Mitchell, D. J. (1995). *W.A.C. Bennett and the rise of British Columbia* (pp. 312–13). Douglas & McIntyre.

161 British Columbia Power, *1961 Annual Report*; British Columbia Power, *1962 Annual Report*.

162 Berkshire Hathaway 1988 Chairman's Letter.

163 British Columbia Power, *1962 Annual Report, 3–4*.

164   British Columbia Power, *1961 Annual Report, 3–5.*

165   Bill Fletcher. (1961, November 18). *The Vancouver Sun*, 26.

166   British Columbia Power, *1961 Annual Report, 10.*

167   British Columbia Power, *1962 Annual Report, 4.*

168   *Moody's Public Utility Manual*, 1961, 1403.

169   British Columbia Power, *1961 Annual Report, 4, 11.*

170   Big majority cash BCE debentures. (1962, June 30). *The Vancouver Sun*; Judgment favors debenture holders. (1963, July 30). *The Province*, 10; Move to redeem BCE debentures. (1962, May 12). *Times Colonist*, 6.

171   Smith, G. (1963, July 30). Utility's seizure is ruled illegal. *The New York Times*, 33.

172   Shaw, R.M. (1963, July 30). Market anticipates judge's valuation. *The Province*, 10; Market price not only guide to share value, Lett rules. (1963, July 30). *The Province*, 10; McAlpine, I., & Vickers, Y. (1963, July 30). BCE takeover was illegal, gov't had no authority. *The Vancouver Sun*, 3; (B.C., 1963) B.C Power v. Atty.-Gen of B.C.

173   A.B. Robertson, Letter to the Shareholders of British Columbia Power, October 1, 1963; Mitchell, D. J. (1995). *W.A.C. Bennett and the rise of British Columbia* (p. 320). Douglas & McIntyre.

174   British Columbia Electric Co., Ltd. *Capital Changes U.S.*; British Columbia Power Corp., Ltd. *Capital Changes U.S.*

175   Warren Buffett, 'The Superinvestors of Graham-and Doddsville', *Hermes* (Fall 1984); Conversation with Charlie Munger on September 28, 2023.

176   Warren Buffett's Partnership Letter, January 18, 1965.

177   Travelers Cheques and Circular Letters of Credit (p. 74). (1921). American Express Company.

178   Miller, N. (1965). *The Great Salad Oil Swindle* (pp. 14-21). Coward McCann, Inc.

179   Miller, N. (1965). *The Great Salad Oil Swindle* (p. 71). Coward McCann, Inc; Grossman, P. (1987). *American Express: The People Who Built the Great Financial Empire* (pp. 247-249, 307-308). Beard Books.

180   Miller, N. (1965). *The Great Salad Oil Swindle* (pp. 17, 21-24, 26). Coward McCann, Inc.

181   Grossman, P. (1987). *American Express: The People Who Built the Great Financial Empire* (pp. 305-307). Beard Books; American Express, *1959 Annual Report*, 4.

182   Grossman, P. (1987). *American Express: The People Who Built the Great Financial Empire* (p. 309). Beard Books.

183   Miller, N. (1965). *The Great Salad Oil Swindle* (pp. 60, 79-80). Coward McCann, Inc.

184   Miller, N. (1965). *The Great Salad Oil Swindle* (pp. 80-81). Coward McCann, Inc.

185   Grossman, P. (1987). *American Express: The People Who Built the Great Financial Empire* (pp. 309-310). Beard Books; Miller, N. (1965). *The Great Salad Oil Swindle* (pp. 71, 80-82). Coward McCann, Inc.

186 Grossman, P. (1987). *American Express: The People Who Built the Great Financial Empire* (pp. 311-312). Beard Books; American Express, *1960 Annual Report*, 2.

187 Grossman, P. (1987). *American Express: The People Who Built the Great Financial Empire* (p. 313). Beard Books.

188 Grossman, P. (1987). *American Express: The People Who Built the Great Financial Empire* (p. 314). Beard Books; Miller, N. (1965). *The Great Salad Oil Swindle* (pp. 105-106). Coward McCann, Inc.

189 Miller, N. (1965). *The Great Salad Oil Swindle* (pp. 134–135). Coward McCann, Inc.; Grossman, P. (1987). *American Express: The People Who Built the Great Financial Empire* (pp. 314–315). Beard Books.

190 Miller, N. (1965). *The Great Salad Oil Swindle* (pp. 135-136). Coward McCann, Inc.

191 Grossman, P. (1987). *American Express: The People Who Built the Great Financial Empire* (pp. 315-316). Beard Books; Miller, N. (1965). *The Great Salad Oil Swindle* (pp. 94, 137-139, 144-145, 147-152). Coward McCann, Inc.

192 Miller, N. (1965). *The Great Salad Oil Swindle* (pp. 80, 137-140, 144, 147-153, 161, 164-169). Coward McCann, Inc; Vartan, V. (1963, November 21). Stock Exchange Suspends 2 Major Brokerage Firms. *The New York Times*, 1; Grossman, P. (1987). *American Express: The People Who Built the Great Financial Empire* (pp. 317-318). Beard Books.

193 Miller, N. (1965). *The Great Salad Oil Swindle* (pp. 89, 145, 179, 216). Coward McCann, Inc; American Express, *1963 Annual Report*, 22.

194 Grossman, P. (1987). *American Express: The People Who Built the Great Financial Empire* (p. 319). Beard Books.

195 Miller, N. (1965). *The Great Salad Oil Swindle* (p. 184). Coward McCann, Inc.

196 Miller, N. (1965). *The Great Salad Oil Swindle* (pp. 217-218). Coward McCann, Inc.

197 American Express, *1963 Annual Report*, 27.

198 Grossman, P. (1987). *American Express: The People Who Built the Great Financial Empire* (pp. 39-41). Beard Books.

199 Grossman, P. (1987). *American Express: The People Who Built the Great Financial Empire* (pp. 45-50, 55-56). Beard Books.

200 Grossman, P. (1987). *American Express: The People Who Built the Great Financial Empire* (pp. 63-65). Beard Books; Massengill, R. (1999). *Becoming American Express: 150 Years of Reinvention and Customer Service* (p. 6). American Express Company.

201 Grossman, P. (1987). *American Express: The People Who Built the Great Financial Empire* (p. 68). Beard Books.

202 Grossman, P. (1987). *American Express: The People Who Built the Great Financial Empire* (pp. 79-84). Beard Books; Massengill, R. (1999). *Becoming American Express: 150 Years of Reinvention and Customer Service* (p. 34). American Express Company.

203 Grossman, P. (1987). *American Express: The People Who Built the Great Financial*

Empire (pp. 79-87). Beard Books; Gross, D., & Editors of Forbes magazine. (1996). *Forbes Greatest Business Stories of All Time* (p. 217). Wiley.

204 Grossman, P. (1987). *American Express: The People Who Built the Great Financial Empire* (pp. 87–92). Beard Books.

205 Grossman, P. (1987). *American Express: The People Who Built the Great Financial Empire* (pp. 92-95). Beard Books; Faltermayer, E. (1964, April). The Future of American Express. *Fortune*, 158–159, 254, 256, 258–260.

206 Grossman, P. (1987). *American Express: The People Who Built the Great Financial Empire* (p. 239). Beard Books.

207 Grossman, P. (1987). *American Express: The People Who Built the Great Financial Empire* (pp. 254-255). Beard Books.

208 Grossman, P. (1987). *American Express: The People Who Built the Great Financial Empire* (pp. 261-264). Beard Books; Mandell, L. (1990). *The Credit Card Industry: A History* (p. xiii). Twayne Publishers.

209 Grossman, P. (1987). *American Express: The People Who Built the Great Financial Empire* (pp. 266-267). Beard Books.

210 Grossman, P. (1987). *American Express: The People Who Built the Great Financial Empire* (pp. 6, 265, 273). Beard Books; Mandell, L. (1990). *The Credit Card Industry: A History* (p. 83). Twayne Publishers.

211 Grossman, P. (1987). *American Express: The People Who Built the Great Financial Empire* (pp. 283-284). Beard Books.

212 Mandell, L. (1990). *The Credit Card Industry: A History* (p. 158). Twayne Publishers; Nocera, J. (2013). *A Piece of the Action: How the Middle Class Joined the Money Class* (p. 15). Simon & Schuster.

213 Grossman, P. (1987). *American Express: The People Who Built the Great Financial Empire* (pp. 283-285). Beard Books; Correspondence with Ira Galtman, March 4, 2024; Rutter, R. (1965, February 8). Personal Finance: The Era of the Credit Card. *The New York Times, 38.*

214 Grossman, P. (1987). *American Express: The People Who Built the Great Financial Empire* (pp. 285-286, 299). Beard Books.

215 Grossman, P. (1987). *American Express: The People Who Built the Great Financial Empire* (pp. 287, 299-302). Beard Books.

216 Grossman, P. (1987). *American Express: The People Who Built the Great Financial Empire* (pp. 302-303). Beard Books.

217 Mandell, L. (1990). *The Credit Card Industry: A History* (pp. xiv, xvi, xx, 28-29, 154). Twayne Publishers.

218 American Express, *1963 Annual Report.*

219 Faltermayer, E. (1964, April). The Future of American Express. *Fortune*, 158–159, 254, 256, 258–260.

220 Faltermayer, E. (1964, April). The Future of American Express. *Fortune*, 158–159, 254, 256, 258–260.

221 Faltermayer, E. (1964, April). The Future of American Express. *Fortune*, 158–159, 254, 256, 258–260.

222 American Express, *1963 Annual Report*, 14.

223 The Company For People Who Travel. (1966, June 7). *The New York Times*, 27.

224 Berkshire Hathaway 1986 Chairman's Letter.

225 Schroeder, A. (2008). *The Snowball: Warren Buffett and the business of life* (p. 867). Bantam Dell.

226 Grossman, P. (1987). *American Express: The People Who Built the Great Financial Empire* (p. 321). Beard Books.

227 Grossman, P. (1987). *American Express: The People Who Built the Great Financial Empire* (pp. 326-327). Beard Books; Miller, N. (1965). *The Great Salad Oil Swindle* (pp. 218-223). Coward McCann, Inc.

228 Faltermayer, E. (1964, April). The Future of American Express. *Fortune*, 158–159, 254, 256, 258–260.

229 Miller, N. (1965). *The Great Salad Oil Swindle* (pp. 222-225). Coward McCann, Inc.

230 Faltermayer, E. (1964, April). The Future of American Express. *Fortune*, 158–159, 254, 256, 258–260.

231 Schroeder, A. (2008). *The Snowball: Warren Buffett and the business of life* (pp. 256-257, 260, 868). Bantam Dell.

232 Faltermayer, E. (1964, April). The Future of American Express. *Fortune*, 158–159, 254, 256, 258–260.

233 Warren Buffett letter to partners, January 18, 1965; Warren Buffett letter to partners, January 25, 1967.

234 Shiller, R. (2001). U.S. stock markets 1871-present and CAPE ratio [Data file]. Retrieved from www.econ.yale.edu/~shiller/data.htm.

235 How Omaha Beats Wall Street. (1969, November 1). *Forbes*.

236 Gramm, J. (2016). *Dear Chairman: Boardroom Battles and the Rise of Shareholder Activism* (pp. 218–219). Harper Business.

237 Schroeder, A. (2008). *The Snowball: Warren Buffett and the business of life* (p. 264). Bantam Dell; Berkshire Hathaway 1994 Chairman's Letter; Warren Buffett letter to partners, January 18, 1964; Warren Buffett letter to partners, July 8, 1964; Author's calculations.

238 Warren Buffett letter to partners, November 1, 1965; Warren Buffett letter to partners, January 20, 1966.

239 Warren Buffett letter to partners, January 25, 1967; Warren Buffett letter to partners, January 24, 1968.

240 American Express, *1967 Annual Report*, 32; Grossman, P. (1987). *American Express: The People Who Built the Great Financial Empire* (p. 327). Beard Books.

241 *Promises to Pay: The Story of American Express Company* (p. 243). (1977). American Express Company; American Express Annual Reports.

242 Mandell, L. (1990). *The Credit Card Industry: A History* (p. xvi). Twayne Publishers; American Express, *1959 Annual Report*, 2; Hammer, A. (1960, February 28). Big Test Passed By Diners' Club. *The New York Times*, 1, 5.

243 Heinemann, H. E. (1968, April 14). American Express Is Back From the Brink. *The New York Times*, 1, 14.

244 Warren Buffett letter to partners, January 25, 1967; Warren Buffett letter to partners, October 9, 1967; Warren Buffett letter to partners, January 24, 1968.

245 Schroeder, A. (2008). *The Snowball: Warren Buffett and the business of life* (p. 298-299). Bantam Dell; Author's calculation based on Warren Buffett's letters to partners.

246 Grossman, P. (1987). *American Express: The People Who Built the Great Financial Empire* (pp. 329-332). Beard Books; American Express, *1968 Annual Report*, 5, 32.

247 Grossman, P. (1987). *American Express: The People Who Built the Great Financial Empire* (p. 7). Beard Books.

248 Mandell, L. (1990). *The Credit Card Industry: A History* (p. xiv, 158). Twayne Publishers; Grossman, P. (1987). *American Express: The People Who Built the Great Financial Empire* (pp. 334-335). Beard Books.

249 Lowenstein, R. (2008). *Buffett: The Making of an American Capitalist* (p. 365). Random House Trade Paperbacks; Lowenstein, L. (1991). *Sense & Nonsense in Corporate Finance* (p. 164). Addison-Wesley Publishing Company.

250 Lowenstein, R. (2008). *Buffett: The Making of an American Capitalist* (pp. 365-366, 412). Random House Trade Paperbacks; Berkshire Hathaway 1991 Chairman's Letter; Berkshire Hathaway 1994 Chairman's Letter; Malkin, L. (1995, February 15). Buffett Quietly Amasses 10% Stake in Amex. *The International Herald Tribune*. https://www.nytimes.com/1995/02/15/business/worldbusiness/IHT-buffett-quietly-amasses-10-stake-in-amex.html.

251 American Express Form 10-K, dated March 31, 1995; Author's calculations.

252 Berkshire Hathaway 1994 Chairman's Letter; Author's calculations.

253 Warren Buffett letter to partners, October 9, 1967.

254 1997 Annual Meeting, Afternoon Session.

255 Bonsall, T. (2000). *More Than They Promised: The Studebaker Story* (pp. 23, 43–44, 53, 70–71, 140–142, 151, 169–171, 183, 250–252, 280, 283–287, 290–291, 443, 459–465). Stanford University Press; Young, J. (2009). *Studebaker and the Railroads: Volume 1* (p. 122). Lulu.com; Studebaker Corporation and Studebaker-Packard Corporation Annual Reports.

256 Studebaker Corporation, *1963 Annual Report*, 3–4.

257 Sandy Gottesman Interview transcript for the *Becoming Warren Buffett* documentary, www.kunhardtfilmfoundation.org/attachment/en/5b64a8a46aa72ce4430396a1/TextOneColumnWithFile/620c06f48cf1a8249a102d60.

258 Studebaker Corporation, *1959 Annual Report*, 3

259 Studebaker Buys Clarke Floor Co. (1960, September 7). *The New York Times*, 59.

260 Studebaker Corporation, *1959 Annual Report*, 5, 13; Studebaker Corporation, *1965 Annual Report*, 10.

261 Studebaker Corporation, *1962 Annual Report*; Studebaker Corp. Sets Acquisition. (1962, October 8). *The New York Times*, 35; Studebaker Buys Appliance Maker. (1962, November 17). *The New York Times*, 29, 34.

262 Studebaker-Packard. (1960, May 3). *The New York Times*, 55; Studebaker Corporation, *1964 Annual Report*, 7.

263 Studebaker Corporation, *1962 Annual Report*, 3.

264 Studebaker Buys Generator Maker. (1960, October 6). *The New York Times*, 59;

Studebaker Corporation, *1961 Annual Report*, 9; Studebaker Corporation, *1962 Annual Report*, 8; Studebaker Corporation, *1963 Annual Report*, 8.

265   Young, J. (2020). *The Studebaker History Corner* (p. 131). Lulu.com; Studebaker Corporation, *1961 Annual Report*, 4; Studebaker Corporation, *1962 Annual Report*, 10; Studebaker Corporation, *1963 Annual Report*, 9; Studebaker Corporation, *1965 Annual Report*, 8.

266   Studebaker Corporation, *1961 Annual Report*, 11; Studebaker Buys Chemical Maker. (1961, March 3). *The New York Times*, 40; Studebaker Corporation, *1964 Annual Report*, 8.

267   Studebaker Corporation, *1964 Annual Report*, 7.

268   Studebaker Corporation, *1965 Annual Report*, 9.

269   Studebaker Corporation, *1964 Annual Report*, 3.

270   Studebaker Corporation, *1964 Annual Report*, 4; Author's estimates.

271   Studebaker Corporation, *1962 Annual Report*, 11; Studebaker Corporation, *1963 Annual Report*, 10.

272   How Omaha Beats Wall Street. (1969, November 1). *Forbes*.

273   STP Corporation, *1968 Annual Report*; Shiller Stock Market Data, accessed via www.econ.yale.edu/~shiller/data.htm.

274   Studebaker Corporation, *1962 Annual Report*, 8; Studebaker Corporation, *1963 Annual Report*, 8.

275   Reckert, C. (1967, December 29). White Industries in Appliance Deal. *The New York Times*, 44.

276   Studebaker Corporation, *1965 Annual Report*, 1; Smith, W. (1966, February 11). Studebaker Reveals Hawaiian Executive Made Bid for Stock. *The New York Times*, 45; Corporations: Tender Invitation. (1966, February 18). Time. content.time.com/time/subscriber/article/0,33009,899046,00.html; Studebaker Corporation v. Allied Products Corporation, 256 F. Supp. 173 (W.D. Mich. 1966).

277   Sandy Gottesman Interview transcript for the *Becoming Warren Buffett* documentary, www.kunhardtfilmfoundation.org/attachment/en/5b64a8a46aa72ce4430396a1/TextOneColumnWithFile/620c06f48cf1a8249a102d60.

278   Hammer, A. (1966, February 17). Who's the Buyer in Studebaker? *The New York Times*, 46; Phalon, R. (1966, February 25). Studebaker Gives 1966 Profit Data. *The New York Times*, 40; Ex-Dissident Joins Studebaker Board. (1966, September 29). *The New York Times*, 76; Studebaker Fight Settled By Court. (1966, December 31). *The New York Times*, 27; Hammer, A. (1966, February 18). Coast Firm Buys Into Studebaker. *The New York Times*, 45; *Studebaker Corporation v. Allied Products Corporation*, 256 F. Supp. 173 (W.D. Mich. 1966).

279   Phalon, R. (1966, February 26). Murphy Concedes Offer to Buy Studebaker Stock Missed Goal. *The New York Times*, 29, 34.

280   *The New York Times*.

281   Studebaker Ends All Auto Output. (1966, March 5). *The New York Times*, 30, 35.

282   Worthington Completes Merger With Studebaker. (1967, November 28). *The New York Times*, 65; Capital Changes U.S., Studebaker Corp; *Moody's Manuals*.

283   STP Shares Offered. (1968, September 27). *The New York Times, 74.*

284   Schroeder, A. (2008). *The Snowball: Warren Buffett and the business of life* (p. 290). Bantam Dell.

285   Lisicky, M. (2012). *Baltimore's Bygone Department Stores: Many Happy Returns* (pp. 45, 58). The History Press.

286   Charles T. Munger testimony, In the Matter of Blue Chip Stamps, Berkshire Hathaway Incorporated, HO-784, Wednesday, March 20, 1975, p. 187; Schroeder, A. (2008). *The Snowball: Warren Buffett and the business of life* (pp. 288–289, 871).

287   Schroeder, A. (2008). *The Snowball: Warren Buffett and the business of life* (p. 289). Bantam Dell; Warren Buffett's letter to partners, January 20, 1966.

288   Warren Buffett letter to partners, July 12, 1966.

289   Schroeder, A. (2008). *The Snowball: Warren Buffett and the business of life* (p. 332). Bantam Dell.

290   Warren Buffett letter to partners, July 12, 1966.

291   Schroeder, A. (2008). *The Snowball: Warren Buffett and the business of life* (pp. 289–290, 871). Bantam Dell.

292   Berkshire Hathaway 1989 Chairman's Letter.

293   Schroeder, A. (2008). *The Snowball: Warren Buffett and the business of life* (p. 876). Bantam Dell.

294   Lisicky, M. (2012). *Baltimore's Bygone Department Stores: Many Happy Returns* (pp. 45–49). The History Press; Martin B. Kohn, "Hochschild, Kohn & Co.—*A Personal Account*," January 1979; Email exchange with Michael Lisicky, January 25, 2024.

295   Hochschild Kohn Financial Statements for the year ended January 29, 1966.

296   Lisicky, M. (2012). *Baltimore's Bygone Department Stores: Many Happy Returns* (pp. 50-55). The History Press.

297   Diversified Retailing Company, Inc., Prospectus, December 18, 1967.

298   Lisicky, M. (2009). *Hutzler's: Where Baltimore Shops* (pp. 15, 34–35). The History Press; Lisicky, M. (2012). *Baltimore's Bygone Department Stores: Many Happy Returns* (pp. 58, 79, 159, 163). The History Press; Email exchange with Baltimore Sun writer Jacques Kelly, June 26, 2023; Email exchange with Michael Lisicky, January 25, 2024.

299   Hutzler Brothers Company Financial Statements for the year ended January 30, 1965; *Hutzler's*. The Department Store Museum. www.thedepartmentstoremuseum.org/2010/06/hutzler-brothers-co-baltimore.html; Lisicky, M. (2012). *Baltimore's Bygone Department Stores: Many Happy Returns* (p. 46). The History Press.

300   *Moody's Manuals* and The May Department Stores Company's *1965 Annual Report.*

301   Schroeder, A. (2008). *The Snowball: Warren Buffett and the business of life* (p. 291). Bantam Dell.

302   *Moody's Manuals* and company annual reports; Howard, V. (2019). *From Main Street to Mall: The Rise and Fall of the American Department Store* (p. 171). University of Pennsylvania Press.

303 Howard Platt Interview, retrieved from the Oral History Collection of the Jewish Museum of Maryland.

304 Schroeder, A. (2008). *The Snowball: Warren Buffett and the business of life* (p. 871). Bantam Dell.

305 Howard, V. (2019). *From Main Street to Mall: The Rise and Fall of the American Department Store* (pp. 8, 193). University of Pennsylvania Press.

306 Hochschild Kohn Notes to the Financial Statements, April 1966.

307 Hochschild Kohn Notes to the Financial Statements, April 1963.

308 Hochschild Kohn Notes to the Financial Statements, April 1966.

309 U.S. Census Bureau.

310 Warren Buffett letter to partners, July 12, 1966.

311 Hochschild Kohn Financial Statements.

312 Lisicky, M. (2009). *Hutzler's: Where Baltimore Shops (pp. 92-94, 134-135).* *The History Press;* Martin B. Kohn, "Hochschild, Kohn & Co.—*A Personal Account,*" January 1979.

313 U.S. Census Bureau.

314 Berkshire Hathaway 1982 Chairman's Letter.

315 Lisicky, M. (2009). *Hutzler's: Where Baltimore Shops* (p. 102). The History Press

316 Lisicky, M. (2012). *Baltimore's Bygone Department Stores: Many Happy Returns* (pp. 149–150). The History Press.

317 Lisicky, M. (2009). *Hutzler's: Where Baltimore Shops* (p. 117). The History Press; Email exchange with Michael Lisicky, January 25, 2024.

318 Warren Buffett talk with students from the University of Kansas, May 6, 2005. Retrieved from rbcpa.com/warren-e-buffett/buffett-talks-to-university-of-kansas-students-on-may-6-2005.

319 Berkshire Hathaway 1989 Chairman's Letter.

320 Berkshire Hathaway 1987 Chairman's Letter.

321 Schroeder, A. (2008). *The Snowball: Warren Buffett and the business of life* (pp. 290–291). Bantam Dell.

322 (1966, January 5). Variety Magazine, 60th Anniversary Edition, (p. 6).

323 Thomas, B. (1999). *Building a company: Roy O. Disney and the creation of an entertainment empire* (p. 239). Disney Editions.

324 Gabler, N. (2007). *Walt Disney: The triumph of the American imagination* (p. 493). Vintage; Thomas, B. (1994). *Walt Disney: An American original* (p. 242). Disney Editions.

325 Gabler, N. (2007). *Walt Disney: The triumph of the American imagination* (pp. 588–589). Vintage.

326 Walt Disney Productions, *1965 Annual Report, 30.*

327 Disney's live-action profits. (1965, July 24). *Business Week*, 78–82; McDonald, J. (1966). Now the bankers come to Disney. *Fortune*, 138–141, 218, 223–224, 226, 228, 230.

328 Author's calculation. Buffett, W. (1991). *Three lectures to faculty, MBA students and undergraduate students.* www.tilsonfunds.com/BuffettNotreDame.pdf; Warren Buffett's letter to partners, January 20, 1966; Warren Buffett letter to partners, July 12, 1966.

329   Financial Organization of the Motion Picture Industry by Floyd B. Odlum; Robertson, J. F. (1981). *Motion picture distribution handbook* (p. 93). Tab Books.

330   Finler, J. W. (2003). *The Hollywood story: everything you ever wanted to know about the American movie business but didn't know where to look* (pp. 19, 51). Wallflower Press; United States v. Paramount Pictures, Inc., No. 1:19-mc-00544-AT (S.D.N.Y. Aug. 7, 2020). https://www.justice.gov/atr/page/file/1302816/dl; United States v. Paramount Pictures, Inc., 334 U.S. 131 (1948), https://www.justice.gov/atr/paramount-decree-review; United States v. Paramount Pictures, Inc., 334 U.S. 131 (Southern District of New York May 3, 1948). https://supreme.justia.com/cases/federal/us/334/131.

331   Sterling, C. H., & Haight, T. R. (1978). *The mass media: Aspen Institute guide to communication industry trends* (p. 372). Praeger.

332   Finler, J. W. (2003). *The Hollywood story: everything you ever wanted to know about the American movie business but didn't know where to look* (pp. 376–379). Wallflower Press; Alicoate, C. (1969). *The 1969 film daily year book of motion pictures: Fifty-first annual edition* (p. 99).

333   (1967, December 8). Hollywood: The Shock of Freedom in Films. *Time Magazine.* content.time.com/time/magazine/article/0,9171,844256-1,00.html; Email exchange with Peter Lev, October 26, 2020.

334   Aaronson, C. S. (1966). *1966 International motion picture almanac.* Quigley Publications, 64A; Finler, J. W. (2003). *The Hollywood story: everything you ever wanted to know about the American movie business but didn't know where to look* (pp. 41–43). Wallflower Press; Monaco, P. (2003). *The sixties: 1960–1969* (pp. 10–11). University of California.

335   Lev, P. (2006). *The Fifties: Transforming the screen, 1950–1959* (pp. 25–26). University of California Press.

336   Barlett, D. L., & Steele, J. B. (2004). *Howard Hughes: His life and madness* (pp. 167–169). W. W. Norton & Company; (1966, January 5). Variety Magazine, 60th Anniversary Edition, (pp. 6, 36).

337   Walt Disney Productions. (1940, April 2). Prospectus: 155,000 shares of 6% cumulative convertible preferred stock; Gabler, N. (2007). *Walt Disney: The triumph of the American imagination* (pp. 57–61. 72–73). Vintage.

338   Gabler, N. (2007). *Walt Disney: The triumph of the American imagination* (pp. 106–112, 118–128). Vintage.

339   Thomas, B. (1994). *Walt Disney: An American original* (pp. 114–116). Disney Editions; Gabler, N. (2007). *Walt Disney: The triumph of the American imagination* (pp. 174–175, 427–432). Vintage.

340   Gabler, N. (2007). *Walt Disney: The triumph of the American imagination* (p. 265). Vintage; Walt Disney Productions. (1940, April 2). Prospectus: 155,000 shares of 6% cumulative convertible preferred stock (p. 25).

341   (1966, January 5). Variety Magazine, 60th Anniversary Edition, (p. 6).

342   Walt Disney Productions, *1944 Annual Report*; Walt Disney Productions, *1945 Annual Report*; Gomery, D. (2005). *The Hollywood studio system: A history* (p. 153). British Film Institute; Gabler, N. (2007). *Walt Disney: The triumph of the American imagination* (pp. 327). Vintage.

343 McDonald, J. (1966). Now the bankers come to Disney. *Fortune*, 224; Gabler, N. (2007). *Walt Disney: The triumph of the American imagination* (p. 519). Vintage.

344 Gabler, N. (2007). *Walt Disney: The triumph of the American imagination* (pp. 492–494, 501–502, 508–509, 527). Vintage; Thomas, B. (1999). *Building a company: Roy O. Disney and the creation of an entertainment empire* (pp. 184–185). Disney Editions.

345 Walt Disney Productions, *1960 Annual Report*, 12; Gabler, N. (2007). *Walt Disney: The triumph of the American imagination* (p. 569). Vintage.

346 Gordon, M. (1958, February 4). Disney's land: Walt's profit formula: dream, diversify—and never miss an angle. *The Wall Street Journal, 1, 12*.

347 Alicoate, C. (1969). *The 1969 film daily year book of motion pictures: Fifty-first annual edition* (p. 97). Film and Television Daily.

348 Monaco, P. (2003). *The sixties: 1960–1969* (p. 44). University of California; Thomas, B. (1994). *Walt Disney: An American original* (p. 315). Disney Editions.

349 Lowenstein, R. (2008). *Buffett: The Making of an American Capitalist* (pp. 92–93). Random House Trade Paperbacks.

350 Buffett, W. (1991). *Three lectures to faculty, MBA students and undergraduate students*. https://www.tilsonfunds.com/BuffettNotreDame.pdf.

351 Gabler, N. (2007). *Walt Disney: The triumph of the American imagination* (pp. 492–501). Vintage.

352 Buffett, W. (1991). *Three lectures to faculty, MBA students and undergraduate students*. https://www.tilsonfunds.com/BuffettNotreDame.pdf.

353 Walt Disney Productions, *1965 Annual Report, 24.*

354 Buffett, W. (1991). *Three lectures to faculty, MBA students and undergraduate students*. https://www.tilsonfunds.com/BuffettNotreDame.pdf.

355 (1966, January 5). *Variety Magazine*, 60th Anniversary Edition, (p. 6).

356 McDonald, J. (1966). Now the bankers come to Disney. *Fortune, 226.*

357 Smith, A. (2006). *Supermoney* (p. 191). Wiley.

358 (1966, January 5). *Variety Magazine*, 60th Anniversary Edition, (p. 67).

359 Buffett, W. (1991). *Three lectures to faculty, MBA students and undergraduate students*. https://www.tilsonfunds.com/BuffettNotreDame.pdf.

360 Universal Studios Inc. V. Francis I. Dupont, 334 A.2d 216 (Supreme Court of Delaware January 20, 1975).

361 Shiller, R. (2001). U.S. stock markets 1871-present and CAPE ratio [Data file]. Retrieved from www.econ.yale.edu/~shiller/data.htm.

362 Thomas, B. (1999). *Building a company: Roy O. Disney and the creation of an entertainment empire* (p. 302). Disney Editions; Thomas, B. (1994). *Walt Disney: An American original* (p. 356). Disney Editions.

363 Walt Disney Productions, *1966 Annual Report*.

364 Finler, J. W. (2003). *The Hollywood story: everything you ever wanted to know about the American movie business but didn't know where to look* (p. 5). Wallflower Press.

365 Berkshire Hathaway 1995 Chairman's Letter.

366 FCIC Interview of Warren Buffett, May 26, 2010. Retrieved from fraser. stlouisfed.org/files/docs/historical/fct/fcic/fcic_interview_2_buffett_20100526. pdf?utm_source=direct_download.

367 Rieser, C. (1959). The Egghead, the Upstart, and Old P. & R. *Fortune*, 84–88, 188–192.

368 Miller, M. (2008, March 5). *Gates No Longer World's Richest Man*. Forbes. www. forbes.com/2008/03/05/buffett-worlds-richest-cx_mm_0229buffetrichest. html?sh=375333313180.

369 Gramm, J. (2016). *Dear Chairman: Boardroom Battles and the Rise of Shareholder Activism* (pp. 218–219). Harper Business.

370 Warren Buffett letter to partners, January 20, 1966.

371 Lowenstein, R. (2008). *Buffett: The Making of an American Capitalist* (pp. 65–66). Random House Trade Paperback.

372 Schroeder, A. (2008). *The Snowball: Warren Buffett and the business of life* (pp. 264, 298–299). Bantam Dell.

373 Berkshire Hathaway 2004 Chairman's Letter.

374 Barbosa, M. (2010). *Interview with Alice Schroeder: The Snowball Warren Buffett and the Business of Life*. web.archive.org/web/20161011022517/http://www. simoleonsense.com/alice-schroeder-the-snowball-warren-buffett-and-the-business-of-life.

375 Berkshire Hathaway 1991 Chairman's Letter.

376 Bianco, A. (1999, July 5). Homespun Wisdom From The "Oracle Of Omaha." *BusinessWeek*. www.bloomberg.com/news/articles/1999-07-05/homespun-wisdom-from-the-oracle-of-omaha#xj4y7vzkg.

377 Zitz, M. (2010). *Giving It All Away: The Doris Buffett Story*. The Permanent Press.

About the Author

A value investor who has worked at multiple investment firms, Brett Gardner has invested across the capital structure. He has also led successful activist campaigns against publicly traded companies. A St. John's University graduate, Brett currently resides in New York City. *Buffett's Early Investments* is his first book.

Printed in the USA
CPSIA information can be obtained
at www.ICGtesting.com
LVHW021212291024
794866LV00005B/20